The Future of
Asian-Pacific
Security Collaboration

The Future of Asian-Pacific Security Collaboration

Sheldon Simon
Arizona State University

Lexington Books
D.C. Heath and Company/Lexington, Massachusetts/Toronto

Library of Congress Cataloging-in-Publication Data

Simon, Sheldon W., 1937–
    The future of Asian-Pacific security collaboration.

    Bibliography: p.
    Includes index.
    1. Asia—National security. 2. Pacific Area—National security. 3. United States—
Military relations—Asia. 4. United States—Military relations—Pacific Area. 5. Soviet
Union—Military relations—Asia. 6. Soviet Union—Military relations—Pacific Area.
7. Asia—Military relations—United States. 8. Asia—Military relations—Soviet Union.
9. Pacific Area—Military relations—United States. 10. Pacific Area—Military relations—
Soviet Union. I. Title.
UA830.S49   1988   355′.03305   87-46296
ISBN 0-669-17074-7 (alk. paper)

Published simultaneously in Canada
Printed in the United States of America
International Standard Book Number: 0-669-17074-7
Library of Congress Catalog Card Number: 87-46296

The paper used in this publication meets the minimum requirements of American National
Standard for Information Sciences—Permanence of Paper for Printed Library Materials,
ANSI Z39.48-1984. ∞™

89 90 91 92 8 7 6 5 4 3 2

To the memory of Judge Jacob Dim, whose wisdom and support are not forgotten

Contents

Figures and Tables

Figures

Tables

Acknowledgments

T his examination of the prospects and pitfalls of Asian security collaboration has been several years in the making. The research trips I made through Asia in 1981, 1982, 1984, 1985, and 1986 provided me with opportunities to discuss such controversial issues as defense burden sharing, the Japanese military role, the future U.S. force structure, and varying national views of threat with governmental, academic, and media analysts throughout the Pacific rim. Both U.S. and Asian officials were generous with their time and candid in their views—in most cases, provided that our conversations would not be attributed.

I also benefited from discussions of the project as it took shape with colleagues in political science at Arizona State University, particularly Robert Youngbood, Stephen Walker, and Pat McGowan. My graduate assistant, David Kravetz, provided superb bibliographic support by his assiduous searches through government documents.

This study could not have been completed without the generous travel support of the Earhart Foundation (Ann Arbor), the U.S. Information Agency, the National Strategy Information Center, and the University of California (Berkeley) East Asian Institute. The last two institutions offered conference opportunities in Southeast Asia where portions of this project were presented.

Finally, a major vote of appreciation goes to the Arizona State University Center for Asian Studies head secretary, Betty Parker, for her patient and careful typing of the manuscript, to the Hoover Institution for providing the grant necessary to write the study, and to my wife, Charlann—an author in her own field—who shared the family study with good nature while we simultaneously worked on major projects.

Introduction

A Global View of U.S. Security Policy

The perspective of this study may be broadly defined as geopolitical.[1] Its two primary actors—the United States and the Soviet Union—are seen as core rival powers that seek security within three concentric fields: (1) a group of close allies or client states, (2) a contingent of potential allies, and (3) a number of volatile peripheral actors that can be either stabilized or subverted depending on their orientations. Each rival's forward bases challenge the security perimeters of the other.

Historically continental and maritime powers frequently have sparked conflict. The latter tend to be mercantile societies oriented toward international trade, while the former often rely on military superiority for domestic control and to protect vulnerable land borders. Sea powers were never the equal of the continental states on land. They tended to compensate for this deficiency by forging alliances that challenged the land power within its continental security zone. Continental states, in turn, objected to their lack of equal access to world sea-lanes. To reinforce their positions, they coerced cooperation along their peripheries, actions that inevitably aroused the fears of sea powers.

Today the dominant insular and continental powers are nuclear armed. Because direct military confrontation must be avoided, the historic rivalry is sublimated through arms-related substitutes for war, including deployments, arms sales, support for proxy and client hostilities, and even arms control negotiations.[2] Traditional geopolitical causes of the rivalry are not resolved, but they are avoided whenever possible.

For the first thirty years after World War II, the Soviet Union and the United States generally allowed each other a free hand in their respective border regions. The United States did not respond militarily to Soviet actions in Hungary or Czechoslovakia nor did the Soviet Union to U.S. intervention in Guatemala or the Dominican Republic. That situation may be changing. The USSR has provided limited arms to its allies in Nicaragua and the United States feels equally justified in supporting the mujahidin in Afghanistan. In supporting the Afghan rebels, the Soviets charge that the United States is threatening a vital security zone. The Reagan administration makes a comparable argument for the Soviet-supported efforts to overthrow the government of El Salvador.

No longer does the United States consider it wrong to support revolutionary movements openly against established regimes if these regimes are pro-Soviet. Washington is less concerned about the maintenance of a general global nonintervention norm than it is with weakening its rival in peripheral areas. Thus the United States in the 1980s has openly supplied rebels in Nicaragua, Afghanistan, Cambodia, and Angola on the grounds that they are "democratic" forces seeking to overthrow nondemocratic governments.[3]

Growing superpower intervention in third world states is a risky and potentially destabilizing undertaking. It encourages counterintervention by other external powers. Moreover, the combination of external dependence and internal vulnerability in these states means that stability and dominance may be transitory at best.[4] The personalization of politics and frequent changes of regime in many third world states means that successor regimes may accept neither stability nor alignment.

Most developing countries confront primarily internal threats exacerbated by support from ethnic or ideological allies across national borders. Thus security is inextricably intertwined with issues of domestic development and the distribution of national production.[5] These issues are inherently difficult for an external actor to influence, much less control.

Evolution of U.S. Containment Doctrine in Asia

There have been three U.S. containment strategies in the Asian-Pacific region since World War II.[6] The first, sustained through the early 1970s, based U.S. security interests on bilateral ties with noncommunist allies—Japan, South Korea, the countries belonging to the Southeast Asia Treaty Organization, and Taiwan—against China. This strategy essentially ignored issues of political democracy and social and economic inequalities within allied states. Under this strategy, the United States fought two wars in Asia and froze its ties with China for more than twenty years.

By the 1970s, the protracted war in Vietnam followed by the withdrawal of U.S. forces from the Asian mainland weakened the strategic U.S. position in the Asian-Pacific region. U.S. allies were left in a militarily and psychologically vulnerable position regarding Moscow and its allies. The shift in Washington's strategic position gradually changed Beijing's view. By the end of the decade, the two came together as tacit strategic partners to counter the Soviet Union's growing political and military presence. This second strategy created the possibility of a broad strategic alignment of the United States, Western Europe,

Japan, and China against the Soviet Union. It thus forced the USSR to face the prospect of a two-front war.

The second containment doctrine lasted until the early 1980s. It foundered on China's fear of excessive dependence on yet another great power, as well as the friction created in U.S. relations with Indonesia and Malaysia, two members of the Association of Southeast Asian Nations (ASEAN) which view China more than the USSR as the long-term security threat to the region. Moscow has shifted its main strategic target in Asia from China to the United States and Japan, permitting China greater diplomatic flexibility to loosen dependence on the United States and promote a limited détente with the USSR. Nevertheless, the U.S. position has not been weakened. Japan has accelerated its rearmament, and Washington is developing better security coordination with its Pacific rim allies. China continues to support Japan-U.S. security ties and has improved relations with ASEAN to balance the Soviet-Vietnam alliance.

The generally favorable results of the third containment strategy are premised on the maintenance of a strong U.S. military presence in the Pacific. Without it, U.S. allies in the region would have sufficient forces to deter neither Vietnam, North Korea, nor, of course, the Soviet Union. The paradox of the third containment strategy, however, is that the fundamental strategic interest of the United States does not coincide with that of most of its Asian allies. For the United States, the regional spillover of the Sino-Soviet conflict in the context of the global Soviet-U.S. rivalry is the major issue in Asia. For most other states, Sino-Soviet relations are peripheral to more immediate and local problems. These local issues, in turn, rank low on the U.S. regional agenda, and Washington is unwilling to allocate resources and political energy to resolve them.[7]

Reagan Doctrine and U.S. Commitments

The Reagan administration seemed to present a new security challenge to the Soviets. Rather than continue to accept the tacit spheres of influence doctrine that had developed as early as the 1950s, rhetorically the administration articulated a worldview reminiscent of the early years of the cold war. After acquiescence to Soviet moves in Afghanistan, the Horn of Africa, and, possibly, Central America under Carter, Reagan's foreign policy took the offensive. Calls for liberation from Communist tyranny echoed in Washington, and the notion of rollback was revived. While in theory the Reagan doctrine could be universally applied, in practice it has focused on third world countries where the Marxist grip is relatively recent and therefore presumably light. The defeat of these governments, in the eyes of the Reagan administration, would right a global imbalance brought about by U.S. weakness in the aftermath of the Vietnam War.

The U.S. invasion of Grenada in 1983 seemed the perfect counterpart of the Brezhnev doctrine in the Western Hemisphere. To demonstrate that communism could be rolled back, U.S. troops quickly toppled a thuggish and plausibly Communist regime with close ties to Cuba and the USSR. For an ideologically minded administration, the Reagan doctrine was born.[8]

Over time the doctrine has been refined to justify aid to anticommunist insurgencies (Nicaragua, Afghanistan, Cambodia) as a proper tit-for-tat rejoinder to Moscow's aid to Marxist insurgencies. Aid to anticommunist insurgents is deemed legitimate because the governments against which the insurgencies battle are unrepresentative and repressive. (Reagan officials did not explain, however, why they continued to support unrepresentative, repressive regimes friendly to the West.)

With a diplomacy directed at challenging the Soviet global position, including, at least rhetorically, Eastern Europe, the stage was set for a massive expansion of the U.S. defense budget. Beginning in 1981, the Reagan administration advanced Five-Year Defense Plans that increased the total spending authority for the Defense Department between 1982 and 1988 from the $1,276.1 billion requested by Carter to $1,768.1 billion. The centerpiece of this budget expansion was the creation of a 600-ship navy, including three new Nimitz-class nuclear-powered aircraft carriers.[9]

Disappointingly, a Congressional Budget Office study noted in 1985 that, with the exception of navy shipbuilding, weapons procurements for the other services were not noticeably greater than during the Carter years. More disturbing was the negative effect of Defense Secretary Caspar Weinberger's big ticket purchases on combat readiness and sustainability. Shortages in airlift, ammunition, and battlefield medical supplies led some high-level army and air force officers to question the U.S. ability to fight for any extended period.[10]

The Reagan administration's fixation on third world revolution also created strains in the Western alliance. Fear of a diversion of resources to peripheral conflicts was combined with the belief that the United States would confront a tar baby situation. By treating revolutionary change in the third world as a crucial component of the Soviet-U.S. global balance, Washington would lock itself into a losing position. Reagan appeared to be reviving the two-camp approach to international politics in which diversity within the global system was minimized and opportunities to work out special relations with Soviet allies and clients ignored.[11]

The Reagan doctrine has taken U.S. security policy back to the cold war model in which commitments are determined not by interests but by the psychology of credibility:

Classical realist model: Interests → commitments → resolve and capabilities → credibility.

Cold war (Reagan) model: Credibility → commitments → resolve and capabilities → interests[12]

The Reagan administration turns the classical realist model on its head. Instead of interests predating commitments to back a particular regime or faction and hence involve U.S. prestige, the Reagan doctrine, in a deep cold war mode, places credibility first. The central concern is the global Soviet challenge. The importance of any particular conflict situation (Angola, Afghanistan, Nicaragua) to U.S. security is less salient for determining Washington's commitment than the belief that these challenges erode U.S. credibility as the leader of world democracy.

The Reagan administration's belligerent posture toward the Soviet Union was supported by the electorate in his first term of office; however, it seems increasingly at variance with public attitudes in his second. A quadrenniel survey of public opinion about U.S. foreign policy reported by the Chicago Council on Foreign Relations in 1987 showed that while Americans still viewed the Soviet Union as their chief adversary, most also favored expanded cooperation with Moscow, that is, the revival of détente.[13] Although coming to power as an opponent of détente, Reagan created a paradoxical result through his success in restoring the perception of a more favorable U.S. military balance. He increased support for détente, thus opening opportunities for negotiated settlements to regional conflicts with the USSR. In 1988, Reagan's last year in office, some political dividends from these earlier investments seemed available. The Intermediate Nuclear Forces Agreement, negotiated in Washington the previous December, for the first time eliminated a whole class of nuclear weapons from superpower arsenals. Moreover, the Soviets appeared to be moving toward some kind of military disengagement from Afghanistan as well as urging Vietnam to compromise over a future Cambodian government of reconciliation.

Both President Reagan and his successor can use these opportunities to try to arrange additional regional understandings with the USSR, increasing stability by creating norms of political engagement. This study explores the prospects for developing new and more stable security relations in the Asia-Pacific region between the United States and its allies and friends and the Soviet Union and its clients. It is dedicated to the search for peace.

Notes

1. This initial conceptual framework is drawn from George Liska, "From Containment to Concert," *Foreign Policy* 62 (Spring 1986): 3–23.

2. Ibid., pp. 15–16.

3. This argument is forcefully made by Evan Luard, "Superpower and Regional Conflicts," *Foreign Affairs* 64, no. 5 (Summer 1986): 1008, 1011.

4. Robert L. Rothstein, "The 'Security Dilemma' and 'Poverty Trap' in the Third World," *Jerusalem Journal of International Relations* 8, no. 4 (1986): 7.

5. For the ASEAN states, this issue is discussed in Sheldon W. Simon, *The ASEAN States and Regional Security* (Stanford: Hoover Institution Press, 1982), chap. 1. For

a more recent assessment of major security issues in Southeast Asia, see chapter 4 of this study and Sheldon W. Simon, "ASEAN's Strategic Situation in the 1980s," *Pacific Affairs* (Spring 1987).

6. For a full discussion, see Guo-cang Huan, "Containment and the Northeast Asian Triangle" and Ulrich A. Straus, "Southeast Asia in the Containment Strategies for the 1990s," both in Terry L. Deibel and John Lewis Gaddis, eds., *Containment: Concept and Policy* (Washington, D.C.: National Defense University Press, 1986), 2: 501–540.

7. Richard H. Solomon, "American Defense Planning and Asian Security: Policy Choices for a Time of Transition," in Daniel J. Kaufman, Jeffrey S. McKitrick, and Thomas J. Leney, eds., *U.S. National Security: A Framework for Analysis* (Lexington, Mass.: Lexington Books, 1985), pp. 363–386.

8. Stephen S. Rosenfeld, "The Guns of July," *Foreign Affairs* 64, no. 4 (Spring 1986): 698–714.

9. James A. Nathan and James K. Oliver, *United States Foreign Policy and World Order*, 3d ed. (Boston: Little, Brown, 1985), p. 427.

10. The CBO study is cited in Robert W. Komer, "What Decade of Detente?" *International Security* 10, no. 2 (Fall 1985): 82–83.

11. Alexander Dallin and Gail W. Lapidus, "Reagan and the Russians: United States Policy toward the Soviet Union and Eastern Europe," in Kenneth Oye, Robert Lieber, and Donald Rothchild, eds., *Eagle Defiant: United States Foreign Policy in the 1980s* (Boston: Little, Brown, 1983), pp. 228–229.

12. These models are taken from Robert H. Johnson, "Exaggerating America's Stakes in Third World Conflicts," *International Security* 10, no. 3 (Winter 1985–1986): 42.

13. The report is summarized in George D. Moffett III, "Survey: Americans Want World Role," *Christian Science Monitor,* March 10, 1987.

1
A U.S. View of Asian Security Issues toward the 1990s—Problems of Burden Sharing

As American strategists look toward the 1990s, two operative concepts are prominently featured: force projection and burden sharing. The latter acknowledges Washington's inability to serve as sole defender of the market-oriented international economy; the former reflects the U.S. belief that it might be required to move military forces rapidly to a variety of global trouble spots. Both assume, however, that the global role of the United States as the predominant actor in world politics will be sustained at least until the turn of the century. Although the United States will continue to exercise its preeminent role in European and Asian regional security, the environments within which it acts have been extensively altered. In Asia the alliances forged in the 1950s are gradually being transformed into relations based on a greater degree of mutuality. U.S. unilateral security guarantees have diminished in scope and value and are being replaced by cooperative political and economic arrangements designed to improve internal stability in friendly states while, it is hoped, reducing the frequency with which military force is used. From a third world perspective, the West is now seen more as a source of arms for the development of indigenous military forces than a guarantor of the status quo through overseas bases and military pacts. The latter are increasingly viewed as outmoded and an insult to third world sovereignty.[1]

Yet the global spread of military capabilities has, unfortunately, been associated with neither a decline in superpower tensions nor commitments to third world clients. For the United States, the bilateral security treaties of over thirty years ago with Japan, South Korea, the Philippines, Australia, and Thailand remain intact, and security cooperation has also been extended to Indonesia, Malaysia, and Singapore. In opposition to these arrangements within the past decade, the Soviet Union is bent on establishing its own Asian military presence, with new clients in Indochina being added to its extensive presence in Northeast Asia, an unprecedented development for the Soviets in this part of the world. The stage appears to be set for either a direct superpower confrontation in Asia within the next several years or a proxy conflict in which Washington and Moscow back their respective clients' regional ambitions.

Is such an outcome inevitable? How will third world nationalisms interact with the continued dependence of regional actors on both the military presence and assistance of the superpowers? Are the security goals of the latter, essentially global in orientation, compatible with the predominantly regional concerns of the Asian states? How effectively does each member of an asymmetrical security relationship use its partner, and how are the costs and benefits divided? Answers to these questions are crucial for an understanding of the dynamics of Asian security and the policies of allies and adversaries into the next decade.

From the U.S. perspective, concerned with the growing gap between commitments and capabilities, a subsequent series of questions emerges:

Do noncommunist states (as represented by the views of political elites) see the USSR as a sufficiently significant threat to build defense forces designed for external protection, as distinct from internal security?

Are noncommunist states willing to collaborate with their neighbors to increase joint defense?

Are noncommunist states willing to coordinate their defense across subregions, with U.S. forces serving as a bridge among them?

How serious are the obstacles (domestic and regional) to the kinds of collaboration suggested above? That is, are regional views of the sources and nature of threats compatible? Even if compatible, can they lead to collaboration?

This study addresses these issues. It is particularly concerned with the compatibility among superpower views of Asian security and those of the regional members. My primary hypothesis is that superpower assumptions of congruity between their global concerns and the goals of their regional partners are overdrawn. As long as the superpowers are willing to provide their clients with military and economic aid for the latter's own purposes while limiting great power demands for policy coordination, relations will appear relatively cordial. But if the superpowers attempt to aggregate their partners' forces to effect an Asian component of a global military posture, incompatibilities will surface, and alliance strains will occur. A corollary to this proposition is that the presence of both superpowers, neutralizing one another, is more acceptable from the viewpoint of many Asian states than the predominance of one, particularly if that one is the Soviet Union.

Asia's Importance to the United States

For the first half of this century, total U.S. world trade averaged less than 4 percent of its gross national product (GNP). Since 1962, however, that figure has reached 17 percent; and if present rates of growth continue, by the year 2000, U.S. foreign trade will account for one-quarter of its GNP—approximately Japan's current percentage. Since 1978, U.S. Pacific trade has surpassed its Atlantic counterpart. In 1986, trade with the Asia-Pacific region was $215 billion, almost 50 percent more than with Europe. Although overall U.S. world trade declined more than 5 percent during the recent world recession (1980–1983), its Asian-Pacific component was down by less than 1 percent. Put another way, in 1983, total U.S. world trade rose 0.5 percent, but trade with the Pacific region grew by 8 percent.[2]

Extrapolation of current production figures shows Asia producing 25 percent of the world GNP by 1990. By adding North America, that figure arises to an astonishing 50 percent. Similar growth patterns have been recorded in Asia's share of world trade, which has increased from 9.5 percent in 1960 to 14.4 percent in 1980 and is expected to reach over 22 percent by the end of the century. Most significant, more than half of this trade occurs within the region itself.[3] At the same time, Asia accounts for more than half the U.S. global trade deficit.

The Asia-Pacific region's economic importance to the United States is reflected not only in its burgeoning trade but also in the region's critical strategic resources, among which are oil, minerals, and rubber. The ever-increasing U.S. demand for these resources, in combination with Asia's increased marketing skills, new manufacturing capacities, and high technology products, ensures that U.S. economic interest in the area will continue to grow.

To protect and nurture this web of regional economic activity requires the maintenance of unimpeded international movement across the sea-lanes of communication (SLOCs). Washington's primary strategic goal for the Asia-Pacific region is therefore to ensure that a sufficient combination of both U.S. and friendly states' naval and air power is available to keep the SLOCs open and to monitor the activities of the only state with the potential capacity and possible motivation to disrupt these sea-lanes, the USSR.

In strategic terms, the USSR has come abreast of the United States over the past decade in military capacities and is for the first time in its history a global power. As a latecomer to many parts of the world, including Asia, the Soviets see themselves as still underprivileged despite their efforts. They lack equal access to—or involvement in—those regions still strongly influenced by the United States. Engaged in catching up, the USSR is very status conscious. It demands recognition as an equal of the United States in Asia, with full participation in all decisions important to the region's future. General Secretary Mikhail Gorbachev's July 1986 speech in Vladivostok outlining Soviet plans for a major Asian political and economic role constituted the most recent expression of Soviet hopes, which may be traced back to Leonid Brezhnev's 1969 call for an Asian collective security arrangement.

Soviet instruments of influence are limited, however. Neither its trade prospects nor political orientation are particularly attractive to market-oriented states in Asia. It relies disproportionately, therefore, on its expanded military might to influence regional political affairs. Soviet armed forces are increasingly observed as its Pacific fleet transits Asian waters, and the USSR has established an indirect presence as well through aid to its Indochina clients. In response, the United States espouses an Asian united front against the Soviets, in the process seeking to incorporate the Asian-Pacific region into its global strategy.

Part of the problem with the U.S. Asian strategy is the prominent role U.S. officials believe China should play. U.S. planners envision a modernized People's Republic of China (PRC) as a substantial counterweight to the USSR, forcing the Soviets to divide their forces at the extreme peripheries of their vast land mass. Yet powerful counterarguments to this strategy exist, frequently emanating from the closest Asian partners of the United States. China has its own goals for Asia, which, over time, are not necessarily compatible with those of the United States, Japan, or Southeast Asia. If the PRC's long-term strategic plans are to exclude the activities of extraregional powers, then Beijing and Washington may still find themselves on a collision course early in the next century.

U.S. experience in Asia, particularly since the attack on South Korea in 1950, has been dominated by warfare and security pacts. The Korean conflict led to the formal arrangements that structure U.S. participation in Asian security affairs to this day: bilateral treaties with Japan, the Philippines, Australia, New Zealand, and Taiwan (the last now transmogrified into the ambiguous Taiwan Relations Act). The failure of the French effort in the first Indochina War (1945–1954) subsequently led to the Manila Pact of 1954 and Thailand's addition to the list of states sheltered under a U.S. security umbrella. Ultimately the U.S. involvement in Indochina resulted in the war in Vietnam, entailing a significant U.S. military effort for over a decade and sensitizing an entire generation of Americans to Asia as a region of dangers and defeats.

Since the generation involved in the second Indochina War (1965–1975) is now moving into civilian and military leadership roles, it is not surprising that they look upon future military commitments in East Asia with considerable caution. If the United States is to sustain its responsibilities to protect the noncommunist Asian states from external aggression, it most certainly will not be willing to do so alone. The growing Soviet military presence and Vietnam's bellicosity toward Thailand, both emanating from Hanoi's occupation of Cambodia, have led U.S. leaders of both major political parties to call upon Japan and the other Asian states to undertake larger responsibilities in their own defense. The question arises, however, whether Asian leaders share the U.S. view of regional security requirements. One recent study suggests the answer is no.[4] By contrast, this study will argue that the potential for collaboration exists but that its realization will depend on economic and political developments in the Asian region over the next several years.

Increasingly U.S. officials are insisting that alliance burdens should be proportional to resources. Now that the U.S. standard of living is no longer far higher than Germany's or Japan's, it becomes increasingly difficult to obtain domestic political support in Washington for the continued allocation of ever larger proportions of GNP to the common defense. The argument that the United States has a unique role to play as a global power is less tenable when all major trading nations rely on open SLOCs for their prosperity.

Earlier, in the wake of the second Indochina War, the Carter administration had hoped that Sino-Soviet rivalry would produce a new regional balance, with Beijing aligned with U.S.-oriented Asian states. USSR-Chinese animosity reduced the ability of each to project power elsewhere in the region and at the same time induced them to seek better relations with noncommunist states, including the United States. This optimistic forecast proved illusory, however, when the Soviets invaded Afghanistan, bankrolled Vietnam's invasion of Cambodia, and began to deploy naval and air forces from Cam Ranh Bay. Once again those states dependent on regional U.S. military deployments called on Washington to reaffirm its interest and will in Asia.

The United States was faced with reconciling the maintenance of its thirty-year-old commitments and a force structure in the early 1980s that included the smallest number of forward deployed military personnel in Asia since 1939. Presumably these forces would be reinforced in the event of crisis through prepositioned supplies at U.S. bases in Japan, Korea, Guam, and the Philippines backed by a growing air and sealift capacity being built during the first Reagan administraton. Critics pointed out, however, that the air and sealift capacities being developed were still insufficient to cover the increased responsibilities of the U.S. Pacific Command (PACOM). Since 1979, in the aftermath of both the Iranian revolution and Soviet occupation of Afghanistan, Seventh Fleet deployment in the Arabian Sea depleted forces ordinarily available in the Pacific. PACOM's responsibilities now covered half the earth's surface and 70 percent of its ocean waters. Could the United States, unaided, keep the sea-lanes open with its Asian forces spread over such a wide expanse?[5] Part of the answer has been the general modernization of U.S. Pacific forces in the 1980s. This includes the replacement of old vessels with Spruance-class destroyers, deployment of new Los Angeles–class attack submarines, replacement of F-4 with F-14, F-15, and F-18 aircraft, and the fitting of B-52s with cruise missiles. Additionally, twenty-four-hour airborne warning and control (AWACs) operate from Japan in the Northwest Pacific and over the Indian Ocean via Malaysia, Singapore, Diego Garcia, and Australia.

The strategic success of the U.S. posture depends on several factors:

1. The continuation of Sino-Soviet enmity (otherwise the threat to the West will grow dramatically).

2. An increase in U.S. defense forces earmarked for Asia so that western Pacific forces can be expanded without reducing the number of units on station in the Persian Gulf. The Gramm-Rudman Act's automatic budget cutting in

deficit years would affect U.S. Pacific capabilities with particular severity. A Georgetown University study estimates that Gramm-Rudman would leave the air force six air wings short of its 1990 goal and the navy with twelve carrier battle groups instead of the fifteen it had planned.

3. The validity of the assumption that the United States will not be required to meet concurrent military commitments in the Pacific, Indian Ocean–Persian Gulf, and Europe. Otherwise the gap between commitments and capabilities is too large and would lead, at minimum, to the sacrifice of one theater to reinforce the others.

4. Convincing Japan that it must accelerate the creation of air and maritime capabilities to reduce some of the U.S. burdens in the northwestern Pacific.[6]

Political Constraints in U.S. Asian Policy

Although Reagan administration officials have sometimes revived the cold war rhetoric of the 1950s, the gap between rhetoric and capacity is apparent to all. Secretary of State George Shultz can exhort Americans about their moral duty to uphold freedom globally, but even within his oratory there lurks a cautionary subtext underscoring limitations on the use of force:

> The lesson of the postwar years is that America must be the leader of the free world; there is no one else to take our place. The nature and extent of our support—whether moral support or something more—necessarily varies from case to case. . . .
> . . . If we shrink from leadership we create a vacuum into which our adversaries can move. Our national security suffers, our global interests suffer, and, yes, the worldwide struggle for democracy suffers.[7]

In the preceding remarks the secretary of state was addressing the loss of consensus on the use of force to uphold U.S. commitments in the third world. One of the most important political legacies for the United States resulting from the Vietnam War has been the loss of national self-assurance in dealing with third world changes deemed inimical to U.S. interests. Even in the more conservative Congress of the 1980s, generally supportive of substantial defense spending, resistance to involvement in third world military actions is strong. Congressional agonizing over Lebanon and Central America illustrates the point. The War Powers Act, passed in 1973 during the Vietnam War to limit presidential discretion, is still very much alive in Congress. Thus even as U.S. naval and air power increase to a level more commensurate with commitments, as former Secretary of Defense James Schlesinger stated in congressional testimony, "there is simply no domestic consensus regarding the prospective use of force":

The likeliest physical challenges to the United States come in the third world—not in Europe or North America. If the more predatory states in the third world are given assurance that they can employ, directly or indirectly, physical force against American interests with impunity, they will bear far less restraint in acting against our interests.[8]

Conditions determining the use of force have given rise to disputes at the very top of the Reagan administration. At a speech before the Trilateral Commission in the spring of 1984, Shultz stressed the importance of the use of force as an instrument of diplomacy (coercive diplomacy): "The broad reality is that diplomacy not backed by military strength is ineffectual. Leverage, as well as good will, is required. Power and diplomacy are not alternatives. They must go together or we will accomplish very little in this world." The reaction of Secretary of Defense Caspar Weinberger, reflecting the views of the uniformed service leadership, most of whom had held battlefield commands in Vietnam fifteen years earlier, was to caution that U.S. forces should be used only as a last resort "when other means have failed":

Employing our forces almost indiscriminately and as a regular and customary part of our diplomatic efforts would surely plunge us headlong into the sort of domestic turmoil we experienced during the Vietnam War, without accomplishing the goal for which we committed our forces.[9]

Going further, Weinberger appeared to reject the notion of the incremental use of force or the orchestration of force with negotiations (employed by both the Vietminh and Americans during the Paris peace talks in the early 1970s). Force should be used "with the clear intention of winning," and there must be "reasonable assurance" of public and congressional support.

Secretary Shultz demurred from Weinberger's all-or-nothing view of force: "The need to avoid no-win situations cannot mean that we turn automatically away from hard-to-win situations that call for prudent involvement. These will always involve risks." In effect, Shultz was arguing that unless the United States was willing to use force in limited contingencies for limited goals, the credibility of its commitment to a number of third world states would be undermined, and the latter might conclude that accommodation with the Soviet Union and its allies would be a wiser policy.

Parameters of U.S. Asian Security Policy

The United States deploys military force to Asia to contend with limited contingencies. In its 1984 statement on "Security and Arms Control," the State Department linked the presence of U.S. land and air forces in Korea and Japan and of the Seventh Fleet in the western Pacific to bilateral and multilateral security agreements with Japan, South Korea, Australia, New Zealand, the Philippines, and Thailand. Specifically these forces are deployed to deter and, if necessary, help the signatory states defend against potential threats from the USSR, North Korea, and Vietnam. (China is no longer mentioned as a source of threat to U.S. allies in East Asia.) Additionally the United States takes responsibility for protecting the SLOCs between East Asia, the Indian Ocean, and the Persian Gulf.[10]

The United States maintains the combat readiness of its Pacific forces by staging regular military exercises in Japan, the Philippines, Korea, and Thailand. It has also exercised with Malaysian forces and conducts naval maneuvers with Australia and, until 1986, New Zealand. As noncommunist Asia's primary guarantor, the United States serves as a common security contact for most of the region's armed forces whose own bilateral contacts—for example, Japan and the Association of Southeast Asian Nations (ASEAN) states or Japan and South Korea—may be limited or nonexistent. Washington's Asian security policy fits into a global doctrine. As part of its Asia commitments, the United States insists that nuclear arms control agreements with the Soviet Union be based on global limits. That is, any reduction of, say, SS-20 intermediate-range missiles in Europe may not be redeployed to Asia. Similarly, in 1987 arms reduction negotiations, the United States urged a zero-zero intermediate-range nuclear forces (INF) removal that included all Soviet SS-20s deployed in Siberia.

Northeast Asia forms the keystone of the U.S. Asian defense. In an important policy statement on December 13, 1983, Secretary Weinberger asserted that "the defense of Japan is as vital as the defense of Europe." He went on to speak of the combined defense efforts of Japan, South Korea, and China as crucial to the maintenance of an Asian regional component to the global security balance.[11] Weinberger's statement reflected Washington's view that China's security orientation toward the United States and Japan had a stabilizing effect on the single flashpoint in Northeast Asia where great power security concerns converge: Korea. By encouraging the United States and Japan to maintain and even strengthen their military posture in the region, the PRC was also communicating its desire to see the status quo maintained on the Korean peninsula.

While U.S. security concerns in Northeast Asia are directly related to growing Soviet military deployments in Siberia and Soviet fleet activities in Vladivostok and Petropavlovsk, Southeast Asia's security generates less anxiety. U.S. priorities include upholding the independence of the ASEAN states and maintaining the freedom of sea-lanes essential for international commerce and the deployment of naval power from the Pacific and the Indian Ocean (figure 1–1). Achievement of these goals depends primarily on the internal political stability of the littoral states. In turn the ASEAN states encourage the United States to maintain a naval presence, supply arms, and sustain economic involvement, particularly to balance Japanese trade and investment.

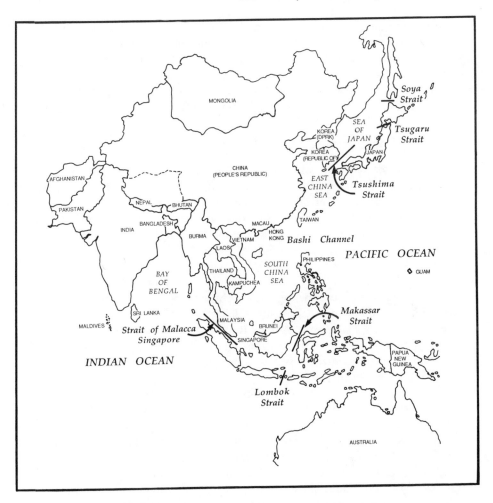

Figure 1-1. Straits in East and Southeast Asia

Southeast Asia is the indispensable back door to the Persian Gulf. If political considerations precluded the use of European transit points to the Middle East, U.S. forces could still be airlifted and supplied from the Philippines and Diego Garcia.[12] Unimpeded transit through the straits of Malacca, Sunda, and Lombok are essential to ensure the rapid deployment of U.S. forces to the southern tier.

U.S. officials believe that the Soviet Union is intent on establishing a "potential choking grip" on Southeast Asian SLOCs through their air and naval deployments at Cam Ranh Bay.[13] Thus one of Washington's security policy goals for the region is to create an ASEAN-China united front against the Soviet

Union and its ally, Vietnam. An effect of this policy, however, has been to reinforce the stalemate over the future of Cambodia. By backing China and encouraging the maintenance of a hard line in ASEAN, the United States hopes to solidify the strategic alignment in Southeast Asia it finds useful in its broader anti-Soviet strategy. This is an important explanation for the relatively low level of U.S. interest in resolving the Cambodian conflict.

A Closer Look at U.S. SLOC Policy

It is difficult to overemphasize the importance of maintaining freedom of the seas in the U.S. global policy. Because capitalist countries must trade to prosper, unimpeded ocean traffic is crucial for market economies' security in the broadest meaning of that term. For example, in 1980 approximately $800 billion of global market economy trade moved by ships, compared with only $40 billion in trade from communist countries.[14]

The primary threat to Asian SLOCs is posed by Soviet submarines in the Northwest Pacific operating from Petropavlovsk. This threat is containable as Japan develops antisubmarine capabilities through the acquisition of P3Cs and surface units while coordinating surveillance with U.S. forces in Japan, the Philippines, and the Marianas. Annual Rim of the Pacific (RIMPAC) war game exercises demonstrate that Soviet submarines could be bottled up in the Sea of Okhotsk and the northern Sea of Japan in the first two or three months of a conventional war.[15]

The Reagan administration's maritime strategy focuses on the Northwest Pacific. It emphasizes the ability to move nuclear carrier battle groups into the northern Sea of Japan to contain the Soviet Pacific fleet in its home waters before it can transit straits and other choke points to the open ocean. A forward-deployed Seventh Fleet would presumably lead the Soviets to withdraw their nuclear-power ballistic missile-carrying and attack submarines to the Sea of Okhotsk for protection, thus reducing the Soviet threat to Asian SLOCs. Therefore the maritime strategy's proponents argue, forward-deployed U.S. forces improve the prospect for open SLOCs by reducing the probability of Soviet maritime dispersion through the region.[16]

Another major U.S. concern with respect to SLOC security is its submarine strategic deterrent.[17] The United States maintains that the invulnerability of SSBNs (the Polaris-Poseidon-Trident fleet) and hence their indispensable role in a second strike depends on their ability to pass through straits and sea-lanes submerged, unannounced, and undetected. In Southeast Asia, the Indonesian straits of Lombok and Ombai-Wetar are crucial for the passage of submerged U.S. submarines. Without unannounced submerged passage, these vessels would have to circumnavigate Australia or double back to the Timor Sea. The point is that neither superpower is willing to announce or request transit permission for its subsurface vessels.

The United States asserts that the navigational provisions of the Law of the Sea Convention (CLOS), though still not ratified by a sufficient number of states to become international law, is part of customary law and hence binding on all states. Washington refers to the provision that treats the oceans between straits as international waters. The irony here is that the United States is arguing for enforcement of the provision of a treaty that its government refuses to ratify on commercial grounds. That is, the United States wishes to benefit from the strategic provisions of the convention without having to abide by its economic provisions, which would create an international authority to regulate seabed exploitation.

So far the U.S. policy of not announcing the passage of its submarines has not elicited any official protests, but the potential for conflict remains. Thailand, Malaysia, and Indonesia claim 12-mile territorial seas, which in some places include straits used for international navigation. The Philippine archipelagic sea claim includes all its straits. By contrast, the United States does not recognize territorial sea claims more than 3 miles from shore and has stated the U.S. Navy will challenge any effort to enforce such claims.

On balance, however, it seems probable that the ASEAN states will tacitly accept the U.S. position. Freedom of navigation through their straits is essential for their own security and prosperity. If the Malacca Strait were interdicted, a majority of Indonesia's exports would be lost, and Japan would have to find alternative routes for 16 percent of its total energy supply. Singapore's economy would be shut down and Malaysia's seriously affected. Scenarios for the future portend massive increases in the flow of energy through the region. Liquefied natural gas (LNG) exports from Indonesia, Malaysia, and Australia could reach 1 trillion, 300 billion, and 800 billion cubic feet, respectively, by 1990.

Because the United States now deploys one carrier task force in the Indian Ocean–Persian Gulf, only two others are available for SLOC protection in the West Pacific. Moreover, the introduction of precision-guided munitions (PGMs), particularly cruise missiles, and the Soviets' SS-20 intermediate-range ballistic missile (IRBM) and TU-26 bomber make sea-lanes even more vulnerable since these constitute a Soviet long-range capability against ocean shipping. Once ships can be attacked from a distant location, the traditional convoy escort may no longer ensure safe passage. Additionally, it should be noted that one of the lessons of the 1982 Falklands War was that smaller nations, if supplied with sea-skimming missiles such as the Exocet, are capable of sinking large ships. If the Soviets or other suppliers provide such systems to Vietnam and/or North Korea, then U.S. forces could be attacked by a Soviet ally rather than the USSR itself. While the Seventh Fleet possesses ample antisubmarine warfare (ASW) for self-defense, it has precious little for merchant convoys. Washington argues the necessity for Japan to expand its maritime capabilities in order to fill the gap between U.S. Persian Gulf commitments and the need to protect the sea-lanes in the western Pacific. Notice the parallel between Japan's commitment to develop the capacity for sea-lane protection within a thousand miles of Honshu and the comparable range of the Vladivostok-based TU-26.

The credibility of Japan's naval buildup is underscored in a 1983 Japanese defense white paper that expresses the intention to defend foreign flag shipping en route to or leaving Japan. The paper implies that under the Japan-U.S. Treaty, Japanese forces could defend U.S. vessels if the former were serving in an escort capacity. A Japan Self Defense Agency top official has interpreted action of this kind to be a legitimate component of SLOC protection. Moreover, if U.S. naval forces were fighting to protect Japan, the self-defense forces would help repel attacks on U.S. forces as part of their joint operations.[18]

The United States maintains significant geopolitical advantages over the Soviet Union in the Pacific. Because Soviet ships must enter and exit from their home waters in the Sea of Okhotsk through one or more narrow straits, submersible vessels can be detected through sonar surveillance systems (SOSUS) of high resolution. P-3 Orions are the primary airborne acoustical surveillance and submarine attack system. They are equipped with mines, depth bombs, torpedoes, and, more recently, the Harpoon missile. The U.S. Navy possesses 524 Orions, which are capable of flying 2,500 kilometers or for four hours and returning to base. Australia, New Zealand, and Japan maintain and are adding P-3s to their inventories.[19] Passive acoustical devices are anchored to the ocean floors in strategic straits or towed by surface ships.[20]

The newest major weapons system being added to U.S. forces in the Pacific is both conventional and nuclear-tipped cruise missiles. With a range of 1,500 miles and the ability to carry a 200-kiloton warhead, these Tomahawk weapons are, in effect, strategic. Because it is impossible to distinguish conventional from nuclear missiles, the introduction of the Tomahawk complicates the task of reaching arms control agreements. By January 1984, flight test successes of the missile were reported to be close to 90 percent; that is, the Tomahawk was delivering its warhead to within 300 feet of the target. By the early 1990s, the U.S. Navy plans to equip 190 of its ships and submarines with 758 cruise missiles.[21] Moreover, the air force plans to deploy 1,763 of the first-generation air version of the cruise missile. Each B-52 and follow-on B-1 is planned to carry twenty air-launched cruise missiles.[22]

The Modernization of U.S. Forces in Asia

Since the late 1970s, the United States has undertaken a number of steps to improve its naval capabilities in the Pacific. Major additions to the Seventh Fleet include a new Nimitz-class carrier, the *Carl Vinson,* replete with the latest model F-18A aircraft, the cruise missile–refurbished battleship *New Jersey,* and its recommissioned sister, the *Missouri.* Three nuclear-powered guided missile cruisers, more Spruance-class destroyers, Perry-class guided missile frigates, the introduction of the Trident sea-launched ballistic missile (SLBM) submarine, three Ohio-class submarines, and more Los Angeles–class nuclear-powered attack submarines have vastly improved fleet capacity in the early 1980s. Additions planned up to the early 1990s include Aegis-equipped guided missile cruisers, two additional nuclear-powered aircraft carriers, and the Arleigh Burke–class guided missile destroyer.[23]

By most measurements of military power, the United States is comfortably ahead of the Soviet Union in Asia. Although the Soviets have a large number of aircraft, U.S. naval and air systems combined provide greater power projection from sea to land and a greater ability to sustain military action over more territory and for longer periods (table 1–1 and figure 1–2). The U.S. emphasis on large surface combatants reflects a sea-control mission, while the smaller number of support vessels is due to the extensive range of shore facilities available to the United States along the Asian littoral. A carrier battle group is configured to maintain control of the air and sea spaces within a 600-mile circumference of its capital ships.

Although the relatively small number of army personnel and tactical aircraft illustrates only a limited U.S. commitment to engage in Asian land wars, the larger number of U.S. amphibious forces reflects the emphasis on power projection and rapid deployment. This goal is also seen in the Defense Department's 1986 military budget request for the purchase of new C-5B and KC-10A cargo planes for the air force and more escort and supply ships for the navy.[24]

The Reagan administration's naval strategy, built around Nimitz-class carrier battle groups, is controversial. Based on the strategic concepts of former Secretary of the Navy John Lehman, the United States sees force combinations as the centerpiece of a horizontal escalation strategy—that is, a capability and willingness to attack the Soviets in locations of U.S. choice, not necessarily at the point of a Soviet provocation. Former Secretary Lehman spoke of sending carrier battle groups to take on the Soviet Pacific fleet in Vladivostok, thus bottling up the fleet in its home port. Most naval strategists, however, view this as a risk-laden endeavor doomed to failure if ever attempted.[25] Large carriers, despite the presence of escorts for protection against submarines, are vulnerable to both land-based missiles and aircraft. (In the Falklands, an Exocet missile sank the British cruiser *Sheffield*.)

Nevertheless, the navy claims that its battle groups have successfully eluded Soviet forces during covert exercises in the North Pacific. At an August 1987 Naval Postgraduate School conference, "The Navy in the Pacific," a spokesman for the commander in chief of the Pacific fleet stated that aircraft from the *Carl Vinson* could have struck targets in Siberia during an August 1986 covert exercise in the Aleutians—maneuvers conducted without Soviet surveillance. The point being made by the navy officer was that carrier battle groups are less vulnerable and more able to evade pursuers than critics contend.

Table 1-1
U.S. Forces in the Pacific, 1985

Region	Ground Forces	Air Forces	Marine Air	Naval Forces
Western Pacific	South Korea: 1 div (155 tks) Japan/Okinawa: 1 MAF (34 tks) 1 MAU 1 bn landing team	South Korea: 48 F-16 ftrs 36 F-4E ftrs 18 A-10 ftrs Okinawa: 72 F-15C/D ftrs 18 RF-4C ftrs Philippines: 48 F-4E/G ftrs	59 ftr and attack aircraft, incl F-4, A-4, A-6 and AV-8B	2 attack carriers 35 cruisers, destroyers, and frigates 13 attack subs (11 nuclear powered) 7 amphibious ships 36 P3C maritime patrol aircraft
Central and Eastern Pacific	Hawaii: 1 div less 1 bde (13 tks) 1 marine bde California: 1 marine div (143 tks)		127 ftr and attack aircraft California: 94 Hawaii: 24 Arizona: 9	4 attack carriers 51 cruisers, destroyers, and frigates 33 attack subs (31 nuclear powered) 24 amphibious ships 72 P3C maritime patrol aircraft 2 Trident SSBN

Source: International Institute for Strategic Studies, *The Military Balance, 1984–1985* (London: IISS, 1985).

Note: div = division; bde = brigade; bn = battalion; MAF = marine amphibious force; MAU = marine amphibious unit; tk = tank; ftr = fighter; sub = submarine.

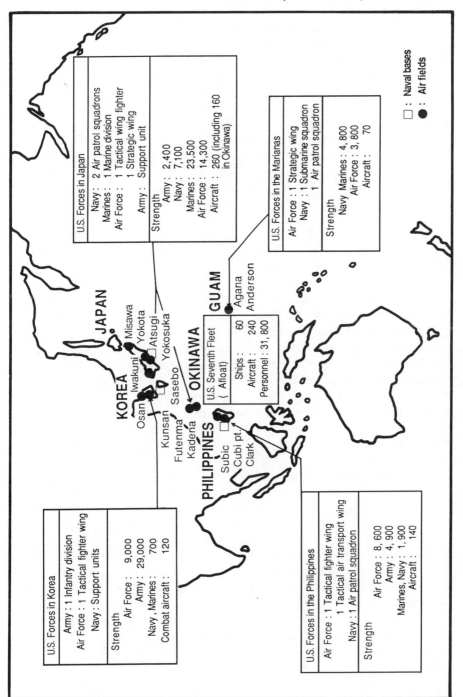

U.S. Forces in Japan

Navy :	2 Air patrol squadrons
Marines :	1 Marine division
Air Force :	1 Tactical wing fighter
	1 Strategic wing
Army :	Support unit

Strength
Army :	2,400
Navy :	7,100
Marines :	23,500
Air Force :	14,300
Aircraft :	260 (including 160 in Okinawa)

U.S. Forces in the Marianas

Air Force :	1 Strategic wing
Navy :	1 Submarine squadron
	1 Air patrol squadron

Strength
Navy Marines :	4, 800
Air Force :	3, 800
Aircraft :	70

U.S. Seventh Fleet (Afloat)

Ships :	60
Aircraft :	240
Personnel :	31, 800

U.S. Forces in Korea

Army :	1 Infantry division
Air Force :	1 Tactical fighter wing
Navy :	Support units

Strength
Air Force :	9,000
Army :	29,000
Navy , Marines :	700
Combat aircraft :	120

U.S. Forces in the Philippines

Air Force :	1 Tactical fighter wing
	1 Tactical air transport wing
Navy :	1 Air patrol squadron

Strength
Air Force :	8, 600
Army :	4, 900
Marines, Navy :	1, 900
Aircraft :	140

□ : Naval bases
● : Air fields

JAPAN
Misawa
Yokota
Atsugi
Iwakuni
Yokosuka
KOREA
Osan
Sasebo
OKINAWA
Kunsan
Futenma
Kadena
PHILIPPINES
Subic
Cubi pt.
Clark
GUAM
Agana
Anderson

Figure 1–2. U.S. Military Deployment in the Western Pacific

Experts inside and outside the navy say that the strategy of carriers going on the offensive within range of the Soviet shoreline would require twenty-four carriers, or thirty-two or thirty-five, not fifteen. George W.S. Kuhn argues in a report published by the Heritage Foundation that a shortage of funding for other ships in each battle group required to protect the fifteen carriers is a serious problem. According to the strategy, the carriers require sixty-one new escorts by 1992, and only twenty-five are planned through 1991. The navy already has some degree of strategy-forces mismatch.[26]

Moreover, at a time when public opinion is cooling toward an unlimited defense budget, the navy's big-carrier building program could be in trouble. Each new Nimitz-class vessel cost $3.3 billion in 1984. A ninety-plane complement would add another $3.8 billion. Because the carrier is a high-value target, defended by aircraft, cruisers, destroyers, frigates, and attack submarines, a new carrier task force as a whole costs approximately $20 billion. Yet the navy plans to have fifteen task forces by 1990.[27]

Naval strategists dispute Secretary Lehman's concept of using carrier task groups to attack Soviet bases in the event of a major war, as distinct from keeping the groups adjacent to international choke points where they can both protect SLOCs and interdict Soviet combatants. The Lehman strategy would place U.S. carriers within F-14 range of Vladivostok. The problem with such a position is that they would also be within range of hundreds of Soviet Backfire and TU-26 bombers in addition to the bulk of the Pacific fleet's attack submarines. The carriers would be in waters where the Soviet fleet is strongest. Furthermore, the Soviets outnumber the Americans three to one in submarine strength, the U.S. price for investing in carrier task forces. Submarines are hard to defend against in large numbers. They can penetrate a target area and leave with great rapidity. (Again recalling the 1982 Falklands War, the British fleet could not locate a noisy ten-year-old diesel submarine that managed to penetrate fleet ASW defenses, release several torpedoes, and escape.)

A U.S. carrier force would carry a complement of thirty-five F-14s armed with two missiles each, but that would hardly be sufficient against, say, a 300-plane attack group from a standoff position of 200 miles. A last defense for a carrier task group under attack would be the newly developed Aegis guided-missile cruiser, which is joining the Seventh Fleet over the next several years. The Aegis computer system can track over 200 incoming missiles and direct surface-to-air missiles (SAMs) to destroy them. However, Aegis test results have been less impressive against target drones. A major problem is the system's inability to distinguish between friend and foe when U.S. and Soviet aircraft are engaged in battle. Additionally, the Aegis is so electronically noisy that its detection and guidance systems would actually assist attackers in locating the carrier task force.

Rather than deploying U.S. carrier task groups to attack the Soviets in their own backyard, Admiral Stansfield Turner recommends a strategy of attrition by which U.S. forces monitor the choke points from the Seas of Okhotsk and Japan and subsequently destroy elements of the Soviet fleet venturing forth through mines, submarines, and carrier-based aircraft. The carriers could also be used in a show of force, that is, as coercive diplomacy, against third world adversaries.[28]

Turner argues, further, that the Reagan administration's emphasis on large carriers and high-performance aircraft may be obsolete. Rather, speed and maneuverability should be manufactured into the missiles they launch. Thus lighter and less costly planes can be carried on lighter and less costly platforms. Since these smaller, lighter aircraft carriers would be considerably cheaper than their Nimitz-class counterparts, more of them could be produced, improving the overall U.S. Navy presence and deployment flexibility. Within ten years, the bomb will be replaced by PGMs, which are fired from planes far from the target area. This development will also reduce the need for expensive high-performance bombers.

Turner's conclusion is that the U.S. Navy is building forces to fight the wars of twenty to thirty years ago. He would establish the following order of priority:

1. Larger numbers of amphibious ships deployed in brigade-sized units so that U.S. Marines and Army forces could be moved rapidly to trouble spots without the need for permanent overseas bases.
2. Many small aircraft carriers with light aircraft and PGMs for sea control.
3. Cruise missiles on submarines and surface ships.
4. Submarine and surface ship escorts for joint defense and sea control.
5. Submarines, mines, and patrol aircraft for attrition operations.[29]

Turner's proposals would move the navy away from its current efforts to carve out a bigger role for force projection against the Soviet's homeland and return it to the more traditional yet highly relevant mission of sea control, more relevant for third world friends and foes. These apparently more mundane activities do not appeal to Secretary Lehman and most of the navy's top strategists, however, who prefer to compete with the air force in strategic warfare.

U.S. forces can concentrate tremendous firepower in the Sea of Japan where most of the Soviet Pacific fleet could be bottled up with limited maneuvering room. A combination of the *Enterprise* and *Midway* carrier groups with air force units from Japan, Korea, and the Philippines can bring 400 aircraft to bear in a region beyond the range of Soviet tactical fighter support. Both big carriers have exercised off the South Korean coast in the annual Team Spirit maneuvers. Regular deployment of a Seventh Fleet carrier in the Sea of Japan and exercises near Hokkaido bring U.S. firepower virtually within hailing distance of Soviet forces in southern Sakhalin.[30]

A serious limitation on the U.S. ability to intervene in crisis situations lies not with seapower but a limited airlift ability, a crucial prerequisite for effective rapid deployment. In 1983, the airforce transport complement of 218 C-130s, 70 C-5s, and 404 C-141s provided a total payload of 24,415 tons. Thus, the maximum airlift across the Pacific from the continental United States would be no more than 2,000 tons per day. This means that it would take more than a week to airlift an armored division to South Korea.[31] Although the air force has arrangements to co-opt civilian air transport planes, it is unlikely these would be used except in a crisis situation of global proportions.

Shifting from Northeast to Southeast Asia, the importance of U.S. facilities in the Philippines (or possible alternative locations in the future) is based on geography. Southeast Asian archipelagoes serve as strategic barriers between the Indian Ocean–Persian Gulf and Japan and Korea to the north. U.S. forces positioned in Southeast Asia can project power in either direction. Moreover, U.S. bases in the Philippines are close to Soviet facilities in Vietnam. Within four flying hours or five sea days, U.S. forces can reach Korea, Japan, Singapore, Guam, or Australia. In double the time, they can reach Diego Garcia in the center of the Indian Ocean. The Pentagon views the Philippine bases as the centerpiece of its forward deployment–containment strategy going back to the Philippine Bases Agreement of 1947.

After the Iranian revolution in 1978 and the Soviet invasion of Afghanistan in late 1979, the Carter administration increased the U.S. naval presence in the Indian Ocean and expanded the capacity of Diego Garcia for prepositioned supplies to accommodate elements of the Central Command (then known as the Rapid Deployment Force). By 1985, additional facilities had become available to the United States in Oman and Somalia. Nevertheless, both Clark and Subic in the Philippines remain essential for resupply of the Diego Garcia depots and the carrier task forces near the Persian Gulf. Additionally the two Philippine bases also house communications equipment to support and coordinate these forces.

The combination of Clark Air Field and Subic Bay naval complex forms the finest naval and air support facilities outside the United States. The former provides airlift capability for the Pacific and Indian oceans, contains a highly sophisticated air combat training facility at Crow Valley, and is also a major logistic center where aircraft are not only maintained but also rebuilt. Clark can routinely handle 3,500 tons of cargo and 22,000 passengers daily. Subic Bay's three major wharves can berth all ship types in the U.S. Navy, including its largest carriers. Its ship repair facility performs 65 percent of all Seventh Fleet repairs. Of equal importance are its labor costs, the lowest in the Pacific.[32] Also significant is Radford Field at Cubi Point, where carrier-based aircraft can practice while their mother ships are being refitted and/or resupplied.

Reagan administration spokesmen defend the maintenance of a U.S. presence at the Philippine bases by arguing that they are an important manifestation of

U.S. power and commitment in East Asia at a time when the USSR is increasing its own regional air and naval deployments. Because of the growth of Soviet capabilities, the ASEAN states openly and China privately urge the U.S. military to maintain a significant air and maritime regional profile.[33] (It should be noted, however, that growing Philippine opposition to the bases may affect their long-term political viability.)

While ASEAN remains generally supportive of U.S. facilities in Southeast Asia, there is some concern that if these bases are used to supply U.S. fighting forces in the Middle East, particularly on behalf of Israel, there could be an Islamic backlash toward both Indonesia and Malaysia that could jeopardize their relations with other Muslim states and exacerbate difficulties already extant in both countries between government and believers.[34]

Burden Sharing

Because of the vast sea areas patrolled by the U.S. Pacific Command from the western Pacific to the Persian Gulf, Washington hopes increasingly to share surveillance responsibilities with allied and friendly states. To encourage burden sharing, particularly with Japan initially, the United States has split its Asian responsibilities into two parts. As summarized by Assistant Secretary of Defense Francis J. West, Jr., in 1982:

> Mr. Weinberger stated that in the Northwest Pacific the United States would provide the nuclear umbrella, offensive projection forces as necessary, and assist the Republic of Korea in the defense of its territory. In the Southwest and Indian Oceans the U.S. would provide the nuclear umbrella, projection forces as necessary, and sealane protection.[35]

By dividing its security role into two distinct regional responsibilities, the United States is encouraging Japan to increase its own capabilities for air and sea control in the northwestern Pacific. Implicitly the Weinberger statement excluded a U.S. commitment to provide SLOC protection in the northwestern Pacific, expecting Japan to assume that responsibility as part of an international division of labor.

The U.S. emphasis on burden sharing is the result of some hard rethinking of the relationship between U.S. commitments in Europe, East Asia, the Persian Gulf, and the Western Hemisphere and the clearly inadequate capability of the United States to fight major engagements in two or more theaters simultaneously. In reviewing the Vietnam War period, military analysts conclude that, though regarded at the time as a half-war, in fact the bulk of U.S. first-line ground and tactical air forces were committed to Vietnam. Had the USSR invaded Europe in 1968, as some feared they might after their invasion of Czechoslovakia, the United States would have been unable to meet its NATO obligations.[36] Jeffrey Record argues that despite real increases in defense spending of over 40 percent between 1980 and 1984, very little military power has been added. There has been no increment to the 19 army and marine corps divisions, and fighter squadrons have increased by only one, from 164 to 165. The exception to this general rule is the navy, which may barely achieve its 600-ship goal by 1990. Nevertheless, the navy is configured around a small number of carrier and battleship groups whose vulnerability in combat is of concern to many specialists.[37] Hence arises the necessity—if commitments are not to be reduced in the face of rising Soviet global capabilities—to rely on greater allied self-defense efforts. Indeed, in the long run, the Reagan administration has stated a hope that the Republic of Korea and Japan would jointly cooperate to bottle the Soviet fleet in the Sea of Japan through coordinated mining of the straits within their territorial waters.[38]

Finally, it should be noted that the United States also foresees a cooperative strategic role for China in helping to contain a growing Soviet Asian military capability despite objections raised by the ASEAN states against U.S. assistance for PRC military modernization. In 1985, Pentagon experts discussed navy-to-navy technological assistance. The Chinese expressed interest in obtaining ship-to-air missiles, radar, and sonar equipment for ASW. They are also looking at gas turbine engines for both new ships and to refurbish existing vessels. While the United States is reported to be willing to sell ASW equipment, there is some hesitation on technological grounds to provide the highly sophisticated gas turbine equipment.[39] Interestingly ASEAN objections to U.S. military aid are focused less on big-ticket items destined for the navy and air force than they are on infantry-type weapons, which could be transferred to insurgents active in Southeast Asia. There is a policy disjunction between the U.S. view of China as a key link in a broad Asian anti-Soviet coalition and a Southeast Asian perspective that sees the PRC more as a future security problem than a partner once the country modernizes.

In sum, while burden sharing has become a major goal of U.S. security policy in Asia, the Reagan administration armed forces buildup undercuts the immediacy of this goal for friendly states experiencing their own economic difficulties. They point to the Seventh and Third fleets with a total of six aircraft carriers, each with eighty-five fighters, ASW planes, fighter bombers, and helicopters. By contrast, the Soviet pacific fleet in 1986 had only two far smaller Kiev-class ships, each of which carries thirty-two helicopters and swing-wing fighters. They conclude that burden sharing may be financially attractive to Washington, but there is little strategic necessity for it in the Asia-Pacific region in the late 1980s.

2
The New Face of Soviet Power in Asia

In the classic treatise from ancient India on strategy, the *Arthasastra*, international balance occurred when countries adjacent to one another were aligned with mutual adversaries. Thus no single country could move with impunity against a neighbor. In many ways, the current combination of East-East and East-West conflicts in Asia fulfills Kautilya's principle. The Soviet bloc is encircled by the North Atlantic Treaty Organization (NATO) on the west and China, Japan, and the United States on the east. China abuts the USSR on the north and the Soviets' ally, Vietnam, on the south. Vietnam faces China on the north and the ASEAN states to the south, backed by the United States and Japan. Moreover, all of the USSR's Asian adversaries are developing mutual trade and investment ties sufficient to create a new sense of regional community, which excludes Moscow. To make matters worse, China has abandoned Mao's policy of autarky, which prevailed from the 1950s to the 1970s, and embarked on a foreign investment and export growth program that promises to integrate the PRC into the Pacific Basin economy. Although three-quarters of the Soviet Union lies in Asia and 30 percent (80 million) of its people live in the USSR's Asia territory, there are, nevertheless, few linkages to the rest of the region.

The best explanation for Soviet population movement to its Asian region has been not economics but security—the desire to protect vast stretches of inhospitable terrain from potential predators, recalling perhaps the 1919 Siberian intervention.

Any Soviet expansionist ambitions in Asia must confront China and Japan, now friendly if not allied countries, backed by the military and economic strength of the United States. The emergence of a Sino-Japan-U.S. coalition has haunted Soviet policymakers since the 1978 Sino-Japanese normalization treaty. A major Soviet strategic goal has been, therefore, to disrupt this coalition through both positive incentives such as trade and investment opportunities (Japan and Siberia) and military intimidation (threats to target Japan in the event of a Soviet-U.S. confrontation and the deployment of over fifty divisions along the Sino-Soviet border).

Interestingly the Soviets have been loathe to employ positive political incentives in dealing with adversaries. A case in point is the territorial dispute with Japan over the ownership of the southern Kuril islands. The return of these islands to Japan would go a long way to ameliorate Japanese bitterness toward the USSR, would undoubtedly elicit Japanese investment on favorable terms for Siberian development, and could even create strains in Japanese-U.S. relations by diminishing the Japanese view of the Soviets as a growing challenge to Japanese security. Despite these potential benefits, however, there is no indication that the Soviets have ever seriously contemplated a change of policy on the southern Kurils. Although strategic considerations account for some of this intransigence—the protection of SSBNs in the Sea of Okhotsk—domestic Soviet politics is the primary deterrent. Any Soviet leader responsible for such a concession of "primordial Russian soil" would create an ideal weapon for politically ambitious elements in the ruling apparatus to use against him. John Stephan explains,

> The Kuriles were "liberated" in 1945 at the cost of Soviet blood and thus fall into the category of the fruits of wartime sacrifices. It would take a bold member of the Politburo to tamper with a situation so intimately bound up with the Great Patriotic War, which in Russian minds has an immediacy and emotional charge far stronger than American . . . collective memories of World War II.[1]

Because of a limited ability to use political persuasion and the general lack of appeal in its economic blandishments, Soviet Asian policies appear disproportionately power oriented. They include:

The development of Siberia's natural resources and establishment of its East Asian territories as a power base from which to project force into Northeast Asia and the North and West Pacific.

The establishment of a strong naval presence in East Asia to control the vital straits near Japan and Korea and to project and protect that presence in the Sea of Okhotsk and Sea of Japan.

Hopes for neutralizing Japan politically. Using its Pacific fleet to intimidate Japan by threatening its SLOCs, the Soviets hope to achieve a more accommodating government in Tokyo and to drive a wedge between Japan and the United States.

The isolation, encirclement, and containment of China while keeping it from becoming a dangerous adversary in the course of its modernization. Alternatively, the Gorbachev regime could follow a more positive policy toward the PRC in the hope of causing it to delay military modernization.

The creation of a new regional military presence in Southeast Asia through the mentorship of a pro-Soviet, Vietnam-led Indochina; at the same time, and contradictory to this, the prevention of security arrangements among ASEAN, the United States, Japan, and possibly even China. A strong Soviet naval presence in Southeast Asia would enable the Soviets to protect their own SLOCs and possibly threaten to interdict the Strait of Malacca and other strategic points in the region that lead into the Indian Ocean.

The projection of a dual, though somewhat mutually contradictory, image of itself as both a revolutionary society and developmental model to the Third World and a formidable superpower dedicated to the orderly advancement of interstate relations and regional stability.[2] While proclaiming peaceful intent, the Soviets continue their Asia military buildup, occupy one nation with armed force, and support an ally's military suppression of another. The net effect is hardly reassuring to those countries the Soviets hope to convince of their desires for regional tranquility.

At minimum, the Soviets are committed to achieving equality with the United States in Asia, which in practical terms means participation in all regional security issues. It is in the hope of buying in to Asian security discussions that the Soviets have announced their plans for zones of peace in the Indian Ocean and Southeast Asia. The USSR is troubled by an inability to devise a doctrine for East Asia comparable to the Pacific community concept, which potentially links the market-oriented economies of the region. Gorbachev has publicized a refurbished version of the old Asian collective security proposal, originally broached by Brezhnev in 1969. In a May 1985 dinner address to visiting Indian Prime Minister Rajiv Gandhi, the Soviet general secretary proposed an all-Asian security conference, presumably to capitalize on the USSR's limited rapprochement with China and its new political position in Indochina. Gorbachev seems to believe that he can apply the same concept he has proposed for European security to Asia, despite vast differences between the two regions.[3]

Beginning with his July 1986 Vladivostok speech and continuing with an extensive interview on its first anniversary with the Indonesian newspaper *Merdeka,* Gorbachev outlined a Soviet Asian policy that cast the USSR in the role of peacemaker. *Izvestiya* summed up Soviet goals for the region in a July 28, 1987, review of Moscow's worldwide policies:

> Broad opportunities for solving the region's problems are opened up by the Mongolian People's Republic's proposals on the conclusion of a convention on nonaggression and the nonuse of force by the Asian and Pacific states, and by the DPRK's [Democratic People's Republic of Korea] proposals on the withdrawal of U.S. troops from South Korea, the country's unification on the basis of peaceful, democratic principles without outside interference, the replacement of the truce agreement with a peace agreement and the drafting of a nonaggression declaration between North and South. The efforts made by Vietnam, Laos, and Cambodia to normalize the situation in their region and the course aimed at establishing good-neighborly relations, trust, and

cooperation with the ASEAN countries, the creation of a zone of peace in Southeast Asia, and the normalization of relations with China on the basis of the principles of peaceful coexistence proceed in the same direction. The struggle of the socialist and nonaligned countries for the speediest convening of an international conference on the transformation of the Indian Ocean basin into a zone of peace is an important avenue of efforts to consolidate peace in Asia.

Gorbachev's *Merdeka* interview stressed Soviet willingness to accommodate both Asian and U.S. nuclear concerns by agreeing to eliminate SS-20s in Asia without insisting on the removal of U.S. warheads in Korea, the Philippines, and Diego Garcia. He also called on the United States to agree to a freeze in nuclear-capable aircraft in the North Pacific and to negotiate a naval separation whereby neither side would approach the coastline of the other within range of their on-board nuclear systems.[4] In effect, the general secretary was hoping to thwart the maritime strategy by appealing to the nuclear fears of Asian allies of the United States. A limitation on naval maneuvers would remove the Seventh Fleet from the Sea of Okhotsk and northern Sea of Japan, which shelter Russian SSBNs.

The Gorbachev idea is the culmination of several different initiatives that portray the Soviet Union as Asian peacemaker. They include a Mongolian proposal for an Asian mutual nonaggression pact, the Indochinese states' call for establishing good-neighborly relations with ASEAN, the Indian Ocean peace zone proposal, and the South Pacific Forum call for a nonnuclear zone. Moscow's promotion of peace is contrasted with U.S. warmongering as embodied in the Reagan administration's "neoglobalism," by which the United States provides "open support for all counterrevolutionary and all opposition forces that are waging a struggle against lawful regimes wherever they might be."[5]

The Soviets portray the Pacific community as an effort to create "a closed regional grouping . . . another militarist bloc," much like NATO. What the Soviets appear to fear most is exclusion from a broader community of Asian-Pacific states following export-oriented, market-based policies. The Soviets believe that the United States wants "to transform the economic structure under creation there into a type of platform or base for stepping up military preparations and military cooperation."[6]

Soviet officials visiting Southeast Asia in the spring of 1986 lashed out at the Pacific Basin community idea and warned that Moscow would oppose any moves to forge "closed economic groupings like the Pacific community." By contrast the Soviet Union would be willing to participate in an all-Asia security conference as a "great Pacific nation."[7]

Soviet Foreign Minister Eduard Shevardnadze made an extensive tour of six Asian-Pacific countries in March 1987, enthusiastically supporting ASEAN's call for a Southeast Asian nuclear-free zone. Notably, however, neither

Shevardnadze nor Gorbachev has indicated any change in the Soviet policy of backing Hanoi's occupation of Cambodia. Better political relations with ASEAN are clearly not worth the risk of antagonizing Hanoi and jeopardizing Soviet access to Cam Ranh Bay.[8]

The Soviet Union has a long history of involvement in conflicts on its Asian periphery. It has fought the Japanese four times in this century. As Donald Zagoria has noted, if Japan had joined Germany in its 1941 attack on the Soviet Union instead of opting for a southern strategy that brought them into a direct confrontation with the United States, the Soviet Union undoubtedly would have been defeated in World War II.[9]

Soviet fear of vulnerability from its Asian sector is understandable. China—the only Asian state with nuclear weapons—is Moscow's most immediate perceived security problem. U.S. forces capable of both conventional and nuclear strikes on the Soviet homeland are based throughout the region and cruise the waters of the Sea of Japan and North Pacific. The country that is arguably Asia's most important, Japan, remains the staunchest U.S. ally outside NATO. Finally, the two most prominent Asian states, China and Japan, identify the USSR as an immediate military threat.[10]

Soviet commentators justify their own East Asian buildup as a counter-balance to U.S. forward-deployed systems. They express apprehension over the possibility of a massive U.S. preemptive strike employing a large portion of the 1,200 nuclear warheads the Soviets claim are available to the United States in the Pacific on carrier and land-based aircraft. Moreover, U.S. plans to deploy Tomahawk cruise missiles on Seventh Fleet submarines and surface vessels are viewed as a major blow to verifiable arm control agreements.[11] Thus the Soviets justify their own inexorable Pacific fleet expansion as necessary to attack the U.S. Seventh Fleet and Air Force, virtually all of whose platforms are capable of carrying cruise missiles.

Soviet analysts refer to the U.S. Navy's new Pacific doctrine of forward deployment from Japan in which U.S. battle groups configured around Nimitz-class aircraft carriers or refurbished battleships, such as the *New Jersey,* would steam into the Sea of Okhotsk to attack Soviet forces at their major bases. Equally threatening is the prospect of U.S. ships mining the Soya and Tsugaru straits, bottling up the Soviet Pacific fleet in the Sea of Okhotsk.[12]

Soviet fears about the vulnerability of its Pacific coast are understandable. Although Siberia offers great strategic depth for the dispersal of key military industries and land-based intercontinental ballistic missile (ICBM) silos, the Pacific seaboard as seen from Moscow is, nevertheless, a distant and vulnerable possession flanked by hostile states (figure 2–1). It dangles at the end of a long and tenuous line of communication, primarily the trans-Siberian railway, which could be interdicted in wartime from China, Japan, or U.S. naval ships and aircraft. The distance from Moscow to the Pacific coast is about 3,000 miles (roughly the distance between the United States and Europe across the Atlantic).

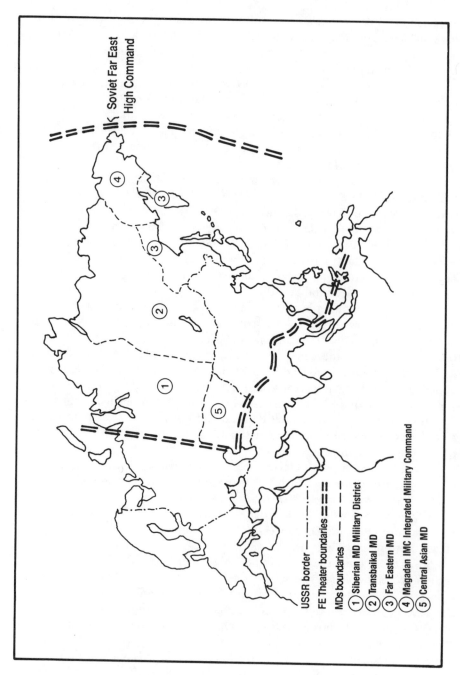

USSR border ———·—··—·

FE Theater boundaries === === ===

MDs boundaries — — —

(1) Siberian MD Military District
(2) Transbaikal MD
(3) Far Eastern MD
(4) Magadan IMC Integrated Military Command
(5) Central Asian MD

Soviet Far East
High Command

Figure 2–1. Soviet Far East Theater of War: Present Boundaries

In recent years, Siberia has received a quarter of the Soviet Union's capital investments, though it has only 10 percent of the country's population. Growing dependence on Siberian resources and the importance of Vladivostok and Petropavlovsk as bases for the Pacific fleet and submarine deterrent led the high command to establish a wartime Far East theater command. This integrates Soviet Asian regions—including the adjoining Pacific Ocean area—militarily and gives it considerable operational autonomy in the event of war. Commensurate with its increased status, Soviet forces in the region have been provided with some of the most modern weapons in the Soviet inventory, including Delta-class SSBNs, Kiev-class very short takeoff and landing (VSTOL) aircraft carriers, a large amphibious ship, the *Ivan Rogov,* MiG-25s, Tu-22M Backfire bombers, and about 135 SS-20 mobile IRBMs, which carry 3 warheads and have a circular error probability (CEP) of within 400 meters.[13] With a 5,000-kilometer range, these missiles could strike northern Thailand, as well as U.S. bases in the Philippines. (Under the December 1987 U.S.–USSR Intermediate Nuclear Force Treaty, however, the Soviets have agreed to remove their SS-20s from their Asian territory as well as from the western Soviet Union.)

Soviet Pacific Forces

Although Soviet ground forces in East Asia more than doubled between 1965 and the early 1980s (from 150,000 to about 435,000), only half of these approximately fifty divisions are considered combat ready. Most are motorized rifle forces with high mobility and good air defense capabilities; and, with the exception of the troops deployed on Sakhalin, Kamchatka, and the Kuril islands, all are oriented toward China. By the mid-1980s, the Soviets had increased their forces to 10,000 in the southern Kurils adjacent to Japan.[14]

The Soviet Pacific fleet, the largest in its navy, has 2 of its 4 Kiev-class ASW carriers and 84 major surface combatants. Of the 130 submarines in the Pacific fleet, 31 are strategic and the remainder attack. Half are nuclear powered. The latter Yankee-class boats patrol all the way to waters off the U.S. West Coast. The Soviets are also estimated to have over 700 sea-launched cruise missiles, an undetermined number of them in the Pacific fleet inventory. The heavy emphasis on attack submarines reflects the missions of destroying U.S. SSBNs, protecting Soviet SSBNs, and penetrating the formidable surface capabilities of Seventh Fleet carrier battle groups.

The Pacific fleet's growth has been a long, gradual process, which can be traced back to the 1960s when Admiral Sergei Gorshkov convinced the Kremlin leadership that advances in nuclear weapons technology required that the Soviets extend their defensive perimeter through sea power against U.S. submarines and carriers (figure 2–2). Between 1964 and the early 1980s, Soviet out-of-coastal area operations grew from 4,000 ship days to 60,000.[16] Moreover, Gorshkov strongly argued that the navy had a peacetime mission to further Soviet foreign policy, including assistance to national liberation movements and deterring "imperialist powers" from threatening "progressive" regimes. These goals implied the creation of force projection and maritime logistics capabilities.[17] By supplying arms and advisers and showing the flag, the Soviets hoped to create dependency relationships in some third world states sufficient to support the USSR diplomatically (India), deny military access to its adversaries, and even accept Soviet requests for military facilities (Vietnam).

Normally a navy projects power in war in three ways: by denying the enemy access to and use of a particular sea area; by controlling a sea area so that its own ships have safe passage; and by using naval assets to conquer or devastate a particular onshore area. The Soviet Pacific fleet, with its emphasis on submarines and land-based aviation, has the ability to accomplish the first task in the Sea of Okhotsk where its SSBNs are located. It is also developing the second capability as it forward deploys elements of the fleet in the South China Sea and Indian Ocean. There is no indication, however, that the Soviets have sufficient naval capacity to attack and occupy territory with amphibious forces far from their home bases. Indeed the absence of sea-based naval aviation and sufficient antiaircraft capability on shipboard is a severe limiting factor in the survivability of forward-deployed units. A second major limitation is the absence of a logistics capability for maritime resupply in the event of war. Only recently, with the introduction of Kirov-class cruisers, have Soviet warships been built with major weapons systems reloads.[18] In all probability, these forward-deployed units are deemed expendable in time of war. Their main missions appear to be political (showing the flag) and intelligence surveillance of U.S. deployments.

It should not be forgotten, however, that Soviet deployments in the South China Sea and Indian Ocean divert elements of the Seventh Fleet from its preferred strategy of containing Soviet forces near the Sea of Okhotsk. By forcing the U.S. Navy and Air Force to spread its assets over a wide range of the Pacific, the USSR can dilute the U.S. threat. On the other hand, because the Soviet Pacific fleet has also detached a South China Sea–Indian Ocean squadron, the USSR could not cover a two-war contingency in both the Sea of Japan and the southern SLOCs.

U.S. naval strategists such as Norman Polmar warn that the Soviets are now building mission-specialized warships to form multipurpose task forces—in short, an emulation of U.S. naval doctrine. When these task forces become operational in the 1990s, the group commander will have more varied capabilities to command and will be more independent of shore control.[19] The Kirov's appearance in 1980 may be the first of this new kind of surface ship for the Soviet navy. Equipped with the long-range SS-N-19 antiship missiles,

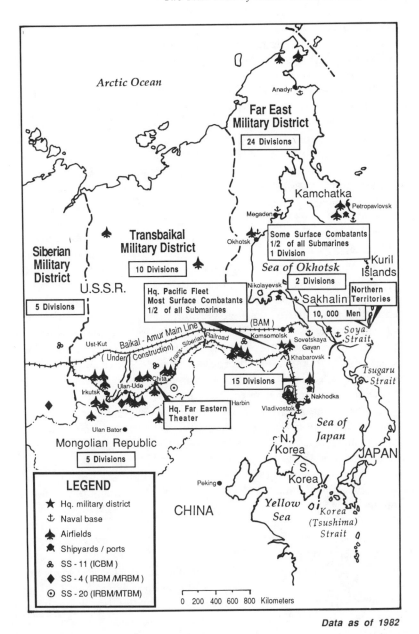

Data as of 1982

Sources: John M. Collins, *U.S.-Soviet Military Balance: Concepts and Capabilities, 1960–1980* (Washington: McGraw-Hill, 1980), pp. 134, 356; *Asian Security 1982* (Tokyo: Research Institute for Peace and Security, 1982), p. 56.

Figure 2–2. Military Buildup in the Soviet Far East

Kirovs will probably join aircraft carriers to supplement their overall defensive systems.[20] The Pacific fleet received its first Kirov cruiser, *Frunze,* in late 1985. Notable is the prospect of task groups consisting of Kiev-class VSTOL carriers protected by Kirov cruisers being used for tactical air operations in forward areas or, in combination with amphibious ships such as the *Ivan Rogov,* even being used for land attacks. (In April 1984, the *Ivan Rogov* was used for joint Soviet-Vietnamese amphibious exercises, the first time Soviet marines maneuvered away from their home territory.) In April 1985, the *Novorossiysk* led an eight-ship task force of Kara- and Kresta-class missile cruisers, as well as two destroyers, on a Pacific cruise—the first on a scale comparable to U.S. Seventh Fleet naval task forces. In August 1986, the *Frunze* led a surface-action group of several ships through the Soya Strait into the North Pacific. Armed with cruise missiles, these ships could be interpreted as a power projection force rather than defense of the homeland.[21]

The Soviet Pacific fleet numbers about 90 surface combatants plus some 700 submarines, auxiliaries, support ships, patrol boats, and landing craft.[22] The primary operational mission of the Pacific fleet is to protect Soviet SSBNs based at Petropavlovsk in Kamchatka and deployed in the Sea of Okhotsk. Much of the remainder of the fleet is committed to countering U.S. ballistic missile submarines and carrier groups in the Pacific and adjacent Asian seas. Only about 10 percent of the fleet's combatants and submarines are normally deployed outside home waters in the Northwest Pacific. They tend to form into two groups, each of 25 ships, one operating from Cam Ranh Bay to the Indian Ocean and the other in the North Pacific.[23] In East Asia, there is normally a patrol ship in the Korea Strait and a naval squadron of four submarines, two cruiser-destroyers, one landing craft, and ten auxiliary ships in the South China Sea. Naval reconnaisance, strike, and ASW aircraft have been deployed at Cam Ranh Bay since 1979, including Tu-95 Bear D and Bear F aircraft. Since November 1983, the USSR has stationed a squadron of TU-16 Badger bombers in Vietnam, half configured for antishipping roles with ASMs, the others for ASW and electronic countermeasure (ECM) missions. In late 1984, the Soviets also began to deploy MiG-23s at Cam Ranh Bay. The combination of MiGs and Badgers constitutes the only Soviet strike aircraft deployed outside the USSR in the Pacific region.

In the early 1980s, the Soviets built five dry docks at Cam Ranh Bay, as well as large-scale electronic facilities to monitor Chinese and U.S. military communications and to communicate with Pacific fleet headquarters in Vladivostok. The USSR has also expanded Kompongsom, the only port in Cambodia, and has constructed an airfield there.[24] In late 1983, as part of a worldwide naval exercise, Soviet forces in the South China Sea engaged in anti-SLOC and convoy operations. Submarine forces operating out of Cam

Table 2–1
Strength of the Soviet Pacific Fleet

Type	1973	1974	1975	1978	1979	1980	1981	1982	1983
SSBN	11	11	11	20	24	23	24	24	24
SSB	8	8	6	6	6	5	8	7	7
SSGN	14	13	12	19	17	17	18	20	20
SSG	10	9	9	6	6	6	4	4	4
SSN	4	7	6	16	13	14	15	19	22
SS	50	44	44	33	44	42	60	47	50
Aircraft carrier	—	—	—	—	1	1	1	1	1
Cruiser, guided missile	3	3	3	6	7	7	8	10	10
Destroyer, guided missile	12	10	9	15	10	11	10	10	10
Frigate, guided missile	—	—	—	—	7	6	7	10	10
Cruiser, light	3	3	3	3	3	3	4	4	4
Destroyer	23	18	18	13	17	15	11	8	8
Frigate	32	27	25	36	49	48	45	50	50

Source: Research Institute for Peace and Security, *Asian Security, 1984*, (Tokyo: RIPS, 1984) p. 65.
Note: After 1979, Kirak I and II are classified as frigate, guided missile.
SSBN = Nuclear Ballistic Missile Submarine
SSB = Ballistic Missile Submarine
SSGN = Nuclear Guided Missile Submarine
SSG = Guided Missile Submarine
SSN = Nuclear Attack Submarine
SS = Nonnuclear Attack Submarine

Ranh Bay were deployed into the Indian Ocean, reemphasizing the importance of this base.[25]

The Soviets station more than 3,000 combat aircraft in their four eastern military districts. Most consist of the latest-model MiG-25 Foxbat interceptors, MiG-23 Flogger fighters, SU-24 Fencer fighter bombers, and supersonic Tu-22M Backfire bombers. These new-generation aircraft far exceed the number of fighters in the combined U.S. Pacific Air Forces. Judging by the location of Soviet air bases and the range of most of the aircraft, their primary target is China. Nevertheless, the new systems provide a wider regional capability as well. The SU-24 fighter bomber, for example, has a combat radius of 1,600 kilometers, and the Backfires can be used for antiship warfare against the U.S. Seventh Fleet since they are equipped with AS-4 long-range ASMs. These Backfires can operate against U.S. naval forces as far away as the mid-Pacific and the Philippines without refueling. During September and October 1982, they were used for the first time in simulated air strikes against two U.S. carrier battle groups operating in the North Pacific.[26]

The Soviet Position in Northeast Asia

As a putative Pacific naval power, the Soviet Union faces several geographic constraints. Its major surface combatants are based in waters subject to interdiction by U.S. air power in Japan and Korea. Moreover, their movement from either the Sea of Okhotsk or the Sea of Japan to the open waters of the Pacific may be blocked at choke points in Japan and Korea. To offset these natural disadvantages, the Soviets have increased the number and capability of their forces on the four disputed islands of the southern Kurils. By the early 1980s, the previous small force of Soviet border troops was reinforced by a full-strength mechanized division of tanks, heavy artillery, and MI-24 assault helicopters. The islands aircraft were upgraded to MiG-23s, and Soviet airborne forces began to exercise on Etorofu, the largest of the islands.[27] While this force buildup could be interpreted as part of a defensive effort to make the Sea of Okhotsk a Soviet lake for the deployment of Delta SSBNs, Japanese defense planners must also consider the possibility of a Soviet attempt to seize northwestern Hokkaido in order to control the Soya Strait and prevent the isolation of its main naval bases at Vladivostok and Petropavlovsk. The Soviet refusal to discuss the possibility of returning the northern islands to Japan, now incorporated into the Sakhalin district of the USSR, must be understood as an integral part of the government's strategic policy for its Far East. Thus, for example, Soviet aircraft operating from the southern Kurils have sufficient range to prevent U.S. aircraft carriers from threatening Vladivostok and other mainland targets. Moreover, Soviet possession of Etorofu increases its own naval access to the Pacific since ships stationed in its deep harbor do not have to go through Japanese choke points.

The Soviets see the militarization of Northeast Asia as an inevitable development based on Japanese rearmament and "necessary" Soviet countermeasures. Tokyo's movement toward the creation of an independent military force is perceived to be a function of simultaneous U.S. pressure for a Japanese arms buildup, the weakening of the U.S. security guarantee, and the shift of U.S. Pacific forces toward the Indian Ocean and Persian Gulf. To counter a combination of Japan's own military buildup in Hokkaido and the U.S. deployment of F-16s at Misawa in northern Honshu, the Soviets have upgraded their own air capabilities on Etorofu and continued to deploy more SS-20s to the Soviet Far East.[28] The Soviets have warned Japan against catering to U.S. interests. Stating that there are no "unsinkable ships," Soviet media aver that the Japanese are leaving themselves open to a "crushing retaliatory blow" if they cooperate with U.S. military plans.[29]

The Soviets have also offered a diplomatic carrot to Japan if it agrees to prohibit the introduction of nuclear weapons into its territory: a treaty that would prohibit the Soviet use of nuclear weapons against Japan. The offer is designed to persuade Japan to prohibit the introduction of U.S. ships with Tomahawk cruise missiles into Japanese waters.[30]

Fundamentally, Soviet policy toward Japan may be judged a failure. There is no peace treaty between the two countries; the Soviets have been unable to thwart the formation of strong political and economic relations between China and Japan; they have not slowed the ever closer military cooperation between Tokyo and Washington; and they have not stopped Japanese rearmament. This dismal record reveals the limited number of mechanisms available to the USSR for influencing Japan. Broad contacts with Japanese society are virtually nonexistent. Even the Japanese Socialist and Communist parties' relations with the Communist Party of the Soviet Union (CPSU) are strained at best. The Japanese economy depends on the Soviet Union for neither significant trade nor investment. Nor can the Soviets budge on territorial issues. The northern islands are too important for the protection of the USSR's sea-based deterrent and the sanitization of the Sea of Okhotsk against U.S. forces in the northern Pacific.

The Soviets are perplexed over new forms of Japan-U.S. security cooperation, particularly in high tech areas of Stealth technology, fiber optics, and laser guidance systems. They tie these technological advantages for future generations of U.S. weapons designs to a new Japanese globalism. That is, the Soviets foresee a situation in which Japan could become a third superpower aligned to the United States militarily and assisting China in developing its own modern military forces early in the next century. The Soviets interpret Japan's active opposition to their actions in Afghanistan and Poland, as well as against Vietnam's occupation of Cambodia, as manifestations of a new world role for Japan. Moreover, they see Japan's remilitarization and anti-Sovietism as inseparable. Japan's participation in U.S.-led RIMPAC exercises and plan to undertake thousand-mile sea-lane defense are examples of incipient imperialist ambitions.

Korea is also of strategic importance to the Soviet Union. Predominant Soviet influence on the peninsula could serve to extend a semicircle around Manchuria to intimidate China. A U.S. military presence could be excluded from the Asian mainland. Soviet domination of Korea would pressure Japan to accommodate Soviet interests. And a number of Korean warm water ports would become available to the Pacific fleet. These desiderata do not translate, however, into any significant support for a military solution to the peninsula's bifurcation. Given the U.S. security treaty with Seoul, Moscow is careful to avoid backing any North Korea claims that could lead to a direct military confrontation. Noteworthy in this regard is the USSR's refusal to proffer even nominal support to repeated calls by North Korea for revolutionary action in the south.[31] Even less attractive to the Soviets would be an open North Korean invasion. That possibility would exacerbate Sino-Soviet relations as each tried to gain control of Pyongyang, virtually ensuring a Soviet-U.S. confrontation and the further buildup of U.S. forces in the Pacific. It could precipitate major Japanese rearmament and possibly even a military alliance of Japan and the Republic of Korea (ROK). In sum, there are compelling reasons for the USSR to support the status quo in Korea rather than to back its reunification.

Nevertheless, North Korea remains important in Soviet strategic considerations. If the Soviets could exercise dominant influence there, they would have forged an important link in the USSR's Asian collective security concept, designed to isolate China. North Korea could provide the Soviets access to ice-free ports such as Nanjin, which would improve the Pacific fleet's deployment opportunities. Additionally, the DPRK acts as a buffer for the soviet maritime province and home of the Pacific fleet. Finally, in the event of war with China, a pro-Soviet North Korea would permit control of the sea routes from Vladivostok to China and the Yellow Sea, rendering China's main coastal zones vulnerable to Soviet attack. Moreover, because of its proximity to the PRC's industrial heartland, North Korea would be an excellent launching point for Soviet strikes into Manchuria.

North Korea is also important defensively. As Japan and China increase their military capacities, a pro-Soviet—or at least friendly—Pyongyang is a major Soviet goal. There is, therefore, a kind of paradoxical relationship between U.S. military support for South Korea and Soviet political leverage in the North. That is, Pyongyang depends on Soviet aid to balance South Korean might. The Soviets appear to fine tune their support so that it is sufficient to maintain leverage over North Korea's military decisions but not so great as to provide the wherewithal for a preemptive attack. Thus, until the mid-1980s, Moscow had refused to supply the DPRK with its most advanced equipment, such as MiG-23s and MiG-25s, even though they have been supplied to the friendly noncommunist states of India, Syria, Iraq, and Libya.[32]

Beginning in late 1984, however, the Soviets seemed to upgrade the DPRK's importance for their strategic assessment. Deputy Foreign Minister Mikhail Kapitsa reportedly discussed the sale of MiG-23s and T-72 tanks with North Korean leaders in a November visit to Pyongyang, according to a Soviet defector who fled to the south at the time. Western diplomats in Seoul believe the Soviets may seek access to North Korean air bases and to Nampo port on the west coast of the Yellow Sea. If these locations are granted, some Soviet ships will have less need to transit the Japanese straits in the event of a crisis.[33]

The intensity of the Soviet courtship increased in 1985 with an August visit to Pyongyang by Soviet First Deputy Premier Geydar Aliyov. His visit coincided with an unprecedented Soviet naval port call and the arrival of first Deputy Minister of Defense Marshal Vasiliy Petrov, the most senior Soviet military official to visit the DPRK since the early 1970s. By mid-1986, the Soviets had given the North Koreans thirty-two of a projected commitment of forty of the previously unobtainable MiG-23s. South Korean intelligence stated that Moscow also intended to supply SAMs to Pyongyang, correcting a long-standing defense deficiency. Soviet access to North Korean ports would be a major breakthrough away from the choke points. There is, however, no indication that Pyongyang is willing to compromise its sovereignty in the same way Hanoi has.

The MiG-23s were probably provided in reaction to the acquisition of F-16 C/Ds by the ROK air force. The South Korean aircraft is a product of 1980s technology with advanced avionics and air-to-air missiles. By contrast, the Soviets have reportedly provided the MiG-23E, which is a less capable version of the aircraft the Soviets use themselves. It became part of the Soviet inventory in the mid-1970s and performs well below the capability of the F-16C/D. The only Soviet aircraft to match the latter would be the MiG-29, and there is no indication that the USSR is prepared to provide its most advanced fighter bomber to North Korea.[34]

In actuality, the Soviet position in North Korea is less secure politically than China's. While jealously guarding his country's independence, Kim Il-sung leans more to Beijing than Moscow. As a staunch member of the Nonaligned Movement (despite its 1961 security treaties with both the PRC and USSR), the DPRK has privately opposed Soviet intervention in Afghanistan and publicly objected to the Soviet-backed Vietnamese occupation of Cambodia. Indeed Pyongyang is a second home-in-exile for the Cambodian Resistance head of state, Prince Norodum Sihanouk. North Korea has also refused to join the Council for Mutual Economic Assistance (COMECON), the Soviet-dominated economic bloc.

The rapid improvement of Soviet–North Korean relations in the mid-1980s stands in marked contrast to the Twenty-sixth Congress of the CPSU in 1981, at which Brezhnev had downgraded the DPRK in his report from a member of the socialist commonwealth, including Cuba and Vietnam, to the category of other socialist states, such as Yugoslavia. In 1985, a new quid pro quo had been struck between Moscow and Pyongyang. In exchange for the MiG-23s, North Korea was permitting Soviet reconnaissance overflights to examine China's heavily industrialized and strategic province of Manchuria. The DPRK also allowed Soviet vessels to visit North Korean ports. This warming trend in Soviet–North Korean affairs may be partially meant by the DPRK to serve as a warning to China to slow its intercourse with Seoul. Indirect trade between the PRC and ROK, for example, is now estimated to exceed Beijing's direct trade with North Korea. While China may hope to draw Pyongyang into fuller relations with the noncommunist world, the North fears that a more open foreign policy would cause it to lose control over the direction of events on the peninsula—hence, Pyongyang's interest in strengthening Soviet ties and Soviet assistance in upgrading the North's military technology.[35]

The Soviet Position in Southeast Asia

As in the United States, Southeast Asia does not hold the highest priority for Soviet strategists. The region's interest to Moscow derives from relations with China and the United States, as well as the Soviet desire to become a global naval power. All three of these objectives are served by Soviet ties to Vietnam. The Soviets have forged a new link in their Asian collective security arrangement surrounding China and have bought into future security decisions for the region. They have also placed a portion of their Pacific fleet and air force opposite U.S. facilities in the Philippines and along the major trade routes between the Middle East and Indian Ocean and the industrial economies of South Korea and Japan.

Cam Ranh Bay's value to the Soviets lies in the base's proximity to China, the U.S. Subic Bay naval facilities in the Philippines, and the multiple straits connecting the SLOCs between the Indian Ocean and the Pacific. The Soviet association with the backing of a Hanoi-dominated Indochina enmeshes Vietnam into Soviet naval strategy, particularly the containment of Chinese influence in the South China Sea. Use of the Vietnam base permits the USSR to sustain patrols along China's South China Sea coast. Soviet ships operating out of Cam Ranh Bay require U.S. Seventh Fleet elements to remain near Subic as a regional counter to these Soviet vessels, thus reducing the number of U.S. ships for both the Northwest Pacific and western Indian Ocean, areas of greater strategic importance for the United States. The presence of five or six attack submarines at Cam Ranh Bay also suggests an interest in blocking the SLOCs in the event of a crisis.

The cost to the USSR has been high but not unbearable given the strategic advantages obtained through its Southeast Asia involvement. In its first postwar aid agreement with Vietnam in October 1975, Moscow agreed to fund 60 percent of Hanoi's Five Year Economic Plan at an estimated cost of $2.1 billion. Since 1978, Soviet economic aid has been estimated at $1 billion per year. By 1987, 70 percent of Vietnam's exports were sent to the USSR as partial payment for Moscow's $2 billion to $3 billion in annual military and economic assistance.[36] By the mid-1980s, Vietnam had been integrated into overall economic planning as a raw material, consumer goods, and labor supplier. An economic dependency relationship had been created every bit as limiting as Indochina's former colonial economic ties to France.

The Vietnamese military machine depends entirely on Soviet assistance for petroleum products, uniforms, and equipment. Between 1979 and 1983, Soviet arms deliveries climbed to about $2.5 billion. An estimated 7,000 advisers operate in Vietnam, 3,000 in Cambodia and 1,500 in Laos.[37]

Beginning in 1979, the Soviet Union rapidly improved the facilities at Cam Ranh Bay. Dry docks for submarines have been built, and underground fuel storage tanks and underground antiaircraft batteries, as well as SAMs, have been installed. Sophisticated electronic intelligence facilities make Cam Ranh Bay one of the most important communication and intelligence facilities outside Soviet territory.

By 1987, the Soviet contingent at Cam Ranh Bay included three to five submarines, ten surface combatants, and ten to twelve auxiliaries in addition to TU-95 Bear and at least fourteen TU-16 Badger reconnaissance and strike aircraft. The VSTOL carriers *Minsk* and *Novorossiysk* have called. Soviet naval infantry are reported to be stationed at Cam Ranh Bay in battalion strength. In December 1984, the Soviets rounded out their military buildup by moving a squadron of fourteen late-model MiG-23 interceptors to Vietnam. When the United States left in 1975, there were two piers. In 1987, five more were added.[38]

While the Bear fly reconnaissance missions throughout Southeast Asia and the Indian Ocean, the Badgers, in addition to their ASW capability, equipped with long-range Kingfish air-to-surface missiles, could attack ship and coastal targets. In effect, the Soviets now have in Vietnam all the elements of a naval surface warfare strategy: cruise missile and torpedo strikes from aircraft, submarines, and surface vessels, coordinated by a land-based communication center. Former U.S. ambassador to the Philippines Michael Armacost claims that Soviet aircraft from Cam Ranh Bay commit "hundreds of violations of Philippine air space while monitoring U.S. military activity from Clark and Subic."[39]

Despite the symbiotic relationship between the USSR and Vietnam tensions and suspicions abound. Vietnamese leaders undoubtedly recall that the Soviets were willing to subordinate Hanoi's interests to relations with the United States in the past and may do so in the future. The Vietnamese are also concerned about improvement in Sino-Soviet contacts for the same reasons. Even the 1978 Soviet-Vietnam security treaty is a limited guarantee to Hanoi, apparently not covering territories in dispute between Vietnam and its neighbors, including China.[40] Thus, there is no guarantee that the Soviet navy would come to Vietnam's aid if there were a military confrontation over the Paracels and Spratlys.

The Vietnamese reportedly resent the arrogance and heavy-handedness of Soviet advisers, and the latter openly criticize their charges for laziness and unreliability. Moscow has also been embarrassed at Vietnamese incursions into Thailand, which began in June 1980 and have continued during each dry season offensive against the Cambodian resistance. Some of the most flagrant occurred in February and March 1985 when Vietnam People's Army (VPA) forces in company strength occupied high ground in Thailand in order to surround elements of Sihanouk's Moulinaka forces. Thai air and artillery strikes were required to dislodge them.

Because of its own economic difficulties, the Soviets cut back economic assistance to Vietnam beginning in 1980. It has hovered at a point below $1 billion annually from a high of $1.3 billion in 1979, despite Vietnam's continued economic needs aggravated by a population growth of about 1 million annually.

Besides reducing food supplies, Moscow also increased the price of refined oil products. Prior to 1980, the Soviets charged only $4 a barrel; after that, they pressed Vietnam to pay the world market price of about $32 per barrel and finally settled for $16, a 400 percent price increase. The Soviet oil price increase and Vietnam's subsequent inability to purchase all the oil it required led to a rice shortage in the north as many of the vehicles needed to transport the south's surplus were idle for lack of fuel.[41]

In 1980 and 1981, the Soviets pushed for even closer control of Vietnam's administrative operations as the price for continued assistance through the acceptance of large numbers of advisers at all levels of Vietnam's ministries, a purge of incompetent cadres from the party, and the replacement of untrained economists with Soviet-trained Vietnamese. The Soviets also used the debt issue to obtain a dominant position in Vietnam's export of coal and grain, preferably used by Hanoi to meet domestic needs or to earn hard currency.[42]

Moscow has insisted on establishing an independent aid position in Laos and Cambodia, unmediated by Hanoi. It has signed aid agreements with both countries that provide for several thousand economic advisers and account for over 50 percent of external assistance to all three Indochina countries.[43] Equally significant are reports of some 1,000 military advisers in Laos and 2,000 Cambodian army and air force personnel receiving training in the USSR.[44] While Hanoi is undoubtedly nervous about Soviet influence in its domain, its leaders are probably confident that their geographic contiguity, long-standing guidance of Laos, and physical control of Cambodia ensure their continued dominance in Indochina affairs.

Hanoi is also concerned about the possibility of a Sino-Soviet understanding over Cambodia, which could lead to a withdrawal of Soviet support. With superficial relations between the USSR and PRC on the mend, Vietnam undoubtedly recalls past collusion between the two against Vietnamese interests at the 1954 Geneva Conference ending the first Indochina War and again in 1962 on the neutralization of Laos. Hanoi fears that history could repeat itself. While these apprehensions are probably overdrawn, Vietnam is alarmed that China insists on the cessation of Soviet aid for Vietnamese forces in Cambodia as a condition of normalization of relations with the Soviet Union. Hanoi reminded the Soviets in the Eighth Indochina Foreign Ministers communiqué of January 1984 that they must continue to reject "the unreasonable demand made by China. . . . The LPDR [Laos People's Democratic Republic] the PRK, and the SRV regard the principled stand of the Soviet Union as important. They view such a stand as a gesture of strong support and important encouragement to them."[45]

The Soviets would most certainly like to maintain their dominant external mentor role in Indochina and establish cordial relations with the ASEAN states simultaneously in order to reduce the latter's reliance on a U.S. security guarantee. Soviet officials regularly offer the hand of friendship to ASEAN. They portray themselves as honest brokers over the Indochina-ASEAN conflict. Deputy Foreign Minister Kapitsa told reporters in Bangkok in March 1985:

"We are not for confrontation. We are for negotiations. We are for appease-ment. We are for détente. And as far as that is concerned, we shall aways be your and Vietnam's friends. . . . We will be able, and we will be ready to take part in a solution in Southeast Asia."[46]

The Soviets hope to play upon differing views within ASEAN of a Soviet regional role to establish the USSR's legitimacy as a regional actor. Moscow seems to be saying that it can control Vietnamese actions by its supply line and also assist ASEAN in containing the "real threat" to its security in the long run, China. Indonesia and Malaysia are potentially more susceptible to this argument. They do not see the USSR as an imminent threat to regional stabil-ity, believe that the U.S. Seventh Fleet is more than sufficient to overwhelm the limited Soviet naval deployments at Cam Ranh Bay, and may be amenable to a Soviet-Vietnam alliance oriented against China as a useful contribution to regional order.[47] An alternate view tends to be held by Thailand and Singapore. They contend the Soviets are engaged in an inexorable military buildup in Southeast Asia and will help further Vietnam's regional ambitions in exchange for continued use of Cam Ranh Bay. This potent combination must be disrupted or ASEAN could find itself in the midst of a new regional con-flagration.[48] Malaysian Foreign Minister Ghazalie Shafie added a new twist to Southeast Asia's view of the Soviet threat when he warned against the sym-biotic relationship between the USSR-Vietnam alliance and an inevitable Chinese response to such a threat on its southern border. This line of reasoning argues that the Soviets constitute an indirect threat to ASEAN because it encourages a Chinese countermove. The Chinese have reportedly set up a training base for a Laos resistance in Yunnan province where ethnic minorities, traditionally hostile to Vientiane, are being trained.[49]

Moscow alternates between carrot and stick tactics toward ASEAN. Sometimes it applauds the association's willingness to incorporate Indochina into regional peace proposals and ASEAN resistance to U.S. efforts at the group's militarization. At others times, Soviet media excoriate ASEAN's appeals to Viet-nam to withdraw from Cambodia.[50] On one occasion, Kapitsa even warned that ASEAN's continued intransigence toward Cambodia could lead to Soviet aid for insurgencies within their countries. His threat backfired, leading to anti-Soviet demonstrations in Malaysia.[51]

While the Soviets have displayed little interest in Southeast Asian communist parties, since they are rather weak and have always looked toward Beijing rather than Moscow for guidance, the Philippines may be an exception. A high-level KGB defector, Stanislov Levchenko, testified before the U.S. House Select Com-mittee on Intelligence that the CPSU was passing money to the illegal Com-munist party of the Philippines (CPP). This allegation was partially corrobated when a Philippine Communist party official told Paul Quinn-Judge of the *Chris-tian Science Monitor* that the Soviets had offered the CPP military aid in early 1985. The offer was rejected, according to the party official, because the Soviets were viewed with as much suspicion as the Americans. Moreover, practical problems of supply to New People's Army (NPA) insurgents, scattered mostly in small units throughout the islands, would be almost insurmountable.[52]

Soviet espionage in Southeast Asia, as in other third world regions, is hardly unusual. In recent years, Soviet officials have been apprehended in Thailand for soliciting information on Thai military installations near the Cambodian border; in Malaysia, a senior aide to the prime minister was identified as a Soviet agent in 1981; and in 1982, a naval attaché was expelled from Indonesia for conspiring to obtain oceanographic data on the Makassar Strait—data that could help Soviet submarines transit between the Pacific and Indian Ocean with minimal chance of detection.[53]

Lest this account of Soviet nefarious activities seem too one-sided, it should be noted that the Soviets have their own security needs in protecting their lengthy trade and supply routes from Vladivostok to the European side of the USSR. Michael Leifer argues that the USSR has more interest in upholding freedom of navigation through international straits than in interdiction:

> As a major maritime power with global naval and commercial interests it would be virtually impossible for the Soviet Union to adopt an isolated discriminate position of denial in respect of any one set of straits used estensively for international navigation, without incalculable repercussions affecting other such straits through which she might wish to deploy. . . . Given the general condition of the global military balance, the Soviet Union in fact possesses an interest in unimpeded passage . . . in order to engage in competitive naval deployments with the United States.[54]

The Soviet merchant marine is, in effect, a hostage if the Soviet Union chooses to engage in sea-lane disruption. Moreover, the most likely situation for such interdiction would be global war rather than a conflict confined to Southeast Asia.

Soviet Military Deficiencies

How serious a military threat is the Soviet Union in East Asia? China responds to this query by regularly sounding rhetorical tocsins in hopes of encouraging a united front among Asian states against the USSR. Typical is the following description of a Soviet war scenario for the region:

> In the event of war, Soviet naval and air units stationed in Cam Ranh Bay can set off eastward and, in cooperation with the Soviet forces stationed in bases at home, launch a two-pronged attack from the southern and northern flanks against the U.S. 7th Fleet and the U.S. military installations in the Western Pacific. By moving southward the Soviet units in Cam Ranh Bay can

promptly seize the Strait of Malacca, the strategic passage linking the Pacific Ocean and the Indian Ocean, and thus cut off the oil supply line to Japan, as well as the link between the U.S. Fleets deployed in the two oceans. By moving northward, these units can blockade China by sea and launch a joint converging attack on the country, with the Soviet ground forces stationed along the Sino-Soviet border moving down from the north. And, finally, by moving westward, the Soviet units from Cam Ranh Bay can enter the Indian Ocean and the Gulf region, join forces with the Soviet Black Sea Fleet, and surround Europe from its flank.[55]

Whether the Soviets have the capacities attributed to them by the Chinese is debatable. Anti-Soviet Cassandras point to the size of its Pacific fleet, noting that it has by far more surface combatants and ten times the submarines of the U.S. Seventh Fleet. The U.S. force, however, packs a much bigger punch per unit, particularly when organized around large aircraft carriers. In this case, numerical disparity masks real capabilities: ASW for the Soviet Union and power projection for the United States. Moreover, the addition of Japan's Maritime Self Defense Force roughly doubles U.S. noncarrier naval power in the Pacific.[56]

The Pacific fleet is hampered in long-range operations by weak air cover and logistics, which rapidly degrade some 200 miles from Soviet shores. Its bases at Magadan, Petropavlovsk, and Anadyr are victims of both geography and the relatively primitive state of development in the Soviet Far East. The bases are unconnected to railways and because they are dependent on supply by sea and air could be interdicted. Sited in the Sea of Japan, the naval headquarters at Vladivostok is subject to blockade and mining operations in the Tsushima, Tsugaru, and Soya straits. Supplies for the more open access base at Petropavlovsk must also pass the Soya and Tsushima straits. Soviet supply ships could use the northern sea route between the Chuki and Bering seas in summer months, but this route is impassable during the winter.[57]

Logistics problems in the Far East exacerbate a more general deficiency in the Soviet navy: its unreliability. At any given time, Western analysts claim, only one in five ships is operational. They tend not to be built for long, trouble-free blue-water voyages but are deployed to protect coastal regions and choke points. Even their numerous attack submarines, which are tasked with cutting SLOCs in time of war, according to U.S. Navy Secretary Lehman, would have to exit through choke points in Japan and Korea. Moreover, states maritime strategist Michael MacGuire of the Brookings Institution, most of these submarines would be held back in a crisis situation to protect Soviet SSBNs in the Sea of Okhotsk.[58]

Despite the steady increase in number of ships assigned to the Pacific fleet in recent years, there is no evidence that Soviet naval doctrine has been altered to take account of its new capabilities. Naval exercises remain confined for the most part to the northwest quadrant in the Sea of Japan and off the Kurils.

These exercises suggest a series of layered defense lines for the Sea of Okhotsk and major bases; that is, they are defensive. At any time, up to 90 percent of the fleet is either in port or close to it.[59]

No significant exercises occurred in the South China Sea until the April 1984 amphibious landings on the Vietnamese coast. Although small scale in comparison to such massive annual U.S. exercises as Team Spirit in Korea or even Cobra Gold with Thailand, the Soviet landings were an unprecedented display of power projection and could be a portent of forthcoming Soviet capabilities if new amphibious vessels are added to the fleet over the next decade. Nevertheless, the April 1984 exercises were more interesting for their political message than any display of new military capability. The Soviets were probably signaling the PRC and ASEAN that their commitment to Vietnam was firm in the event of any PRC attempt to repeat the 1979 march into its neighbor's northern provinces. The Soviet Union's ability to deter China has given it considerable leverage in consolidating its use of Cam Ranh Bay. In 1984, the USSR increased the number of Tu-16 Badgers based there to between fifteen and twenty and added a squadron of MiG-23 interceptors. Nevertheless, in wartime, Soviet forces based in Vietnam could be rapidly destroyed through U.S. attacks from the Philippines or Guam. This fact alone is sufficient to make the point that the Soviet use of Cam Ranh Bay as an intelligence and patrol base for the South China Sea and Indian Ocean depends on the maintenance of peace.

Reinforcement of Soviet contingents in the south in time of war is equally unlikely. Ships leaving Vladivostok would have to travel more than 2,000 miles, transiting straits and waters dominated by the United States and Japan. Nor do the Vietnamese facilities themselves have sufficient storage capacity to supply protracted operations.

In sum, the primary operational mission of the Soviet fleet is to protect the Soviet SSBN force in the Sea of Okhotsk. Much of the rest of the fleet is committed to countering U.S. SSBNs and carrier groups in the Pacific. Only about 10 percent of the fleet's principal surface combatants and submarines are deployed outside home waters; only about 15 percent of SSBNs are normally on alert, compared with 55 percent of U.S. submarines.[60]

The major weaknesses of the Pacific fleet are lack of air cover outside home waters (VSTOL carrier-based Yak-36 Forgers have only a 16-minute flight time), absence of forward bases with facilities to supply protracted warfare needs, and a noisy and relatively old submarine force, which, although greatly outnumbering U.S. submarines, is vulnerable to superior U.S. ASW techniques. (These submarines are being replaced in the late 1980s, however, by newer and much quieter models.) Because most Soviet submarines in the Pacific would remain in the north in the event of war, only a handful would be available for the interdiction of ports and sea-lanes in the entire Pacific and Indian oceans. It is highly improbable, then, that the Soviets possess the capability to sever these lanes for any extended period. Rather, in the event of war, the best Soviet ships would probably be kept in home waters where they could be protected by land-based aircraft.

It appears that the main role for the Soviet Pacific fleet is political: to demonstrate that the USSR is an Asian actor and therefore must be involved in any decisions concerning the future of regional order. At some time in the future, the Soviets might also offer themselves as a protector against a growing Chinese blue-water navy to those states that perceive Beijing as a greater long-term threat than Moscow.

General Secretary Gorbachev has brought a new style to the USSR's Asia policy. His Vladivostok address of July 28, 1986, provided a blueprint "for integrating the Asian-Pacific region into the general process of establishing a comprehensive system of international security proposed at the 27th Congress of the CPSU." From a regional perspective, the most interesting features of the initiative were the emphasis on normalization of Sino-Soviet relations as a way of settling the Cambodian conflict and an appeal for limitations on naval activities. For the latter, the Soviets hope to create zones free of ASW activity, in all probability to protect their SSBNs in the Sea of Okhotsk. In the former, the even-handed treatment of China and Vietnam did not include the standard endorsement of Hanoi's position on the irreversibility of the Cambodian situation. Gorbachev also hinted at a possible trade-off between Soviet facilities in Vietnam and termination of the U.S. air and naval presence in the Philippines. This could be an effective propaganda tack when the Philippine bases come up for renegotiation beginning in 1988.[61] Under Gorbachev, the Soviets appear to be creating a new image: that of a major player in Asia, one that initiates policy rather than merely reacts to others.

3
Is There a Japanese Regional Security Role?

Japan's view of its world security role is shaped predominantly by economics, particularly the relationship of international trade to prosperity. Four geographical areas are deemed especially important for both military and economic reasons: Northeast Asia, Southeast Asia and Australia, the Persian Gulf, and the United States. Northeast Asia blends both military and economic concerns. The Soviet Union and China dominate the region. Economically Japan has become an important contributor to Chinese development and is the largest single market for Chinese petroleum. The potential for Siberian development still interests Japanese businessmen, though strained political and security relations have reduced the prospects for a significant Japanese role since the Soviet invasion of Afghanistan and its military buildup on the northern islands. Korea and Taiwan are major trading partners and locations for Japanese investment.

Southeast Asia and Australia are important essentially for economic reasons, the latter as a supplier of coal, iron ore, and uranium and the former as a major export market. Japanese investors constitute the primary foreign business presence in the region ($11.6 billion cumulative investment in mid-1983, or 48 percent of total foreign investment in ASEAN).[1] Indonesia, Malaysia, and Brunei supply Japan with about 20 percent of its oil. Southeast Asia also straddles the SLOCs linking the Persian Gulf to Japan. The Persian Gulf's importance to Japan is based entirely on oil. Over 75 percent of the country's petroleum needs are met from sources in this region.

The linchpin for Japan's security in economic and military dimensions is the United States. Japan's security treaty with the United States is a guarantee of its physical integrity in a Northeast Asia dominated by the USSR. The U.S. alliance permits Japan to maneuver between Moscow and Beijing and stabilizes regional relations by supplementing Japan's own limited military capabilities. Larry Niksch of the Congressional Research Service has noted: "The alliance is one basis for an American role in Southeast Asia and the Indian Ocean as well as the Pacific that protects Japan's economic interests and sea transport routes."[2]

Since 1945, insofar as Japan had any conscious strategy, it was to ensure the continuation of the U.S. security umbrella. Because the United States is committed to the maintenance of a worldwide competitive market economy, Tokyo's economic security could be comfortably based on U.S. military guarantees. The doctrine developed by a succession of Liberal Democratic party (LDP) prime ministers to rationalize this policy was deemed comprehensive security. Edward Olsen wryly observed, it is "mostly a rationale for Japan to do as little as possible militarily in order to focus on economic progress."[3]

Comprehensive security was a sensible policy for a highly vulnerable state with a great power protector and limited military establishment constrained by constitutional prohibitions against overseas deployments. Japan is dependent on the cooperation and goodwill of a variety of trade partners and raw material suppliers. Resource dependency means that the country can ill afford to alienate major suppliers. Hence Japan tries to remain aloof from international frictions in which association with any given side would lead to economic sanctions from others. Alternatively Japan will try to mediate among disputants to resolve conflicts that could be costly to it (the Iran-Iraq war).

Until this decade, open discussion of defense was virtually taboo. In 1978, for example, Self Defense Forces (SDF) Chief of Staff Kurisu Hiroomi's criticism of the SDF's lack of independent authority to resist an attack on the home islands led to his dismissal, though a year later Tokyo authorities heeded his advice and rectified the situation. Kurisu was also the first high-level SDF officer to question the distinction made between offensive and defensive strategies, a political minefield that no public official wished to traverse but a distinction that had to be operationalized if Japan was to develop a sensible force structure. Since neither military nor civilian defense officials were tasked until quite recently with developing strategic options, there has been little basis for order-of-battle purchases other than U.S. pressure.[4]

Washington has unilaterally devised strategies, defined each partner's role, and invited Japan to increase its share of the burden. Not surprisingly such actions have been only marginally successful because there is little indication of a true mutuality of interests. The latter cannot occur until Tokyo and Washington see the Asian threat environment in a congruent way and Tokyo acknowledges the necessity of a larger role for itself. Part of the problem is the United States itself. Its policymakers send mixed signals to Japan, urging an increased defense capacity but ambivalent over the desirability of a greater regional military role.

Japan's Strategic Situation

Japan's geographical situation—an arc of islands east of China and south of the Soviet Union—renders it difficult to defend against a hostile power. The nation's high degree of urbanization and limited territory render a defense in depth impossible. Japan has therefore pursued a kind of rolling economic security, maximizing markets and sources of supply, being as nonprovocative as possible militarily to neighbors, and becoming economically indispensable by virtue of its technological superiority. Japan's first explicit postwar strategic doctrine was shaped not out of any systematic assessment of threat but rather because increasing fiscal constraints impelled the government to come up with a justification for defense expenditures. Known as the National Defense Program Outline (NDPO), this concept was adopted in 1976 and used to justify a force of only minimum size to repel a "limited and small scale aggression." The notion was one of threshold deterrence—that is, the capacity to force the adversary to attack at a high enough level to trigger automatically the U.S. security guarantee. The NDPO, which called for no substantial increase in Japanese forces, had the positive effect of creating a public opinion consensus in support of the government's defense policy.[5]

This cautious position began to change only in the late 1970s as the culmination of a variety of changes in Japan's environment. First, the Carter administration's plans to phase down U.S. ground forces in Korea caused a number of Japanese officials to question U.S. reliability. Then the Soviet military buildup in the Far East, including the deployment of SS-20s and Backfire bombers along with the deployment of an army division on the northern territories, refocused Japanese attention on the imminence of a Soviet threat. As these developments were unfolding, the USSR invaded Afghanistan and bankrolled the Vietnamese occupation of Cambodia in 1979, demonstrating for the first time that it was willing to use military force in Asia just as it had in Eastern Europe.

The Japanese government under Prime Minister Zenko Suzuki responded to this more threatening environment when it promised the United States in 1981 to expand its defense efforts to include the sea space and airspace adjacent to Japan. Noteworthy was an explicit departure from the NDPO, which had not provided for increasing air defense capability. Thus, in the summer of 1982, the Suzuki government raised the number of F-15s it would purchase from the United States from 100 to 155 and of P3C antisubmarine patrol planes from 45 to 74 by 1988.[6] Suzuki officials also interpreted the NDPO sufficiently broadly to state that it was permissible for the Maritime Self Defense Force (MSDF) to share sea-lane defense west of Guam and north of the Philippines. This decision, in turn, provided the strategic rationale for a naval buildup. By early 1983, Prime Minister Yasuhiro Nakasone had expanded Japan's sea-lane role to include the possibility of blockading the straits around Japan in cooperation with the U.S. Seventh Fleet. This decision elicited a new domestic political controversy: whether Japan would violate its constitution in a combined U.S. blockade action by engaging in "collective defense."[7]

Japan-U.S. Security Cooperation

Although the United States quite correctly urges an increase in Japan's military capabilities and willingness to share regional defense burdens, Japan's indirect contribution to Washington's Asian security posture should not be overlooked. To a considerable extent, the U.S. military presence in the western Pacific and Indian Ocean relies on Japanese bases. The home porting of the aircraft carrier *Midway* in Yokosuka and the U.S. Third Marine Division in Okinawa constitutes an important contribution to the Asian force projection of the United States. Moreover, Japan spends well over a billion dollars annually to defray U.S. costs in maintaining these forces in country. Nevertheless, a growing number of American critics are impatient with Japan's reluctance to become more directly involved with U.S. Asian defense efforts. Edward Olsen has complained: "In effect, in return for granting the United States the privilege of using bases in Japan, Tokyo gets U.S. gratitude for the dubious honor of assuming Japan's duty to defend its home islands and its foreign interests."[8] Thus one of the reasons behind Japan's enthusiastic welcome for the Reagan administration's Asian buildup was the relief it provided from the fear that Tokyo might have to pick up the slack behind a retrenching U.S. military policy.

Prime Minister Nakasone has been the first Japanese leader willing to discuss burden sharing openly. He explicitly promised Washington that Japan would help meet the Soviet threat in the contiguous straits by monitoring the sea-lanes and also referred to Japan as an "unsinkable aircraft carrier." Uncharacteristically Nakasone is a leader willing to move ahead of Japanese public opinion on this issue in the hope of shaping it. He has implicitly challenged the assumption of the NDPO that there are no direct military threats to Japan by stressing the Soviet force buildup on the northern islands and the deployment of SS-20s and Backfires in East Asia. These systems are aimed at U.S. forces and bases in the region; therefore Japan must be a priority target in the event of a U.S.-Soviet confrontation even if Japanese forces are not directly involved in action against the Soviets. (See table 3–1).

In effect, initially with Prime Minister Suzuki's promise to extend sea-lane defense to a thousand-mile radius of Honshu and subsequently with Prime Minister Nakasone's open description of the defense relationship with the

Table 3–1
Ratio of Defense Expenditure to GNP

	1965	1970	1975	1980	1981	1982
USSR	4.6	11.7	8.4	12.0	15.0	a
United States	8.0	7.8	5.8	5.7	6.1	6.5
Britain	6.8	4.9	4.9	5.1	5.3	5.3
France	4.6	4.0	3.9	3.9	4.1	4.2
Germany	5.7	3.3	3.7	3.2	4.1	4.1
Japan	1.3	0.8	0.9	0.9	0.9	0.9

Source: International Institute for Strategic Studies, *The Military Balance, 1984–1985* (London: IISS, 1984).

[a]No precise figures are available, but some Western estimates range from 10 to 20 percent.

United States as an alliance, an important psychological barrier has been breached. The new relationship presupposes joint fleet operations in areas outside Japan's territorial waters—in other words, collective security, which is forbidden in Japan's Constitution. While some controversy arose over both Suzuki's and Nakasone's commitments, it caused no political damage to the LDP, and Japanese public opinion appears to have accepted the military buildup toward sea-lane defense.

The Reagan administration has urged Japan to abandon the NDPO and double its procurement plans for sea-lane and air defense. At the Japan-U.S. Security Treaty consultative committee meeting in Hawaii in June 1981, Washington insisted that Japan develop sufficient capacity to cope with the Soviet fleet as well as its Backfires.[9] Because the Seventh Fleet deploys one to two carrier task forces in the western Indian Ocean, Japan's utility as a barrier against Soviet naval egress from the Seas of Okhotsk and Japan looms ever larger in joint strategic planning. If Japanese forces can block the Soviet navy from the Tsugaru (between Hokkaido and Honshu) and Tsushima (between Japan and Korea) straits, the Soviet Pacific fleet will be denied access from its headquarters at Vladivostok to its only major ice-free facility on the Kamchatka peninsula, Petropavlovsk. Japan already has a permanent naval patrol on the Soya Strait separating Hokkaido from Soviet Sakhalin.[10]

In case of emergency, Nakasone has claimed that Japan would be entitled to block the major straits even if it were not yet under direct attack. Japan's ability to effect this policy unaided is another matter. The MSDF lacks SAM and SSM missiles and still has minimal mine-laying capability. Moreover, the sheer quantitative growth of Soviet naval and air power in the region could overwhelm any independent Japanese effort to close the straits. More reasonably, Japanese air and naval efforts should be seen as an extension of U.S. Seventh Fleet capabilities—particularly intelligence, surveillance, antisubmarine warfare, and air defense. These help prevent Soviet Backfires and attack submarines from intercepting the Seventh Fleet as its assists in Japan's defense.[11]

Noteworthy in this regard is U.S.-Japanese joint planning under which officials from both countries are studying sea-lane defense, defense against a hypothetical Soviet invasion of Japan, and reaction to a conflict on the Korean peninsula. The MSDF has participated in the annual RIMPAC exercises with the United States since 1980. In addition to U.S. ships, these exercises in recent years have also included Australian, New Zealand, British, and Canadian vessels. Even the South Korean navy has been involved indirectly with the MSDF by bilaterally and simultaneously exercising with Seventh Fleet forces. Thus, Seoul and Tokyo can claim that they are training only with U.S. ships when in fact the three navies maneuver together.[12] In 1984, U.S. Marines exercised with Ground Self Defense Forces (GSDF) troops on Hokkaido in a scenario designed to repel a Soviet invasion. Communication arrangements have been improved to permit Japanese ships and planes to communicate directly with U.S. control centers.[13]

In September 1982, Japan approved a U.S. plan to deploy over fifty F-16 fighter-bombers at Misawa air base in northern Honshu beginning in 1985. These aircraft balance the Backfires stationed in Vladivostok. They could intercept the Backfires close to Soviet territory before the latter could fire their air-to-surface missiles (ASMs).[14] From the Soviet perspective, the Misawa deployment is seen as an offensive change by which the United States develops a capability to bomb Soviet Pacific fleet bases, since the F-16s could fly to the Siberian coast from Misawa.[15] Once again, the stationing of attack aircraft in Japan places the country directly in harm's way in the event of a Soviet-U.S. crisis. Japan's willingness to accept increased U.S. firepower in and around the home islands constitutes a recognition that despite the military buildup, the Japanese military could not by itself withstand the combined firepower of the Soviet fleet, SS-20s, and Backfires. Ironically, however, the Reagan administration's decision to increase Seventh Fleet and Pacific Air Force strength around Japan may be counterproductive to the acceleration of Japan's own defense buildup. If the United States appears to be accepting the main responsibility for defending the home islands once again, the need for Japan to pull more of its own weight proportionately diminishes.

Although defense analysts generally agree that at Japan's current rate of defense spending—approximately 1 percent of GNP—the SDF's ability to defend the home islands and surrounding sea-lanes may not materialize until the turn of the century, progress is tangible.

December 1984 joint exercises in the Sea of Japan with both the *Midway* and the nuclear-powered carrier *Carl Vinson* included Japanese F-15s with Sidewinder air-to-air missiles intercepting twenty-six Badger bombers that flew down the west coast of Japan. In September, U.S. and Japanese navy exercises had involved 90 MSDF ships and 125 Air Self Defense Force (ASDF) aircraft in an eight-day operation designed to exploit Soviet vulnerability in the Sea of Japan.[16] Similar exercises were held in 1986, incorporating the recommissioned battleship *New Jersey*. These joint exercises close to Japanese home waters could be the initial stage of broader U.S.-Japan security deployments if the MSDF is willing to engage in joint patrols with the Seventh Fleet within the thousand-mile radius Japan has promised to cover. U.S. officials believe that the continued Soviet buildup in the North Pacific could make such joint deployments politically acceptable to Japanese public opinion.[17] Public opinion polls do not, however, reinforce this optimism. An October 1984 *Yoimuri* poll showed that only 2 percent of the respondents agreed that Japan should absorb more of the costs of stationing U.S. forces in Japan. The same poll revealed only a 5.4 percent agreement that Japan should strengthen its defense forces to meet U.S. demands.[18]

One area in which agreement seems to exist is the contribution of Japan's electronics and communication skills to mutual security. The September 1983 Korean Airline (KAL) shootdown demonstrated the sophistication of Japan's electronics surveillance. A greater sharing of underwater, surface, and airborne intelligence gathering with U.S. command centers could be a significant addition to Seventh Fleet operations. Japan is planning to build an over-the-horizon (OTH) radar, which will cover the Korean peninsula, the Soviet coastline along the Sea of Japan, and Sakhalin island, as well as the Kuril islands. In cooperation with planned U.S. OTH radars in the Aleutians and Guam, all Soviet air and naval movements along the Asia-Pacific rim can be monitored.[19]

Although China is reluctant to promote an anti-Soviet trilateral entente in Northeast Asia, Beijing recognizes that U.S.-Japan cooperation is in the PRC's interest for it permits Chinese leaders to concentrate their own resources on economic modernization. China and Japan have even agreed to share intelligence on Soviet military movements.[20] Moreover, while not openly endorsing Japan-U.S. cooperation and sea-lane defense, the Chinese have expressed no opposition to it. PRC analysts see the Japanese defense buildup as an "understandable" response to Soviet actions in Siberia and on the northern islands.[21] Thus, Japanese and U.S. cooperation protects China in the same way that NATO protects France.

In all probability, Japan-U.S. defense cooperation will continue to improve. It will be driven by the common external threat of growing Soviet air and naval deployments in the vicinity of the home islands on the one hand and the effect of the U.S. defense burden on Japan-U.S. economic relations on the other. Washington's budget and balance of payments deficits are directly related to its large defense outlay, much of which goes to the navy, which in turn is a major factor in Japan's defense. At the same time, high U.S. interest rates to finance the deficit inflated the dollar's value until 1987, which debilitated the competitive position of U.S. exports while improving opportunities for Japanese goods to penetrate the U.S. market. Americans boosted their purchases of Japanese goods by 51 percent between 1982 and 1984. The U.S. merchandise trade deficit with Japan in 1984 was $36.8 billion, about 30 percent of the total U.S. deficit.[22] Japan must contribute more to defense cooperation, then, to ease the U.S. defense burden and lower the tension level in economic relations with its main partner.

Legally Japan's Constitution appears to prohibit collective security. The country is permitted, nevertheless, to defend itself. Thus, Japanese forces, in deploying with U.S. units, can engage in joint actions if Japan's defense is at stake. Employing this logic, Japan can cooperate with the United States to blockade the three straits since these are vital for the protection of the home islands. Sea-lane defense may be on shakier legal ground, however, since combat far from national territory may not be so clearly related to its defense.[23] By articulating a thousand-mile sea-lane defense doctrine, Japan has accepted the U.S. position that the U.S.-Japan Security Treaty entails regional as well as bilateral responsibilities.

The Midterm Defense Program Estimate (1983–1987), which outlines the country's weapons procurement plans, however, has been disappointing to U.S.

observers. There is little improvement in sustainability of forces at sea, and there is no evidence of a new doctrine beyond the 1976 NDPO home islands orientation. Moreover, there may be another problem on the horizon as the United States equips many of its Seventh Fleet combat vessels with Tomahawk nuclear-capable cruise missiles. Given Japan's nonnuclear principles, the question arises whether Japan can defend U.S. convoys if they are equipped with nuclear weapons. Prime Minister Nakasone has stated that the U.S. use of nuclear weapons in joint U.S.-Japanese operations would be warranted if Japan's survival was in danger—the most flexible interpretation of Tokyo's nonnuclear policy yet provided by a Japanese leader.[24]

JSDF Capabilities

Six months into the first Reagan administration, the U.S.-Japan security subcommittee met in Hawaii. Secretary Weinberger presented an estimate of what Japan would need to carry out joint defense plans in terms of additional air and naval capabilities. During discussions in 1982, Weinberger claimed that Japan would almost have to double its annual defense budget increments to achieve its sea-lane defense goals by the early 1990s. The Ministry of Finance overrode the Defense Agency, however, and the NDPO remained operative. U.S. defense analysts urged Japan to accelerate purchases of F-15s to improve the country's leaky air defenses and build up at least a sixty-day ammunition supply. (In late 1982, there was only a four- to five-day supply.) It should also extend the reach of its early warning air system, including the modernization of its radar and purchase of additional E-2Cs and P3Cs to cover the thousand-mile sea-lane commitment.[25]

In fact, Japan's radar warning system—which had performed so ineptly when a defecting Soviet's MiG-25 slid underneath it in 1976—has been updated. Its sites have been hardened and cryptographic facilities made more secure. Japan's E2Cs are now feeding data into BADGE, along with satellite and electronic intelligence.[26] Japan's ability to eavesdrop on Soviet military information traffic was impressive in the aftermath of the KAL shootdown in September 1983. It will be interesting to see whether Japan will move in the future to acquire an AWACs capability in addition to the E2Cs it is adding. AWACs has over a ten-hour flight capability compared to five hours for the E2C. The latter's radar is also more easily jammed. AWACs thousand-mile coverage ensures greater warning time against Soviet Backfires, which could launch ASMs from 150 miles out. In short, if Japan is serious about developing a thousand-mile sea-lane surveillance, AWACs is a necessity.[27]

It is seldom understood that despite Japan's low priority for defense affairs, it is virtually self-sufficient in military production, manufacturing 80 percent of its hardware, with the exception of aircraft and some missile systems.

On the cutting edge of high technology, Japanese achievements in fiber optics, gallium-arsenide semiconductors for smaller and more powerful computers, and microelectronics have led to U.S. demands for technology transfer.[28] Japan has developed its own ground-to-air short-range missiles, high-speed gunboats, supersonic jet trainers, and battle tanks. Some 300 companies engage in defense production, although only 0.5 percent of overall industrial output is defense related.

Much of this military potential could be put into Japan's new (1981) defense commitment: sea-lane protection. Initially the government stated that the MSDF and ASDF would be tasked with escorting vessels, including U.S. ships, carrying goods to Japan along two sea-lanes: the Tokyo-Guam route and Osaka-Bashi Channel (between Taiwan and the Philippines). Subsequently, however, JSDF officials seemed to make this commitment more open-ended, stating that sea-lanes are not necessarily limited to particular widths and that their defense is based on the requirements of antisubmarine patrols, sea-lane escort activities, and straits protection. This broader interpretation has led to the controversial conclusion that Japan may assist U.S. naval vessels within their defense perimeter and that closing the Japanese straits, presumably as a way of blocking Soviet access to the Pacific, is a legitimate right of self-defense if the country is faced with imminent attack.[29]

Although Japan's new ships are being equipped with such up-to-date equipment as the Phalanx air defense gun and chaff launchers, SM-IMR missile systems, ASW improvements such as the AN/SQR-18A towed array sonar, and the MK-46 mod. 5 ASW torpedo, it is unlikely that these additions will provide Japan with an independent ability to protect against a Soviet Pacific fleet that has as many submarines as Japan has destroyers and undoubtedly possesses complete data on Japan's vulnerable ports and lack of sufficient escort vessels and aircraft. In sum, Japan's larger maritime role in East Asia depends on coordinated, joint efforts with the U.S. Seventh Fleet and continued political cooperation with Washington. Only if the United States authorizes the sale or license of new systems being introduced into the U.S. Navy to Japan can the MSDF effectively meet its sea-lane defense commitments.[30]

Even then, Japanese procurement levels under the 1976 NDPO would be insufficient. Japanese analysts believe that the MSDF would have to increase its destroyer force by half, procure an additonal hundred ASW aircraft, and acquire four or five more squadrons of F-15s to be able to maintain open sea-lanes, interdict the straits, and cope with a Soviet contingency in the north. Given the country's overall budget austerity in recent years, it is improbable that these forces will be acquired before the mid-to-late 1990s.[31]

A glance at table 3–2 reveals that only in two areas—replacement of the GSDF's SAM system and introduction of the F-15 fighter to replace the F-104—does the midterm achievement rate reach the plan level of 40 percent after two years. Moreover, the price inflation of such systems as the F-15, costing

Table 3–2

Achievement Rate for Orders of Major Equipment under the 1983–1987 Program Estimate, as of 1984

	Orders in 1983–1984	Targets	Achievement Rate	Shortfall	Total Strength at Completion of Plan
GSDF					
Type 74 tanks	120	373	32%	253	850
New 155 mm howitzers	58	176	33	118	176
AH-1S antitank helicopters	10	43	23	33	56
Surface-to-air missile system (improved Hawk)	2 groups	3 groups	67	1 group	8 groups
ASDF					
Destroyers	5	14	36	9	60
Submarines	2	6	33	4	15
P3C anti-submarine patrol planes	15	50	30	39	72
MSDF					
Operational planes	39	120	33	81	400
(F-15 fighter interceptors)	(30)	(75)	(40)	(45)	(138)

Source: Ikeuchi Fumio, "The 1986–90 Medium-Term Defense Plan," *Japan Quarterly* (November–December 1984): 392.

$40 million per unit in 1984 as opposed to $29 million in 1978, and the P3C up from $31 million in 1978 to $47 million in 1984, may reduce procurement levels, thus postponing NDPO goals even further. Revealing, too, is the absence of reserves in the current program. Even if achieved, stockpiles of ammunition and spare parts would be depleted in fewer than thirty days if a war broke out.[32]

There may be some cause for guarded optimism, however. Under the 1986–1990 defense program, Japan plans to increase its destroyers to 60 and its P3C aircraft to 100. (See table 3–3.) These figures are three and five times as many, respectively, as the U.S. Seventh Fleet deploys. By 1990, moreover, the ASDF will be spearheaded by 200 F-15s and 100 F-4s, more than the U.S. Air Force has in Japan, Korea, and the Philippines combined. Equally important, the logistics budget is to increase by 20 percent, markedly improving sustainability.[33]

Table 3–3
Increased Capabilities Needed for Defense of Japan
and Thousand-Mile SLOC

	Number Needed in Addition to 1983 Force Level
Equipment	
F-15 fighter aircraft	300
AWACs equivalent aircraft	8–10
KC-10 tanker aircraft	10–14
Tactical jet aircraft	60–90
SAM groups	3–7
Attack submarines	10–12
Frigates-destroyers	20
P3C ASW aircraft	130
Personnel	
Active	25,000
Reserves	30,000

Source: Thomas B. Modly, "The Rhetoric of and Realities of Japan's 1000-Mile Sealane Defense Policy," *Naval War College Review* 38, no. 1 (January–February 1985): 31.

Most threats to Japan's SLOCs from the USSR by air or sea must either pass through or near Japan's airspace or the Japanese straits. Yet the JSDF is woefully unprepared to meet these threats even if the NDPO is fulfilled (table 3–3). Moreover, if one probes further to examine JSDF training procedures, the picture looks even bleaker. Because of concern for the fishing industry, there are strict limitations on areas where mine laying, sweeping, and ASW training may occur. The best waters must be shallow, but these are off-limits since they are fishing zones. Japanese pilots train less than half the time of their American counterparts; and air-to-air missiles are so scarce that many ASDF pilots have never fired one. Integrated operations between the MSDF and ASDF are virtually unknown. Because there is no unified command system, coordination with U.S. forces in an emergency becomes needlessly complicated. Nor is there a standard procedure for ASDF protection of the fleet in the event of war.[34]

To sum up, in the mid-1980s, despite efforts to add some modern systems, particularly guided missile cruisers, the MSDF is ill equipped to deal with a Soviet air or naval threat. Its primary weapon against submarines, the Mark 44 torpedo, is obsolete. Most of its surface vessels lack SAMs and SSMs, as well as modern electronic equipment. The MSDF is essentially an ASW force, possessing neither interceptor nor attack aircraft. Japan's much publicized willingness to mine the three major straits in the event of a crisis appears less reassuring when Japan's experts state that under present conditions it would take six months to close the passages between the Sea of Japan and the Pacific Ocean.[35] Moreover, Japanese officials have also affirmed that they will not preempt the straits. That is, there are no plans to close the straits until Japan is attacked. In all probability, this policy is militarily worthless since in the event of war, the Soviets would seize control of the straits as one of their earliest actions.

Strategically, Japan's position is understandable, however. Rather than engage in a Don Quixiote-like gesture against the USSR, the Japanese say to the United States that if Washington believes it is necessary to block the straits, the U.S. Navy should proceed to do so. Japan, however, will not engage in such a venture by itself.

A Closer Look at the Japan–Soviet Straits and Northern Islands

The geographical obstacles confronting Soviet naval access to the open ocean from Vladivostok place Japan automatically in an adversarial position. Tokyo's security relationship with the United States only exacerbates this opposition. The Soviets reacted to the warming of Sino-Japanese relations beginning in the late 1970s and the Midterm Defense Buildup of the JSDF in the 1980s by increasing their own activities on the disputed northern islands of Kunashiri and Etorofu. Radar installations, runways of sufficient length to handle MiG-23s, helicopters, and SAMs were all introduced by the early 1980s along with a permanent garrison of some 13,000 motorized infantry. A new airfield on Kunashiri is probably capable of handling Backfire bombers.

With these installations in place, the USSR turned to harassing Japan in hopes of intimidating its more modest military. Soviet warships regularly interfere with Japanese military and civilian shipping. Soviet aircraft from the northern islands frequently violate Japanese airspace. (See figure 3–1.) Indeed control of this airspace would be crucial for Soviet domination of the Soya Strait in wartime as a quick access route to the Pacific.[36] Japanese officials are well aware that they lack the capability to defend northern Hokkaido if the Soviets wanted to seize the land bordering the Soya Strait. Instead Japan has developed an intelligence network in the north capable of eavesdropping on the USSR and North Korea. With six radars in Hokkaido, Japan keeps track of air and sea traffic in the Sea of Okhotsk.[37]

Just as Soviet control of the Soya Strait would require occupation of northern Hokkaido, so Japanese dominance necessitates the occupation of southern Sakhalin or at least its neutralization through massive air strikes. The JSDF does not have the force structure in the north to accomplish this. Politically it is equally inconceivable that Japan would initiate hostilities in this region. To do so would invite massive retaliation from the USSR. Japanese forces could be effective only as adjunct to a U.S. command. The question arises, Would Japan be willing to confront the Soviets as a result of a U.S.-Soviet showdown, say, in the Middle East where Japanese interests were not directly at stake?

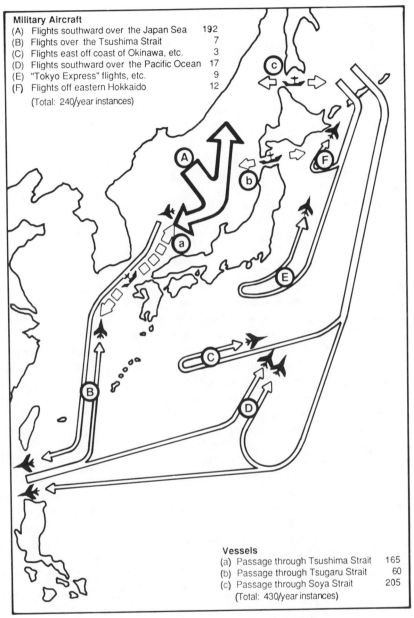

Military Aircraft
(A) Flights southward over the Japan Sea   192
(B) Flights over the Tsushima Strait   7
(C) Flights east off coast of Okinawa, etc.   3
(D) Flights southward over the Pacific Ocean 17
(E) "Tokyo Express" flights, etc.   9
(F) Flights off eastern Hokkaido   12
      (Total: 240/year instances)

Vessels
(a) Passage through Tsushima Strait   165
(b) Passage through Tsugaru Strait   60
(c) Passage through Soya Strait   205
      (Total: 430/year instances)

Source: Defense Agency, Japan, *Defense of Japan 1982*, (Tokyo: Japan Defense Agency, 1982), p. 35.
Note: Number of ships and instances indicates average figures from 1977 to 1981.

Figure 3–1. Outline of Soviet Naval Activities and Military Aircraft Movements around Japan

Another way of phrasing this question is, How willing will Japan be in the future to subordinate its security policy to U.S. global concerns when the latter could lead to a military confrontation with an overwhelmingly powerful neighbor? In fact, the question may be moot. In both Middle Eastern and European war scenarios, even if Japan chose to remain neutral, it would probably be unable to do so. The Soviets would move to control the Soya Strait immediately in order to free up passage for its Pacific fleet into open waters.

If Japan is to put up a reasonable defense of northern Hokkaido and presumably the Soya Strait as well, it must increase the number of F-15 squadrons in the Northern Air Defense Force beyond those allotted under the NDPO. F-15s are critical for intercepting Soviet Backfires with their standoff missile capabilities. To achieve this buildup would require raising defense spending to about 2.5 percent of GNP.[38] According to U.S. government estimates, Japan needs 70 destroyers, 25 submarines, 125 P3Cs, and several hundred F-15s to defend its straits and sea-lanes. In 1983, it had 49 destroyers, 14 submarines, 6 P3Cs, and 20 F-15s.[39]

Japanese officials are ambiguous about the conditions under which they would either blockade the straits themselves or permit a U.S. blockade. The only clear condition would be after a Soviet attack. Such a policy would be an exercise in futility, however, since the Soviets would undoubtedly have gained control of the sea passages as a prelude to any assault on Japan. More ambiguous would be the case where a Soviet attack seemed probable. In February 1983, Prime Minister Nakasone stated that a U.S. action to blockade the straits might be acceptable if there were an imminent threat to Japan's security. This formulation was repeated by Hisashi Owada, director general of the Foreign Ministry's Treaties Bureau, a year later.[40]

One Japanese defense analyst, who requested confidentiality at a Naval Postgraduate School conference, "The Navy in the Pacific," in August 1987, states that there is a strategic disjunction between the GSDF and the MSDF. The former train to secure northern Hokkaido and are prepared to move two-thirds of their forces to northern Japan in a crisis. However, the MSDF is not prepared to escort U.S. carrier battle groups in the northern Sea of Japan to interdict the Soviet Pacific fleet before it reaches the Soya Strait. Instead, the MSDF stresses thousand-mile sea-lane protection, a task of limited use in the event of a Soviet-U.S. showdown.

The MSDF's reticence in becoming an adjunct ASW force for the U.S. Navy may be a nationalist objection to serving U.S. strategic interests rather than Japan's. Moreover, the MSDF cannot declare its main task to be the escort of U.S. carrier battle groups, for this could be construed as a violation of the Japanese Constitution's prohibition on collective self-defense. Thus, during 1987 joint exercises, the U.S. Navy and the MSDF seemed to engage in different scenarios. While U.S. ships maneuvered in the northern Sea of Japan and even entered the Sea of Okhotsk (the Soviet bastion), the MSDF conducted amphibious operations designed to recover a captured Hokkaido, not to assault the Kuril islands and secure the Soya Strait. The MSDF sees the U.S. maritime strategy as dangerous and escalatory. It appears unwilling to cooperate with it. By contrast, GSDF officials accept the maritime strategy and train to play a ground force role within it, that is, the securing of northern Hokkaido.

The U.S. decision to deploy F-16s at Misawa air base in northern Honshu in the mid-1980s combined with the permanent patrol of Japanese vessels in all of the straits could be the harbinger of a new straits control strategy whereby Japan provides electronic intelligence on Soviet ship movements, and, in a crisis situation, U.S. airpower and sea power would be employed to deter, preempt, or attack. With Seventh Fleet Tomahawk cruise missiles and Harpoon antiship missiles, the Pacific fleet would be vulnerable as they lined up to transit each strait bottleneck.

The Korean Connection

Since World War II, Japan has had a "free ride" on Korean security. For the most part, this situation has suited all parties. The Japanese and Koreans share a historical antipathy comparable to the Greeks and Turks or Turks and Armenians. Koreans see Japan as a brutal conqueror, which trampled their traditions from 1895 through 1945 and sold their young men into slavery. Japanese, until quite recently, viewed the Koreans as rustic upstarts. The large Korean minority in Japan continues to suffer social and economic discrimination.

Nevertheless, both countries realize that Korean stability is important for the security of each and that Japan may well have to make some contribution to it, since the United States may not be willing to bear all the burden of external guarantor indefinitely. Thus Japan goes out of its way not to target Korea's major industries as rivals but instead facilitates the growth of Korean giants in steel, petrochemicals, and, more recently, automobiles. An economically strong South Korea is not likely to seek unification with a halting, debt-ridden North. As Edward Olsen puts it:

> Were Korea to be peacefully unified, the resultant state, regardless of its political coloration, could rather easily become a threat to Japanese interests. Such a Korea would have a combined population of about 55 million, would combine the productivity of the south with the indigenous resources of the north, would possess armed forces in excess of one million, and would share a common antipathy toward Japan.[41]

Japan is equally concerned about one Korea or the other attempting to reunify the peninsula by force. U.S. defense of the ROK in the event of a northern attack would inevitably involve bases in Japan and could conceivably bring the war to Japan as well—for example, through the bombing of U.S. facilities.

Moreover, given the small number of U.S. forces in Korea (about 40,000), war could even lead to the use of battlefield nuclear weapons, a military psychological barrier the Japanese are particularly loath to cross since it would lead to a nightmare situation: local nuclear war on Japan's border, with fallout spreading east by prevailing winds.

It is unsurprising that Japan is so enamored of the status quo in Korea. Under current conditions, Japan has the best of all worlds in Korea: the peninsula is divided, and the United States looks after Tokyo's strategic interests. Yet reliance on tactical nuclear weapons is neither comfortable nor prudent. Washington, Seoul, and Tokyo should do more to ensure that defense of the ROK shifts entirely to conventional force. Indeed there is some doubt that U.S. public opinion would tolerate the use of nuclear weapons in Korea with its implication of crossing a hitherto forbidden line and risking escalation with the USSR.

Japanese security cooperation with the ROK would be no easy task to accomplish. It would appear to violate the constitution's Article IX to send Japanese forces to Korea even if Seoul were willing to receive Japanese troops, a politically inconceivable act for the foreseeable future. There are less volatile actions Japan could take in support of South Korea's security. Increased air and naval cooperation would not require the stationing of Japanese forces in Korea. However, it would require a change in Korea's political attitude toward Japan. The vision of the militarily swaggering Japanese imperialists would have to be laid to rest if genuine security cooperation is to develop.

A logical location for trilateral cooperation (U.S.-Japan-ROK) to begin is the Tsushima Strait flanked by the South Korean naval base at Chinhae and the U.S. base at Sasebo, Japan. Tsushima could be an effective choke point against the Pacific fleet. Soviet ship passages through this strait averaged about 170 per year between 1976 and 1983.[42] Japanese P3Cs could become an important component of a trilateral surveillance network against Soviet submarines in the area. Indeed, the Japanese and ROK navies by themselves in 1983 constituted a combined force of 42 destroyers (many with Harpoon SSMs), 25 frigates, 14 submarines, 40 minesweepers, and 17 P3Cs. Japan's navy and air force expansion plans would add another 40 to 50 F-15s, 125 more P3Cs, 3 more destroyers, 70 additional frigates, and 24 more submarines by the early to mid-1990s.[43]

The potential for tripartite naval security cooperation is enhanced by the existence of bilateral security treaties between the United States and Japan and the United States and the ROK. The U.S. Fifth Air Force and the Seventh Fleet have command structures that treat South Korea and Japan as a single region. For example, the Fifth Air Force has one air division at Japan's Kadena Air Base and another at South Korea's Osan Air Base. In 1984, Japan's ASDF conducted a joint training exercise with the U.S. F-16s stationed in the ROK. North Korean media also claimed that JSDF officers participated in the ROK-U.S. 1985 Team Spirit exercise as observers.[44]

In 1980, JSDF counsellor Atsuyuki Sosa stated that joint exercises with South Korea would be legal. Three years later, U.S. Under Secretary of Defense Fred Ikle also expressed a desire to see tripartite exercises centering on the Tsushima Strait. According to one Japanese analyst, the logical time to have moved toward a tripartite alliance would have been after the Soviet-Vietnam Treaty of Friendship in 1978 and the building of Soviet military bases beginning soon after on the northern islands.[45] However, no new arrangements have been made to coordinate the service branches of the three countries. Japan's fear of violating its constitutional prohibition against collective security and the historical antipathy between Korea and Japan prevail over any military advantages that might be derived from joint planning and deployments in the Sea of Japan. If the Soviet fleet continues to grow and if Japan-ROK relations continue to improve through such gestures as the 1984 "apologies" of the emperor and Prime Minister Nakasone to General Chun-Doo Hwan for Japan's brutal occupation of Korea between 1895 and 1945, prospects for military collaboration seem brighter in the 1990s.

Japan and ASEAN

ASEAN's economic dependence on Japan is well documented. In the early 1980s, 45 percent of Indonesia's trade, 34 percent of the Philippines', and 29 percent of Thailand's all went to Japan. Yet the highest Southeast Asian share of Japanese world trade was the oil and gas from Indonesia at 4.2 percent; all other ASEAN states' trade was 2 percent or less.[46] ASEAN's importance to Japan is reflected in other data, particularly the fact that about 60 percent of Japan's Official Development Assistance has gone to ASEAN states for several years and that 50 percent of all economic aid going to ASEAN in the mid-1980s originates in Japan.[47] The ASEAN states have also become a major industrial platform for those products no longer cost competitive if fabricated in Japan, such as textiles and small-scale electronics.

Fear over Japanese economic domination and the belief that Tokyo was unwilling to increase value-added imports from the ASEAN states to alleviate growing balance of payments deficits led to anti-Japanese riots during Prime Minister Kakuei Tanaka's tour of the five states in January 1974. Since that time, as an important component of omnidirectional diplomacy, Japanese leaders have paid considerable attention to ASEAN economic concerns. Prime Minister Takeo Fukuda, in a similar ASEAN visit in 1977, spelled out the new Fukuda doctrine, which offered a massive $1 billion aid package to help develop ASEAN-wide industrial projects. In a major diplomatic initiative, Fukuda also offered Tokyo's good offices to ASEAN if they desired Japan to serve as an intermediary in establishing better relations with Vietnam. As events played out, neither the individual $200 million country industrial projects nor Japan's diplomatic proposal were achieved. The latter was resented as political in-terference in Southeast Asia affairs, and the former led to intra-ASEAN bickering over which country should take responsibility for particular projects. Never-theless, in December 1987, after the third ASEAN summit meeting in Manila, Prime Minister Norboru Takeshita proffered a $2 billion aid package consisting primarily of loans for new private sector ventures. Once again, the ASEAN states have an opportunity to absorb Japanese capital for their own developmen-tal programs.

Both Japan and ASEAN are reluctant to discuss mutual security. Each prefers that the United States remain the dominant external military guaran-tor in the ASEAN region. The status quo is quite comfortable for Tokyo in that Washington bears the cost of patroling the sea-lanes so essential for Japanese trade from Southeast Asia through the Indian Ocean to the Middle East. Of the 150 ships passing through the Strait of Malacca each day, 44 per-cent of those over 30,000 tons are Japanese.[48] Japanese officials were un-doubtedly reassured by Secretary Weinberger's March 1982 statement in Tokyo that the United States would continue to ensure freedom of transit between the Pacific and Indian oceans. To enforce this commitment, the U.S. Navy ex-ercises regularly with the littoral states.[49]

Although the MSDF is gradually increasing its capacity to monitor sea-lanes over 1,000 miles from Honshu, Southeast Asian observers are skeptical over whether this coverage would have any meaning in an East Asian confron-tation with the USSR. Moscow could neutralize Japan with attacks on its ports and airfields, thus greatly reducing the latter's ability either to project or monitor forces in Southeast Asian waters. Only timely and direct U.S. involvement in Japan's defense might deter Soviet preemption.

Aside from the question of Japan's capabilities in a regional military showdown, ASEAN views of a growing Japanese force projection capability—although becoming more positive—remain ambivalent. Singapore and Thailand are the most openly supportive of a Japanese thousand-mile sea-lane defense, arguing that Tokyo must assist the United States to increase overall regional security against the Soviet threat.[50] Indonesia and the Philippines are less en-thusiastic. Former President Ferdinand Marcos publicly voiced concern about whether Japan still harbors ideas of domination. In his 1982 visit to Japan and the United States, President Suharto argued that sea-lane defense should be better left to the cooperative efforts of the states of the region.[51] Malay-sian analysts seem to take a middle position with respect to the desirability of a Japanese security role. Ahmad Zakaria, formerly of the Malaysian Institute of Strategic and International Studies, believes that Japan will play a larger security role in Southeast Asia as time goes on, and ASEAN should watch these developments carefully.[52] Malaysia's concern centers on the belief that Japan will find the thousand-mile sea-lane perimeter insufficient and as it develops greater capability will choose to extend it.

The idea that Japan should increase its defense efforts within its own domain—a thousand miles south and east of Honshu—appears acceptable to ASEAN. It will make U.S. tasks easier to perform by permitting more of the Seventh Fleet to locate in the South China Sea and Indian Ocean. Unacceptable, however, would be a Japanese presence in the ASEAN area. If Japan is to do more for ASEAN security, it should provide military aid for the ASEAN states' own buildup. As President Marcos put it during Prime Minister Suzuki's visit to Manila in February 1981: "[The Philippines] has no fear of a resurgent military Japan providing the United States maintains its military presence in Asia." Singapore has gone furthest in actually proposing a collective defense arrangement with external powers, including Japan. Finally, even Indonesian analysts, whose government is the most reticent of the six in welcoming external forces, have written that a gradual Japanese defense buildup is acceptable as long as Japan consults ASEAN regularly and the buildup is conducted as part of a joint U.S.-Japan arrangement. This arrangement is seen by Indonesians as an interim development until the ASEAN states build sufficient forces to be responsible for their own region.[53]

In my discussions with midlevel foreign policy officials in the Philippines, Malaysia, and Singapore during the spring of 1984, long-range projections were somewhat at variance with statements by governmental leaders. A number of government analysts perceived that by the mid-1990s, Japan would have a significant naval presence in Southeast Asian waters and that this presence would be tolerable to ASEAN if it were part of a joint U.S. force. The analysts agreed, however, that the one exception to this generalization would be Indonesia. Jakarta feels strongly that no other state should be responsible for monitoring its sea-lanes. The U.S. presence is tolerated for the time being but presumably only until Indonesia has sufficient naval forces to conduct its own surveillance and control.

Nevertheless, after Nakasone's visit to Jakarta in May 1983, bilateral security consultations were initiated at Indonesia's request. Indonesia is probably interested in intelligence sharing and possibly technology transfer. Both are island countries with problems of sea-lane defense.[54] These regular security talks belie Jakarta's complete rejection of a Japanese security role in the region.

ASEAN public opinion seems to indicate a growing level of trust in Japan. A Japanese Foreign Ministry poll taken in 1983 shows an increase in trust toward Japan from the last such poll in 1978: from 76 to 87 percent in Indonesia, from 71 to 78 percent in Malaysia, from 66 to 78 percent in Thailand, from 75 to 77 percent in the Philippines, and from 60 to 74 percent in Singapore. On the other hand, fears of Japanese militarism were expressed by 54 percent, 37 percent, 35 percent, 28 percent, and 19 percent, respectively, of respondents in Thailand, Malaysia, Singapore, the Philippines, and Indonesia. The overwhelming proportion of respondents wanted Japan's role in Southeast Asia to remain exclusively economic.[55]

Finally, ASEAN is less than enthusiastic about Japan's policy toward China. During Prime Minister Suzuki's visit to the region in 1981 and President Suharto's trip to Tokyo in 1982, ASEAN concern was expressed over Japan's preferential treatment for China's modernization. Industrial loans were provided by Beijing on easier terms than those provided to ASEAN, though the latter were more important as trade and investment partners to Japan. In a 1982 visit to Thailand, the director-general of the JSDF stated that Vietnam, not China, was a greater security threat to ASEAN. Japan also argues that its assistance to China is a stabilizing factor in Asian politics, which should be welcomed by ASEAN.[56] Nevertheless, the predominant ASEAN view is that Tokyo is helping to build an economic rival to ASEAN exports and investments designed to drive terms of trade and business opportunities even further against the Southeast Asian group of six.

The U.S. hope, then, is not that Japan becomes an independent regional military power—anathema to such neighbors as China, the Philippines, and Korea—but that Tokyo develops the capacity to fulfill its pledge to defend the surrounding sea-lanes. Japan would not stand in for the United States in this region; rather, its forces would augment the Seventh Fleet by subjecting Soviet naval and air movements to close surveillance. The concept of Japanese forces being additive to U.S. forces implies, of course, that the United States has abandoned its swing strategy to Europe in the event of a crisis. Reassurance of U.S. Pacific allies, including Japan, that the ASDF and MSDF will not be primarily responsible for western Pacific defense is essential if an expanded role for these forces is to be politically acceptable in Asia.

U.S.-Japan joint exercises are increasing in scope and number, with the biannual RIMPAC '86 also involving the Australian, Canadian, and British navies. Nevertheless, unlike NATO, the United States still has no joint command structure with Japan. Current plans state that in the event of imminent attack on Japan, the two governments will conduct closer liaison; no joint command is planned, even for air defense where rapid task coordination would be essential. The reason for this anomaly is Article IX's prohibition on collective self-defense. Thus, joint defense beyond territorial waters and airspace is problematic. Within Japanese airspace and sea space, however, the LDP government interprets the constitution in a manner that permits Japan to respond to an attack on U.S. forces, arguing that such a response falls with individual or national self-defense. Thus, Japanese ships can protect U.S. ships within Japanese waters, though the chain of command would be through the MSDF and not the U.S. fleet.[57]

Basically the JSDF, while desiring full participation with U.S. forces in Japan, hopes to avoid having to justify that participation in the Diet—hence, the ambiguity surrounding the Japanese commitment to defend U.S. forces and the insistence that Japanese and U.S. forces are not integrated. The JSDF has been more concerned with defusing joint defense as an issue in domestic politics than with devising more effective security arrangements.

4
Southeast Asia, the Subregional Crossroads

A Brief ASEAN Overview

Perhaps the most successful example of regional organization in the third world, ASEAN was formed in 1967 among the states of Indonesia, Malaysia, Singapore, Thailand, and the Philippines. Brunei adhered to the association in 1984 after independence from Great Britain. Formed during the dark days of the second Indochina War and during a period of considerable intramural strife among its members, few observers predicted the political success that lay ahead for the five neighbors. Within fifteen years of its inception, the ASEAN states were compiling some of the most impressive economic growth statistics in the world. Relying essentially on international market forces and foreign capital investment, even during the recent world recession when most nations were experiencing zero growth or worse, the ASEAN states—with the exception of the Philippines—were chalking up annual GNP increments of 6 to 8 percent. Agreeing to settle peacefully or paper over differences among themselves, by the early 1970s, the ASEAN five began to coordinate their regional economic positions with industrial partners. Annual dialogues with the United States, the European Economic Community (EEC), Australia–New Zealand, and Japan were inaugurated in the late 1970s in the course of which the five would press for preferential market access and encourage loans and investments.

Although somewhat successful as a consultative mechanism toward third countries, ASEAN has no illusions about becoming another EEC. Its economies are more competitive than complementary, and less trade in percentage terms occurred among the six in 1986 than it did when the association was formed. Attempts to develop ASEAN-wide industries have not reached fruition. Rather, economic nationalism has dominated regional policymaking, most recently illustrated by the failure of a long-discussed ASEAN automobile project and the decision by Malaysia to develop its own national car.

Despite only modest successes in economic coordination, ASEAN has become a major force in Asian international politics, particularly after the Vietnamese invasion of Cambodia in late 1978. The movement of some 180,000

Vietnamese troops into Cambodia with subsequent annual spillovers of refugees and combat onto Thai soil led ASEAN to rally around its front-line member. The association discovered that it had both political prestige and influence in such international conclaves as the United Nations and the Nonaligned Movement. Overwhelming majorities in the UN annually back ASEAN resolutions condemning the Vietnamese aggression in Cambodia and calling for their withdrawal and internationally supervised elections. Currently ASEAN takes the lead in annual strategy planning for the UN debates on Cambodia and also serves as primary interlocutor in negotiating with Vietnam over Cambodia's future. The major capitalist states defer to ASEAN on Southeast Asian security issues at the same time they coordinate their own regional security plans with the association.

Reasons for ASEAN Security Cooperation

Although not a problem-solving organization with hierarchical decision mechanisms to arbitrate member disagreements, ASEAN may be more accurately termed a conflict-avoidance system in which conscious efforts are made to contain interstate disputes.[1] There are no central structures or delegations of sovereignty. Rather, experience in cooperation on political and economic issues within the association and in common fronts toward external partners and adversaries has created over time a series of norms, procedures, and expectations. These norms affect which issues are moved on and off agendas, determine which activities are legitimized, and influence which, when, and how conflicts are resolved. Since the Vietnamese invasion of Cambodia, these patterns of diplomatic cooperation now openly include defense and intelligence matters.

ASEAN's interest in regional security owes much to Indonesia's inspiration. In the wake of Jakarta's confrontation (1963–1966) against Malaysia, ASEAN was formed to promote regional reconciliation and to manage intramural disputes. Two ancillary objectives were to prevent the diversion of resources from economic development to the members' militaries and to create a mechanism by which external powers would be discouraged from interfering in Southeast Asia. The latter aspiration found expression in the 1976 Bali Declaration of ASEAN Concord, which endorsed a regional peace zone. A subsequent Treaty of Amity and Cooperation was made available for accession by non-ASEAN states of the region, with Indochina particularly in mind.

The emergence of Vietnam by 1979 as the dominant power in Indochina based on a Soviet alliance thwarted ASEAN's strategic conception of a region free of great power security activities. On the other hand, Indonesia was undoubtedly relieved that Sino-Vietnamese antagonisms ensured Indochina would not become part of a Chinese sphere of influence. Still, Indonesia's inability to draw Vietnam toward ASEAN's view of regional order prior to Hanoi's movement into Laos and Cambodia was a keen disappointment. Hanoi's insistence that a dominant position in Cambodia and Laos was a matter of national security was diametrically opposed to Thailand's: that an independent Cambodia remain as a neutral buffer against Vietnam. Indonesia sacrificed a longer-term goal (a greater ASEAN) for the short-term necessity of unifying the association's current membership over a vital security issue to its frontline state, Thailand.

Southeast Asia's history over the last thirty years illustrates that its members have consistently sought to escape incorporation into either communist or Western blocs. Radical nonalignment was an early policy against the vestiges of Western colonialism as embodied in Indonesian President Sukarno's late 1950s distinction between the new emerging forces (NEFO) and the old established forces (OLDEFO). It was no random choice that the Indonesian city of Bandung became the location of the first meeting of the third world states bent on proclaiming their independence from great power controls in 1955. In more recent years, although political radicalism has disappeared from the foreign policies of the ASEAN states, strong identification with third world positions on North-South issues persists. For Muslim countries, such as Indonesia and Malaysia, there is the further pull of Middle Eastern issues, varying from the Arab-Israeli conflict to alleged Libyan support for Muslim separatists in the southern Philippines. In the North-South dialogue, although ASEAN is among the more moderate of the Group of 77, the association's members identify with third world demands for preferential access to the markets of developed states and a curbing of the latter's protectionist policies.

The ASEAN states see their primary security problems as internal to each society, requiring a combination of policies to achieve economic growth, more equitable distribution of income, political participation, and the integration of diverse ethnic groups. Nevertheless, external threats are attracting more concern as the Soviet-Vietnam alliance solidifies and China continues to associate with the ASEAN position on Cambodia. ASEAN leaders are concerned over the Soviet naval and air presence at Cam Ranh Bay, which was upgraded in late 1984 to include MiG-23s, an attack aircraft that could reach much of the region from Vietnam. However, the ASEAN states are generally much more relaxed about the Soviet potential for influence or subversion elsewhere in the region than is the United States. Although the Soviet Union is seen as an enemy of the ASEAN system, it is one with few significant capabilities to affect it. For some, Moscow may even be a useful counterweight to Beijing when the latter develops its own regional naval capacity.

Donald Weatherbee has identified four distinct levels of threat in the ASEAN region:[2]

1. Threats internal to the ASEAN states such as revolutionary insurgencies, ethnic dissidence, and religious strife. Each ASEAN state has faced some

form of internal warfare. Their armed forces have historically been structured to meet this kind of challenge.

2. Intra-ASEAN threats arising from persistent political and jurisdictional disputes such as the Sabah issue and overlapping maritime claims. The processes of ASEAN itself have served to mediate threats of this nature as ASEAN has become a security community, in Karl Deutsch's sense, in which there no longer is an expectation of the use of force by one member against another.

3. Threats originating from non-ASEAN regional sources. The most apparent threat of this nature would originate in the regional polarization marked by ASEAN's confrontation with Vietnam. It is in meeting this threat that the ASEAN states have reoriented and modernized their militaries.

4. The threat of great power intervention in the region. There is little militarily the ASEAN states can do about this level of threat. The ASEAN policy response has been rhetorically to exclude great powers through the brandishing of the symbolic framework of the Zone of Peace, Freedom, and Neutrality (ZOPFAN) while realistically encouraging the operation of a regional balance of power.

Although the ASEAN states repeatedly demur that they have not formed a military alliance, they readily acknowledge bilateral and trilateral security arrangements outside the framework of the association, which in fact interrelate all of their military establishments in some fashion with each other. (The exceptions are the Philippines and Malaysia, which do not exercise with each other because of the unresolved Philippine claim to Sabah.) Not only do ASEAN militaries exercise together regularly, but they exchange intelligence information and military officers among their war colleges too. External powers are also linked into ASEAN defense activities. Thailand and the Philippines have formal defense ties to the United States, and Malaysia and Singapore are linked to Britain, Australia, and New Zealand through the Five Power Defense Arrangement (FPDA). Moreover, it could be argued that the FPDA goes beyond the ASEAN-Commonwealth countries to include U.S. assistance in a crisis because under ANZUS, Washington is committed to aiding Australia if its forces come under attack. In some ways, ASEAN enjoys the best of both security worlds. On the one hand, the six can claim representation in the Nonaligned Movement since its largest member, Indonesia, is a founding member. Simultaneously, the association is part of the democratic states' Pacific defense system.

ASEAN's insistence that regional problems are the primary responsibilities of its members is exemplified in its practice of the frontline state concept. When a particular issue is more important to one state than another, the former takes the policy lead. Muslim fundamentalism is left to Indonesia and Malaysia; Cambodian policy is given primarily to Thailand, though beginning in 1983 Indonesia was selected as the major interlocutor because of its historical ties to Hanoi. On the question of the U.S. bases, the Philippines sets the association's tone, though here too other ASEAN states have informally urged Manila not to jeopardize the bases' future in the light of the growing Soviet regional presence.[3]

Lest it appear that ASEAN is merely a figleaf for a Western security arrangement, as the Soviets sometimes charge, its members' ambivalent attitudes toward external security links should be discussed. The ASEAN states have no desire to be pawns in a U.S. crusade against the USSR or Vietnam. Nor are they comfortable with a balance of power in which the United States, ASEAN, and China are rigidly aligned against the Soviet-Vietnamese camp.[4] Southeast Asian governments still see their major security concerns as internal economic and political issues that can be solved only through economic development. Insofar as the United States is invited to play a larger regional security role, in all probability the Soviets will increase their activities as well, forcing ASEAN states to direct an increasing share of their national budgets to external defense and away from internal development. ASEAN would prefer, then, a reduction of tensions between Washington and Moscow rather than a further escalation of hostility.[5] The latter offers additional opportunities for great powers to interfere in the affairs of their regional partners.

ASEAN's 1971 endorsement of Malaysia's ZOPFAN proposal has been an effective diplomatic device to project a regional image of neutrality while maintaining the guarantees of friendly external powers. The zone concept acknowledges the existence of alliance arrangements and base rights but refers to them as temporary. As a carrot to the Indochinese states, ASEAN proffered the possibility of regional nonaggression pacts through the 1976 Treaty of Amity and Cooperation, which came out of the Bali Summit Conference of that year. The institutional mechanism put in place to resolve intra-ASEAN disputes by the treaty is a high point for Southeast Asian regional collective security insofar as that term refers to peaceful settlement procedures.[6] Nevertheless, the Indonesian-Malaysian view of ZOPFAN has not been effective in curbing the military buildup of either the United States or Soviet Union in Southeast Asian waters as each seeks to protect its sea-lanes from the other's predatory intentions. Nor has ZOPFAN in its most recent manifestation—a call for a nuclear-weapons-free zone—elicited any guarantees from the United States and USSR that their forces in the region would not be equipped with nuclear arms.

For the foreseeable future, ASEAN will remain closer to the ANZUS countries and Japan than to either the USSR or PRC. While the presence of the latter two is regarded as unavoidable, ideally that presence should be regulated through the principles of ZOPFAN.

Pending the admittedly long-term realization of ZOPFAN, the ASEAN states must decide separately and collectively how to deal with the interests and activities of the major powers. The United States is either a formal (Thailand, Philippines) or informal ally (Malaysia, Singapore) with four of

ASEAN's six members and is viewed by the other two (Indonesia and Brunei) as a friendly state whose economic and military presence in the region remains essential for the association's autonomy. Nevertheless, the United States is seen as an inconstant friend, one whose foreign policy has changed mercurially from deep military involvement during the second Indochina War (1965–1975) to general indifference in the war's aftermath (1975–1980) and more recently to a renewed security concern with Southeast Asia derived from its geostrategic location (1980–   ). While the buildup of U.S. air and naval power in East Asia is welcomed, Washington's political will is still suspect, particularly to the extent that ASEAN leaders perceive that the United States must rely on China to deal more effectively with the USSR. Southeast Asians are not enamored of U.S. support for the Chinese position in the Cambodian conflict. They believe this stiffens Beijing in its campaign to bleed Vietnam, solidifies China's intrusion into Southeast Asian security affairs, and further justifies the continuation of the Soviet-Vietnam alliance.[7] In sum, U.S. political reticence translates into opportunities for other, less benign external actors to involve themselves in regional affairs.

This fear applies also to U.S. interests in a regional role for Japan. Rather than augmenting U.S. capabilities, a Japanese military presence in Southeast Asian waters is seen by Indonesia as an excuse for the United States to do less and, still worse, as an additional provocation to the USSR.[8] ASEAN states differ on a future Japanese role. Singapore's Prime Minister Lee Kuan Yew has openly advocated multinational naval task forces for the region incorporating U.S., Japanese, Australian, and New Zealand ships.[9] In effect, this arrangement could be interpreted as one way of guaranteeing ASEAN autonomy through the protection of friendly forces, though it would not provide the balanced external guarantees envisioned in the Malaysian view of ZOPFAN.

Every ASEAN state is concerned about the long-term intentions of the USSR. All are convinced that the Soviets intend to increase their military presence in Southeast Asia through their use of Vietnamese bases. While ASEAN militaries see the Soviet naval buildup as a security threat, the Indonesian and Malaysian foreign ministries seem less convinced, according to Robert Tilman's interviews. The Indonesians and Malaysians believe that Vietnam eventually will loosen its ties to the USSR since the current close relationship is out of character for an independent-minded Vietnam. The Thais, however, are not persuaded by this argument. They see Indonesia far removed from the Cambodian conflict and desirous of casting Vietnam in the role of a long-term buffer against China. The Thais further point out that Malaysia is actually changing its orientation over time away from the more optimistic view of Vietnam's intentions articulated in the 1980 joint Indonesian-Malaysian declaration at Kuantan and toward a view closer to Thailand's: that the Soviet-Vietnam alliance is permanent and bodes ill for any practical plan to convince either the Soviets or Vietnamese to alter their security orientation. Mutual benefits are simply too great.[10]

It is important to understand that although the ASEAN states are concerned about a growing Soviet military presence in Southeast Asia, for the most part they do not see that situation as their responsibility. Rather, the Soviet buildup is seen as part of the Soviet-U.S. global superpower game in which the Soviets are attempting to place their military assets in every region in which there is a U.S. presence. As two prominent Indonesian analysts put it: "Soviet capabilities in Southeast Asia have . . . been intended primarily to collect intelligence data, to develop a capability to project power in the region and into the Indian Ocean in time of crisis, to balance the U.S. Seventh Fleet at Subic and Clark Field [*sic*] and to balance the PRC along its southern borders. Thus, an increase of U.S. Seventh Fleet presence in the Asian-Pacific region is needed as a counterbalance."[11] Although Indonesia would prefer that neither superpower deploy near its waters, if the Soviets are there, the United States must be provided facilities to offset them.

An acceptance of the U.S. military presence, however, should not be equated with an endorsement of the Reagan administration's efforts to enlist the ASEAN states in an anti-Soviet crusade. ASEAN's comparatively relaxed view of the USSR is based on the belief that there are virtually no vulnerable political targets for subversion in Southeast Asia (though a deteriorating Philippine polity with a growing Communist insurgency could tempt the Soviets to become more active in those islands). ASEAN leaders find it virtually impossible to conceive of scenarios in which the Soviets would use military power against the six. Rather, Soviet forces are seen as facing China and the United States as well as Japan.

From the standpoint of ASEAN diplomacy, one of the most disturbing features of the Soviet-Vietnam alliance has been the necessity for the association to move toward the United States and China, thus compromising its preferred nonaligned posture. Moreover, because Indonesia and Malaysia hoped that a Soviet presence could be manipulated by ASEAN to balance China's military growth over the next decade or two, ASEAN's current adversarial role is doubly uncomfortable. If U.S. military aid helps China develop a force projection capability, the ASEAN states may hope to retain some kind of future Soviet option. Rather than Washington's providing China with the most modern weapons for use against the Soviets, ASEAN fears it will sell systems that help to build the PRC's conventional strength, particularly in transportation and communications. It is just such conventional equipment in China's hands that the smaller Asian states fear most. For Indonesia, there is the additional concern that a militarily powerful and economically modernizing China will ultimately challenge Jakarta for leadership in Southeast Asia.

The primary disjunction in ASEAN security views lies between Thailand and Indonesia, with Singapore aligning more with Bangkok, Malaysia leaning toward Indonesia, and the Philippines and Brunei located more or less in the middle. Thailand historically has been concerned with land-based threats from the west (Burma) and east (Indochina). Since World War II, the latter has been the only significant source of threat to Thailand's territorial integrity, initially through large numbers of Vietnamese and Laotian refugees from the first Indochina War (1948–1954), followed by Vietnamese and Laotian assistance to the Thai communist insurgents in the 1960s and early 1970s. Finally is the most disturbing prospect of all—the presence of 160,000 regular Vietnamese forces in neighboring Cambodia and an additional 40,000 to 50,000 in Laos. For Thailand, China has become an important security guarantor against Vietnam by demonstrating its willingness to put pressures on Hanoi's northern border whenever the Vietnam People's Army (VPA) attacks the Cambodian Resistance on the Thai frontier.

Indonesia, by contrast as an island country, faces no direct security threat and hence prefers a foreign policy based on regional neutralization (ZOPFAN) rather than reliance on external mentors. Recalling their own anticolonial struggle against the Dutch, Jakarta's leaders believe they understand Vietnam better than any other ASEAN member. Vietnam is not seen as a hostile state in the long run—unlike China—but rather one whose security concerns can be met through accommodation with ASEAN as reflected in the Kuantan principles enunciated by Malaysia and Indonesia in March 1980. A Vietnam, independent of the Soviet Union even if hegemonic over Laos and Cambodia, could play an important part in containing China and in the realization of ZOPFAN.

To its credit, Jakarta has subordinated its own security preferences to Bangkok's for the larger goal of ASEAN solidarity and to honor the frontline state principle. Other members of ASEAN, in turn, have designated Indonesia as the association's interlocutor with Hanoi. Thus, from late 1983, Indonesia has pursued a kind of two-track diplomacy toward Vietnam. The Foreign Ministry sustains a united front behind Thailand, while a prominent military leader, General Benny Murdani, meets Vietnamese officials and reassures them that Indonesia understands Hanoi's security needs. Although Indonesia opposes Vietnam's reliance on the Soviet Union, it understands Hanoi's reasons. By relying on Moscow, Hanoi strengthens its primacy in Indochina and its autonomy from the PRC. Both of these objectives are more important to Vietnam than either a more pristine version of nonalignment or even the acquisition of Western credits for economic growth. Jakarta accepts the utility of a strong Vietnam arraigned against China's People's Liberation Army (PLA) whose future plans may turn to the south. If Indonesia can convince Vietnam that Hanoi's interests are compatible with ASEAN's ZOPFAN aspirations, a regional order evolving from the joint actions of the two major blocs within Southeast Asia becomes possible for the first time.[12]

Malaysia, too, prefers an equidistance strategy toward external powers as the only sure way to protect Southeast Asian integrity. Deputy Prime Minister Dato Musa Hitam stated the long-term ZOPFAN goal in March 1984:

Malaysia believes that we must seek to ensure against the rise of two power blocs in Southeast Asia. There must be accommodation of each other's legitimate interests. There should be an independent Vietnam and the reduction of Soviet influence in Indochina and an independent and non-threatening Indochina. All the countries of the region should adopt policies of friendship to all and a reasonable equidistance from all the external big powers, whose legitimate interests must be accommodated. The countries of Southeast Asia must not only seek noninvolvement in the Sino-Soviet and U.S.-Soviet conflict, but also act to prevent hegemonism whether it be Soviet or Chinese or American.[13]

Statements such as Musa Hitam's are rhetorical devices that can be used to justify the presence of U.S. bases and Australian forces within the ASEAN region as temporary in nature while emphasizing that their presence "does not in any way affect the sovereign capability of a host country to exercise her full freedom to formulate and execute policy of her choice."[14] In effect, the rhetoric of nonalignment facilitates the political acceptability of external guarantors because the latter are said to be in the region at the sufferance of its members.

ASEAN's most troublesome immediate security issue originates neither in external military deployments nor the fear of cross-border military incursions but rather in the deteriorating political and economic situation of one of its members, the Philippines. Although this study consciously eschews a focus on domestic security concerns because of its main interest in linkages within and among Asian regions, the importance of the Philippines for regional security necessitates a brief discussion of its domestic situation. The Philippines' initial interest in ASEAN is found in the opportunity it presented for full-fledged membership in an unequivocally Asian club, thus helping to resolve its regional identity crisis, given the presence of large U.S. bases in the islands.

At ASEAN's inception in 1967, the Philippines was viewed as one of the more promising prospects for economic growth and political stability. It had a large educated population, reasonably good infrastructure, and a lively competitive democratic political system with the most outspoken press in Asia, and it attracted considerable external investment, particularly from the United States. By the mid-1980s, this bright picture had been totally repainted in hues of grey and black. The rule of Ferdinand Marcos for over fifteen years, most of it under martial law, had emasculated political democracy and so corrupted the economy that foreign investors were staying away in droves, while those still present in the islands were unable to obtain the foreign exchange they required to keep their businesses in operation.

By the mid-1980s, even the essentially pro-Marcos Reagan administration was pressing the Philippine government to enact major political and economic reforms designed to alleviate military repression, tighten profligate government spending on showcase projects unrelated to economic development, and dismiss incompetent, corrupt cronies from major positions in the economic sector. In the aftermath of the assassination of Benigno Aquino in August 1983, the situation had become grave indeed. The political opposition polarized into a fragmented group of former parliamentarians who could agree on neither a single leader nor a common program and a much better organized left opposition led by the Communist party of the Philippines (CPP) through rural and urban cells. The party employed a united front format to increase its political appeal to noncommunists. The economy had so stagnated that in 1984 and 1985 the Philippines may have experienced a net decline in living standards at a time when most other ASEAN states were charting annual growth rates up to 6 percent. And a growing communist insurgency focused in the south and rural areas was rapidly spreading to cities with their thousands of unemployed as well as sympathetic clergy, students, and intellectuals.[15]

Corazon Aquino's "peaceful revolution" in the aftermath of Marcos's effort to steal the February 1986 presidential election has provided the first ray of hope for political and economic recovery in the Philippines in over a decade. President Aquino faces the herculean tasks of attracting new foreign investment to turn the economy around, obtaining sufficient new credits to meet interest payments on the Philippines' $21 billion international debt, and negotiating a solution to both the Muslim Moro rebellion and that of the communist NPA. To her credit, Aquino has approached these tasks with energy and perseverance. Talks with Muslim leaders in Mindanao in the summer of 1986 have led to at least a temporary truce with the Moros.

Efforts to negotiate with the communists have been less successful, however. By 1986, they were operating in all regions of the Philippines and considered to be a power in areas of sixty-two among the seventy-three provinces. The NPA's armed strength is estimated at between 16,000 and 22,000 by U.S. and Philippine officials, while the latter acknowledge that about 400 towns and cities and 7,000 hamlets are infiltrated by the NPA.[16]

The Philippine military and NPA distrust each other in the negotiations. Each side insists the other must cease patrols first. The army opposes a cease-fire in place for fear that it would lead to a de facto recognition of NPA control over parts of the country. Aquino appears to be siding with the military, insisting there can be no compromise over the integrity of the country under a single, elected government. While this position is important for retaining the loyalty of the armed forces, it appears to give the communists little incentive to stop fighting.

ASEAN Military Capabilities

ASEAN military budgets have experienced remarkable growth since the Vietnamese occupation of Cambodia in 1979 (table 4–1). Aggregate military spending had exceeded $8 billion by 1982, an increase of over 200 percent since

Table 4–1
ASEAN Military Expenditures, 1975–1984
(millions of U.S. dollars)

Year	Thailand	Malaysia	Singapore	Indonesia	Philippines
1975	531	688	325	1,399	712
1976	632	647	380	1,370	757
1977	745	849	464	1,419	728
1978	800	723	442	1,404	556
1979	942	778	457	1,784	643
1980	1,100	1,006	598	2,100	779
1981	1,310	1,447	707	2,690	862
1982	1,437	2,077	852	2,936	878
1983	1,562	1,976	n.a.	2,527	n.a.
1984	1,715	1,792	857	2,420	504

Sources: *World Military Expenditures and Arms Transfers 1971–1980* (Washington, D.C.: U.S. Arms Control and Disarmament Agency, March 1983), pp. 52–69; *The Military Balance 1980, 1981, 1982, 1983–1984, 1985–1986* (London: International Institute for Strategic Studies).

1975 and more than 70 percent since 1978. Yet ASEAN's total combined armed forces was still less than Vietnam's 1.2 million member army; and defense expenditures declined after 1982 as budgets were affected by the world recession. The ASEAN states were under no illusion that, as the Singapore Defense Minister Goh Keng Swee put it in 1979, "In any military contest between the two sides—assuming there is no third party intervention—the outcome would be quick and decisive."[17]

While differences over the source and imminence of long-term threats to the region persist among ASEAN's members (Soviet Union and Vietnam versus China), a consensus has developed that the regional balance regarding Vietnam should be redressed. In 1980, the ASEAN armed forces began to emphasize external force capabilities, particularly air forces and navies, for the first time. Although these forces would have little ability to deter or defend against a great power, they could provide a measure of self-defense against a regional enemy, especially if multinational military cooperation continues to grow.

It may be useful to examine each ASEAN state's security situation briefly to determine the extent to which regional capacities are being developed. Unsurprisingly, the government least affected by this trend is the one facing the most serious internal insurgency, the Philippines. External security is largely conceived as coming under the U.S. security umbrella in any event. Both the size of the Philippine Armed Forces (AFP) and its budget have ballooned, from 60,000 men in 1971 to 150,000 in 1985. In a country with a deteriorating economy, the military budget doubled from $1 billion in 1980 to $2 billion in 1984. Over two-thirds of the military are ground forces. Deployment is divided between Luzon and the southern island in an effort to control the bitter NPA insurgency. The rapidly expanding armed forces has stretched the military's ability to train and supply its personnel to the limit, with a subsequent erosion of military values, command and control, and civil-military relations. Enlisted ranks in particular were expanded through rural conscription with little personnel screening. The quality of training varies widely from region to region. It is poorest in the constabulary and civilian home defense forces, units disproportionately associated with depredations against the local population.

The AFP suffers from deficiencies in mobility and communication equipment, lacking sufficient numbers of trucks, helicopters, and radios. As the army adopted a more aggressive posture in NPA-infested areas, it deemphasized civic action programs of rural construction and medical care, which were so successful in the anti-Huk campaign of the 1950s. It remains to be seen whether the Aquino government will reinstate civic action as a component of its program of a negotiated resolution to the NPA rebellion. Although the AFP clearly outnumbers the insurgents, the latter have been recruiting at such a rapid rate that the military has not maintained a sufficiently favorable force ratio against the guerrillas.[18]

Although Philippine naval and air force officers gaze somewhat enviously at the new systems for regional defense being acquired by their Malaysian and Indonesian counterparts, they are reconciled to the priorities of counterinsurgency warfare in their own country. Thus, the Philippine navy's essentially World War II vessels continue to approach the operational end of their lives with little prospect for replacement. In effect, the Philippines lacks not only any capability to withstand an ocean-borne threat unaided but cannot control even the smuggling of contraband and arms, particularly to its strife-ridden southern islands.[19]

Insofar as the Philippines confronts a regional external threat, it lies in the South China Sea off Palawan where Manila claims sovereignty over some of the eastern Spratlys. Because the United States is not committed to defending Manila's claims, the AFP has augmented its own base on Palawan to support its small deployments in the Spratlys. Three Exocet-armed attack craft along with a squadron of F-5s are at Palawan keeping watch over Vietnamese activities on adjacent islands.[20] They are probably sufficient to give a good account of themselves against the small number of forces currently in the area but would be unable to fend off a serious Vietnamese effort to occupy all the eastern Spratlys.

As in the Philippines, the Thai military's primary concerns also center on ground warfare. Before the end of the 1970s, this warfare was devoted to counterinsurgency efforts in the north and northeast against the Thai Communist party (CPT) and in the south against Malaysian communists seeking refuge in a convenient border location. These Thai security concerns rapidly diminished in the early 1980s as CPT terrorists were both won over to the government side through generous amnesty offers and lost their sanctuaries and supplies in Laos and Vietnam because they had been aligned with China since the 1960s. Paradoxically, the Sino-Soviet conflict solved a serious Thai security problem as the Vietnamese turned away Thai insurgents who had received sanctuary and succor over the previous decade and a half. As government-to-government relations with Thailand deteriorated, Hanoi nevertheless abandoned one of its most important levers of influence in Thailand by ceasing to support the CPT.

Freed from the necessity of dispersing its forces over long stretches of the Cambodian and Laotian borders, the Thai military faced a new and historically more worrisome danger: the presence of VPA troops just beyond the Cambodian frontier. The centuries-old policy of maintaining a buffer against the Vietnamese, a primary reason for the Thai decision to align with the United States during the second Indochina War, was in jeopardy. Thailand's response has been to beef up the military even further, this time with a heavier conventional warfare capability designed to keep Vietnamese soldiers as far from the border as possible. Thus, in 1983, Thailand acquired 155-millimeter howitzers from the United States. The military budget for 1984, including funds for internal security, reached 25 percent of the total government budget, the highest proportion of any other ASEAN state.[21] Weapons acquisition plans, designed to create a more credible deterrent against a land thrust by Vietnam, include 200 M-28 medium tanks, as well as antiarmor rockets and missiles. The army is the favored service in this scenario, receiving more than half of the budget in 1984. Thus, the Vietnam threat has reinforced the traditional pattern of intramilitary political power.[22]

The Thai navy is less impressive, essentially a coastal defense force equipped with Exocet and Gabriel SSMs. It is deployed in the Gulf of Thailand, lacking the electronics for sea surveillance. The air force, too, has been oriented primarily to counterinsurgency and border protection with ten of its thirteen squadrons configured in a ground-support mode.[23]

One of the most interesting developments in Thai military aid sources has been China's offer of medium tanks and 130-millimeter artillery at approximately 10 percent of their market price with a ten-year grace period before repayment. Given a stagnant Thai defense budget, the Chinese sales are particularly welcome, although they have probably not been enthusiastically greeted by Indonesia and Malaysia. China also sold 400 armored personnel carriers to the Thai army on similar terms, assisting its current program to mechanize as many infantry divisions as possible. In July 1987, the PRC broadened the scope of its military aid by adding antiaircraft missiles and submarines to the systems it would sell to Thailand at "friendship prices."[24]

Although Singapore maintains the highest per capita defense spending in ASEAN, its military forces are small, with little regional capability unless integrated into a large, cooperative air and naval defense arrangement with its neighbors Indonesia and Malaysia.

Malaysia, as in most of the other ASEAN states, had organized its armed forces primarily for counterinsurgency on both the peninsula and Sabah.

Through the 1970s, this strategy had been successful for the most part, especially when combined with bilateral border control operations with its Indonesian and Thai neighbors. As the internal security threat waned, the Vietnamese invasion of Cambodia and subsequent Soviet deployments out of Cam Ranh Bay created a new regional security situation for Malaysia. The Malaysian armed forces began to move toward the development of a conventional warfare capability. Thus, whereas defense expenditures between 1975 and 1979 remained essentially flat, between 1979 and 1982, they almost tripled, with the lion's share going to the navy and air force as the primary components of a regional capability.[25]

Beginning in 1981, 75 percent of the army's training shifted from counterinsurgency to conventional warfare with the acquisition of 26 British Scorpion light tanks and 450 West German Condor personnel carriers. The emphasis was on mobility so that the army could shift to either coast depending on the location of any external threat. The navy is acquiring new West German Kosturi frigates, which will vastly expand its ASW, antiship, and at-sea command and control. It also has initiated a coproduction agreement with South Korea for fast attack craft. Several Italian-built minesweepers have also been ordered.[26] Air force expansion is based on the delivery beginning in 1984 of 88 refurbished A-4 Skyhawks. By 1985, two Skyhawk squadrons were added to the existing two F-5E squadrons. All of these capital purchases mean that Malaysia spends about 10 percent of its GNP on defense—a high proportion for a country in which the military is not a significant domestic political actor and for which there is no imminent external threat. Noteworthy, however, is the identification of Indochina as the source of Malaysia's security concerns. Donald Weatherbee has observed that Kuala Lumpur's military planning and exercises are based on an adversary with the command structure, disposition, and tactics of the Vietnamese.[27]

Budgetary constraints brought on by the world recession since 1982 have entailed a significant cutback and delay in acquisitions. The major casualty has been air base planning for Gong Kedak near the Thai border on the east coast, only an hour's flight from Vietnam and positioned to provide rapid assistance to Thailand in the event of a military attack. Defense development in 1985 was pegged at $183 million, 23 percent less than 1984, which, in turn had been cut 15 percent from 1983.[28]

Malaysian security relations with Thailand are close and cooperative both through coordination of actions against the Malayan Communist party (MCP) and Malay irredentism in the Thai south and because of Malaysian fears that if Thailand capitulates to Vietnamese pressure, Malaysia itself would be the next frontline.[29] Malaysia is also worried about Thai dependence on China. The longer the Bangkok-Beijing relationship continues, the more deeply China becomes a de facto security partner to ASEAN. Some Malaysian analysts fear that Thailand might be pressured by China to stop cooperating with Malaysia against the MCP.[30]

While an augmented navy and air force will undoubtedly help protect Malaysian interests in the South China Sea, Malaysia cannot face the Vietnamese and/or Soviets alone. The navy, even with its new ships, can monitor only a small portion of the country's 200-mile exclusive economic zone (EEZ), while the Skyhawks will probably not even be used for ocean surveillance because they lack the necessary electronics.[31]

As in the other ASEAN states, Indonesia too has had markedly increased defense expenditures since the Vietnamese invasion of Cambodia. Jakarta has added F-5Es and Skyhawk A-4 and TA-4 fighter bombers. In 1986, the air force announced it would purchase twelve F-16s. The navy is becoming one of the region's more diversified, with the acquisition of three Dutch-built Fatahilah-class corvettes armed with Exocet missiles and two new frigates. The latter have a range of 4,500 nautical miles and will be equipped with Harpoon SSMs, superior to the Exocet. Two type-209 submarines from West Germany have entered service, with another two on order. The navy's large patrol contingent has expanded with some fourteen new vessels either recently commissioned or planned for purchase. Two new minesweepers have been ordered from the Dutch.

Indonesia's major maritime combat acquisition over the next ten years is the coproduction agreement announced in 1983 with Boeing Marine Systems. In all probability, ten jetfoils will be built by the mid-1990s. Operating in conjunction with three Boeing 737 maritime patrol aircraft delivered in 1983, the Indonesian navy will have the best coastal surveillance capability in Southeast Asia, although it also has the largest archipelagic sea space to cover in the region.[32]

Although Indonesia does not anticipate a direct Vietnamese attack, it is concerned about the potential for conflict in the South China Sea around the Natuna Islands. Vietnam has not challenged Indonesia's occupation of these islands, but there are disputes over ownership of the possibly oil-rich seabed near them. This South China Sea conflict motivated much of Jakarta's hardware purchases. Noteworthy, too, were two large-scale military exercises held in 1980 and 1981 in which the Indonesian army was deployed to repel an invader whose tactics closely resembled Vietnam's.[33]

Indonesia is deploying combat aircraft to Sumatra within range of the Natunas. The government also announced that a $5 billion naval base is to be constructed in Sumatra to provide a permanent capability to protect the country's South China Sea and straits approaches to the archipelago. To exercise tighter control over its airspace and territorial waters in the north, Indonesia acquired several Thompson radars in 1986. The radars have detected numerous violations of Indonesian airspace by Soviet carrier-based planes, TU-16 Badger fighter bombers, and TU-95 Bear reconnaissance aircraft flying from Cam Ranh Bay. The U.S. Congress agreement to sell Indonesia F-16s was based in part on this information about Soviet overflights.[34]

Donald Weatherbee has noted the ambiguity in Indonesia's air force doctrine. Should it play a predominantly support role to the more favored army and navy or develop an independent capability to attack external targets?[35] General Benny Murdani, the armed forces (ABRI) commander, insists on an air support emphasis and has stated that the air force should be reduced in size though upgraded in sophistication. He has unfavorably compared Indonesia's 27,000-man and 100-plane air force to Singapore's 7,000 men and 160 aircraft. Yet while insisting that the air force remain a support service, Murdani was a prime mover behind the Indonesian decision to buy F-16As.

ASEAN Military Cooperation

The ASEAN states have been cooperating along their common land and sea frontiers for several years on a bilateral and trilateral basis.[36] One of the most successful examples of this kind of cooperation has occurred on the Thai-Malaysian border since 1949 for purposes of controlling communist operations on both sides. Over the past twenty years, both governments have administered border control operations through cabinet-level joint border committees, which plan and monitor the joint activities of the two countries' armies and police forces in the border areas. Despite periodic suspicions by each side that the other may not be cooperating fully for its own domestic political reasons, the overall situation along the border has improved remarkably since the late 1960s. CPT activities are at a low ebb, as are MCP operations in Thai enclaves. Insofar as tensions exist, they focus on Thai suspicions that the Malaysians permit separatists whose goal is an autonomous Muslim region in southern Thailand to operate in Malaysia. While Malaysia claims it does not support these aspirations, there is some evidence to suggest that Kuala Lumpur has an arrangement whereby it does not harass the dissidents in exchange for intelligence on MCP activities in southern Thailand.[37]

The most common forms of ASEAN military cooperation are air and sea exercises. All ASEAN navies and most of their air forces have conducted joint training on a multilateral basis, with the exception of Malaysia and the Philippines because of their unresolved dispute over Sabah. ASEAN newcomer Brunei also takes part in these arrangements by providing training grounds for the Singapore army.

While the ASEAN armed forces are no match for Vietnamese ground forces, naval modernization since 1980 has created an aggregate of new ships that far surpass Vietnam's ability to control regional sea-lanes. (See figure 4–1). Singapore's purchase of an E-2C Hawkeye airborne warning system combined with Indonesia's Boeing 737s create the capability for a regional air and naval surveillance system that could be used to coordinate air and sea defense among Indonesia, Malaysia, Singapore, and possibly Thailand if the

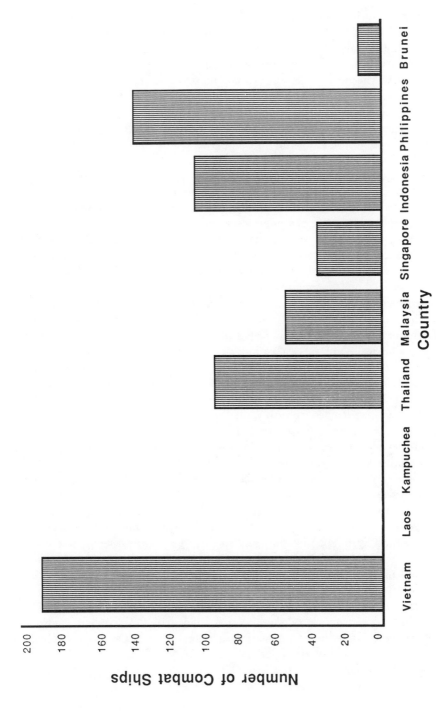

Source: James R. Caswell, "ASEAN and Indochina: A Strategy for Regional Stability in the 1980s" (Master's thesis, U.S. Naval Postgraduate School, 1984), p. 34.

political decision were made. (An early indication of such planning would be trilateral sea surveillance exercises employing the AWACs systems.)

As of the mid-1980s, ASEAN civilian leaders had still not formally discussed defense cooperation among all six members, although there is some belief that the need to develop capabilities to patrol overlapping EEZs and jurisdictional disputes with Vietnam could provide an incentive to move further toward collaboration.[38] Nevertheless, maritime joint planning has not yet gone beyond limited joint exercises. There is, for example, no naval equivalent of the regular joint ground force operations on the Thai-Malaysian and Malaysian-Indonesian land frontiers. However, arguments have been made by both the Malaysian air force and navy that offensive-retaliatory capabilities are needed to meet the enemy before it reaches one's homeland.[39] The Malaysian navy, particularly, is acquiring ASW equipment, including helicopter-carrying corvettes that can minesweep the straits and search for submarines.

Perhaps the most significant development in Southeast Asian regional military cooperation in the first half of the 1980s was the growing sense of confidence by ASEAN's two Malay states (Indonesia and Malaysia) in its Chinese neighbor (Singapore). In the summer of 1987, the Malaysian and Thai defense ministries agreed to set up joint naval and air patrols for the first time in their Joint Development Authority area in the Gulf of Thailand. The Joint Development Authority was created in 1986 to develop gas resources in the two countries' common sea boundary. Although the patrols may have been motivated by Malaysian concerns over Thai fishing violations, the joint patrol could be a useful precedent for combined South China Sea surveillance.[40] (See tables 4–2 and 4–3.) In 1984, a Malaysian officer joined the Singapore Staff College as a student. Reciprocally, the Malaysian army's combat training center at Pulada accepted a Singaporean officer. Joint air and naval exercises were held over Singapore for the first time since 1965. Nevertheless, Singaporean land forces still do not train in the nearby jungle warfare school at Johore, though they exercise in both Thailand and Brunei and as far away as Taiwan and Australia.[41]

Singapore is intensely interested in collaborative ASEAN defense arrangements, particularly with its closest neighbors. While both Malaysia and Indonesia fully accept Singapore's independence—as contrasted with the situation in the mid-1970s when the city-state was viewed as a Chinese Trojan horse—they remain loath to enter into more formal security arrangements beyond the FPDA. Both Indonesian and Malaysian officials acknowledge that effective security around the straits must include all three countries.[42] Thus, the three agreed on the two-week April 1985 deployment of a squadron of Singapore F-5Es at Butterworth air base in northwest Malaysia for maneuvers with Malaysian counterparts under the FPDA.[43]

One of the more interesting issues raised in recent years with the standardization of F-5 aircraft across ASEAN air forces is the possibility of joint procurement

Table 4–2
Fast Attack Naval Craft in Southeast Asia

Ship Class	Country of Origin	In Service with	Tonnage	Maximum Speed (knots)	Maximum Range (mi/kts)	Main Armament
SHERSHEN	UR	VN	180	45	850/30	4 × 30mm 4 × torpedos
OSA II	UR	VN	210	36	800/30	4 × 30mm 4 × Styx
PERDANA	FR	MY	234	37	800/25	1 × 57mm 1 × 40mm 2 × Exocet
RATCHARIT	IT	TH	235	36	2,000/15	1 × 76mm 1 × 40mm 4 × Exocet
SPICA-M	SW	MY	240	38	1,850/14	1 × 57mm 1 × 40mm 4 × Exocet
PSMM	SK	ID/PI	120	35	2,000/17	2 × 30mm 2 × Exocet
FPB 57	SG	SG	410	38	1,300/30	1 × 76mm 2 × 40mm
WASPADA	SG	BR	150	32	1,200/14	2 × 30mm 2 × Exocet
PRABRARAPAK	SG	TH	224	41	2,000/12	1 × 57mm 1 × 40mm 5 × Gabriel
TNC/FPB 45	SG	SG	225	38	2,111/12	1 × 57mm 1 × 40mm 5 × Gabriel
Type A/B	SG	SG	100	32	1,300/30	1 × 40mm 2 × 20mm

Sources: *Jane's Fighting Ships 1983–84* (London: Jane's Publishing Co., 1983); Jean Labayle Couhat, ed., *Combat Fleets of the World 1982/83* (Annapolis: Naval Institute Press, 1982).
Note: UR = Soviet Union; FR = France; IT = Italy; SW = Sweden; SK = South Korea; SG = Singapore; VN = Vietnam; MY = Malaysia; TH = Thailand; ID = Indonesia; PI = Philippines; BR = Brunei.

and storage of spare parts. A central ASEAN parts depot would make sense economically, for it could lead to reduced unit costs through bulk purchases. (This would be even more true if the ASEAN air forces upgrade over the next decade to the F-16.) So far, the proposal has not gone beyond the discussion stage because of fears that a centralized arrangement would be viewed as a first step toward an ASEAN military alliance and also because there is no agreement on the location of the proposed depot. Singapore, Thailand, and Indonesia have expressed interest, although Jakarta is adamantly opposed to any dependence for armaments on Singapore.[44]

In 1986, Bangkok and Washington discussed the possibility of establishing a war reserve stockpile in Thailand. U.S. Secretary of Defense Weinberger agreed

Table 4–3
Joint Exercises of ASEAN States, 1983

Period	Participating Countries	Type of Exercise	Where Conducted	Participating Units	Exercise Name
April 26 –May 11	Philippines United States	Maritime	Central Philippines region	15 vessels	Balicatan Tanjunt Flash '83
April 28 –May 1	Singapore Malaysia Australia	Air	South China Sea		
May 20 –May 29	Indonesia Malaysia Singapore United States	Maritime	Strait of Malacca		
June 3 June 12	5 British Commonwealth nations	Maritime	South China Sea	18 vessels 16 aircraft	Starfish '83
July 6 July 27	United States Thailand	Maritime/ air	Gulf of Siam		Cobra Gold '83
August 1 August 9	Malaysia Australia	Land/ air	State of Kedah, Malaysia		
August 4 August 13	Malaysia Thailand	Maritime	South China Sea Gulf of Siam		Thaly Sec III
August 20 August 31	Malaysia Indonesia	Land	Kota Kinabalu, Malaysia		Tatar Malindo Dua
August 22 August 31	Indonesia Thailand	Maritime	Java Sea Sunda Strait		Sea Garuda IV
November 25 December 25	United States	Air	Thailand		Commando West 6

Source: Research Institute for Peace and Security, *Asian Security 1984* (Tokyo: RIPS, 1984), p. 169.

to the project during an April visit. U.S. weapons would be prepositioned in Thailand for use only in a nation-threatening emergency by Thai armed forces. The stockpile will probably be disbursed among several Thai bases. Its appeal at this time is directly related to Thailand's position as a frontline state against Vietnam.[45] The stockpile will upgrade the Thai logistics system, making it more compatible with that of the United States, thus allowing the Thai armed forces to plug directly into the U.S. supply network. The agreement also permits Thailand to stockpile $50 million worth of munitions without paying for them unless they are needed.[46]

ASEAN Military Links with External Powers

The ASEAN states have a long history of military ties with external partners, including Great Britain, Australia, and New Zealand via the FDPA with Malaysia and Singapore and bilateral mutual security agreements between the United States and the Philippines and Thailand and Great Britain and Brunei. Only Indonesia has no formal security link to a state outside ASEAN. (See table 4–3.)

The two sets of security arrangements are connected through ANZUS by which any attacks on Australia, New Zealand, or U.S. forces in the Pacific could elicit assistance from the others on the basis of their constitutional processes. This is particularly important as a way of buttressing the small Australian and New Zealand contingents in Malaysia and Singapore. That is, an external attack on these two countries in which ANZAC forces were involved could lead to U.S. military assistance under ANZUS, assuming the concurrence of Kuala Lumpur and Singapore. (New Zealand's role in this arrangement could be compromised because the United States has withdrawn its security guarantee to New Zealand as a result of the Lange government's prohibition of U.S. Navy port calls.)

Although the Southeast Asia Treaty Organization (SEATO) has been moribund since 1976, its framework—the Manila Treaty—remains operative. Under the treaty's terms, the U.S. Air Force and Navy could have access to Thai bases to help Thailand repel an external attack. Australia and New Zealand could provide similar assistance. The same terms would apply for assistance to the Philippines, though U.S. facilities are already there.

Even Indonesia, concerned about the growing Soviet naval presence in the region, sent a large defense delegation to Washington in 1982 and sought closer defense ties through the purchase of U.S.-made equipment. Units of the U.S. Seventh Fleet regularly maneuver with units from Singapore, Indonesia, and Malaysia, as well as its Manila Pact partners. The purpose of these exercises is to protect South China Sea sea-lanes.[47]

American foreign military sales (FMS) to ASEAN for fiscal year (FY) 1984 were $206,500,000, about 2.5 percent of the five countries' aggregate defense expenditures of about $8 billion. While the FMS program is not composed of credits, it does provide U.S. government guarantees for seven-year commercial bank loans. U.S. grants for the ASEAN states are much smaller—$12 million in FY 1984, $5 million of which was designated for Thailand. (See table 4–4.)

The ASEAN states openly acknowledge the necessity not only of the maintenance of a U.S. military presence throughout East Asia but also the utility of joint exercises with U.S. forces. This is a far cry from the rhetorical support still given ZOPFAN. Malaysia, the concept's country of origin, has been quite open in accepting the reality of ZOPFAN's postponement. As Foreign Minister Ghazalie Shafie put it:

Table 4–4
FY 1984 U.S. Security Asistance Programs
(thousands of dollars)

Country	Foreign Military Sales Guarantee	Economic Support Fund	Military Assistance Program	International Military Education and Training Program
Thailand	94,000	5,000	5,000	2,400
Singapore	0	0	0	50
Philippines	50,000	50,000	0	1,300
Malaysia	12,500	0	0	500
Indonesia	50,000	0	0	2,700

Source: Guy J. Pauker, *Security and Economics: The Military Expenditures of the ASEAN Countries* (Santa Monica: Rand Corporation, P–6880, May 1983), p. 17.

There may be the need for us in ASEAN to update our conception of the ZOPFAN proposal in the light of the realities of the 80s. For instance, there is at least the need for a rationalization of the principles of ZOPFAN with the reality of foreign bases in the Southeast Asian region which while temporary in nature are likely to stay for sometime to come. *What needs to be emphasized in this context is that the presence of foreign bases does not in any way affect the sovereign capabilities of a host country to exercise her full freedom to formulate and execute policy of her choice.* [Emphasis added][48]

In other words, the military presence of friendly foreign states does not necessarily compromise a third world state's integrity as long as the latter's policies are determined through an independent assessment of its own interests. Moreover, since there is still no external guarantee by major powers for ZOPFAN, "a U.S. military presence is welcome and indeed seen as an insurance against the threat of external aggression in the region."[49]

The Future of the Philippine Bases

The credibility of an external security guarantee for ASEAN is intertwined with the complex questions surrounding the future of the Philippine bases. As a major domestic issue enveloped in nationalist rhetoric, the Aquino government is approaching the bases' renewal in 1991 cautiously. Those who support the continuation of a U.S. air and naval presence in the Philippines—such as former Defense Minister Juan Ponce Enrile—see it as a significant contribution to regional security in the light of the Soviet military buildup across the South China Sea at Cam Ranh Bay.[50] They also point to the positive impact of U.S. expenditures on the depressed Philippine economy and view the bases as the best means of ensuring the continuation of a special relationship with Washington. Those who oppose the U.S. presence take the negative on all of these reasons. Rather than contributing to regional security, the bases would draw a Soviet attack; the local economy has become a neocolonial dependency of U.S. service spending; and the special relationship is a euphemism for Philippine subordination to U.S. strategic interests.

The physical and financial advantages of the Philippine bases cannot be overemphasized. The United States maintains six major operational facilities in the Philippines, together with several smaller supporting installations. The two major bases are the Subic Bay Naval Complex (which includes the naval station at Port Olongapo, the ship repair facility, naval supply depot, and naval magazine at Camayon Point, the Zombales and Tabones training grounds, and the Cubi Point naval air station) and Clark Air Base (which includes the highly automated Crow Valley gunnery and bombing range, where U.S. pilots fly against "Soviet adversaries," and the Camp O'Donnell communications facility). Subic Bay is one of three forward naval bases in the western Pacific (the other two are at Yokosuka and Sasebo, Japan) and contains the largest U.S. naval facilities west of Hawaii. It handles two-thirds of all ship repairs for the Seventh Fleet and constitutes the largest naval supply and POL depot in the world. The Clark complex has facilities for supporting and repairing 200 aircraft, a large supply and ordnance depot, and a 43,600-acre bombing and gunnery training range. Clark also houses important links in the sophisticated global antisatellite surveillance system (ASAT) and Strategic Air Command global communication system, and the TACOMO aircraft nuclear missile submarine communication system.

U.S. facilities dwarf their Soviet counterparts at Cam Ranh Bay across the South China Sea, although the continuing buildup of Soviet Badger, Bear, and, most recently, MiG-23s as an air defense contingent underscores the need to maintain U.S. forces in the region.

The Philippine bases are key transshipment points for U.S. logistics throughout the western Pacific, Indian Ocean, and Persian Gulf. They ensure freedom of the SLOCs among these bodies of water, particularly through the Southeast Asian straits. Located in the heart of the region, the bases are force multipliers in that contingents can be deployed to trouble spots much more quickly than if they had to come from Japan or the mid-Pacific. Guam is six ship-days from the Malacca Strait. Its harbors have one-quarter the ship berthing capacity of Subic. Although Singapore has the harbor capacity, U.S. forces would have to share with the ships of many other countries, hardly a secure situation. Labor costs are high, and in the event of a major crisis, the Singapore Strait could be blocked. Only Andersen Air Force Base on Guam could handle the largest U.S. aircraft in the Pacific inventory. The rest would have to relocate back to Japan or Hawaii. Labor costs after such a transition would be enormous.

Although President Aquino and her advisers prefer to keep their options on the Philippine bases open until negotiations for their renewal begin in 1988, the majority of the delegates she appointed to the Philippines' Constitutional Commission (Con-Com) charged with drafting a new basic charter for the country are opposed to the bases in their present form. In hopes of preempting the president, the Con-Com voted against extending the bases agreement after 1991 and for the declaration of the Philippines as a "zone of peace, neutrality, and nuclear free [sic]." The commission had decreed that any new bases agreement will require the approval of the Philippine senate.[51]

Even those who take a less extreme position on the bases' future prefer to see the conditions of their use brought under greater Filipino control. Ambassador Narciso Reyes proposed in the Con-Com that the United States not be permitted to send forces from the bases into any combat area unless specifically authorized by the Philippines.[52] While the Con-Com's recommendations are not binding on the Aquino government, they carry considerable political weight. Aquino could use them for political leverage to negotiate a more favorable bases package, or they could become the rationale for the bases' termination.

From the Philippine perspective, the principal utility of the bases has been economic rather than military. Indeed, the Philippines faces no imminent external threat. Insofar as the country may be at risk, it is because of the presence of the U.S. bases. Undoubtedly some of the Siberian-deployed SS-20s and Vietnam-based Badgers have the Philippine bases as their targets in the unlikely event of a Soviet-U.S. confrontation.

Economically the bases comprise a significant boost for the Philippines. They provide employment directly to 40,000 Filipinos and an annual cash infusion of $200 million, approximately 5 percent of the country's GNP. That total is expanded through both a multiplier effect and additional spending by 16,000 U.S. military and civilian personnel and their 25,000 dependents, as well as direct military procurement of goods and services in the country's economy.[53]

Military planners acknowledge that the importance of the Philippine bases will diminish toward the end of the century as the U.S. Navy deploys a new generation of warships that are lighter, more fuel efficient, and with lower maintenance and repair requirements. Repair will be increasingly accomplished at sea, in smaller port facilities, or simply less frequently in Japan and Hawaii. These new vessels will be able to cruise farther away from target areas without degrading their ability to defend against unfriendly forces. However, if the U.S. Navy and Air Force were to leave Clark and Subic, the political impression of regional disengagement might well be created even if there was no diminution of military capacity. This latter point is particularly important as the Soviets continue to increase their deployments from Cam Ranh Bay. It could be argued that a rollback of the U.S. military presence could encourage a Finlandization of ASEAN and a reconsideration by the PRC of its security ties to the United States. In other words, unless a change in the U.S. military status in the Philippines is clearly shown to degrade neither U.S. military capabilities nor its political will, such a change could be destabilizing and encourage both Soviet and Vietnam adventures.

Despite these caveats, the United States is examining alternative arrangements for those forces tasked with patrolling the South China Sea to the Persian Gulf. There are at least theoretical advantages to some of the ideas. Decentralization of bases would render the United States less vulnerable in the event of war. Airfields on Guam could accommodate all aircraft types currently using Clark. Additional facilities might be obtained in Japan and Australia, including the large naval base on the Indian Ocean at Cockburn South. Other possibilities include the reconstruction of the old World War II air bases on Palau and Tinian in the Marianas, as well as the possibility of renting space at the Sembawang base in Singapore.[54]

There are problems with all these alternatives. Singapore, despite its excellent location and ship repair facilities, is vulnerable in time of crisis and lacks the fuel storage capacity available at Subic with the latter's ability to handle over 1 million barrels a month. Nor would Singapore be able to duplicate Subic's warehouse facilities, which stock over 150,000 items. Moreover, the expansion and construction of bases on Guam and the Marianas would require at least a decade. Costs may be $3 billion to $4 billion, and neither location would have a sufficient labor force.[55]

Tengah Airfield in Singapore can accommodate all aircraft in the U.S. inventory. P3C Orions currently use Tengah to patrol for Soviet submarines in the Indian Ocean. U.S. ships and aircraft also have limited access to Australian bases in Darwin, Learmoth, Tindal, and Townville, as well as Cockburn Sound. These bases would be particularly useful in supporting Diego Garcia if the Australian government would agree to an expansion of U.S. military activities.

The commander of the U.S. Thirteenth Air Force was reported to have stated that F-15s could provide the same amount of regional coverage from Guam as from Clark with one inflight refueling. C-5A and C-141 cargo transports could also fly from Guam to Diego Garcia. Thus, sea-lane surveillance, defense, and supply need not be degraded if U.S. air forces were to shift to the mid-Pacific. Guam also has dry docks capable of handling aircraft carriers.[56]

The Sembawang shipyards in Singapore can accommodate any ship in the U.S. Navy, including Nimitz-class carriers. Modern frigates with underwater sonars can be handled in their new dry docks. Sembawang also maintains large storage facilities, which can supply most ship types. Australian, New Zealand, and British naval vessels are provisioned and repaired at Sembawang.[57]

While alternatives to the Philippine bases may be technically feasible through the decentralization of facilities to other parts of East Asia and Australia and the introduction of a new generation of naval vessels that require less frequent maintenance, are these alterantives politically practical? I asked this question in an extensive tour of the region in May and June 1984, speaking with government officials and research analysts from think tanks and academia.[58] Not surprisingly, responses were mixed. Going from most-to-least consensus, virtually all those interviewed throughout ASEAN preferred to see the U.S.

bases remain in the Philippines. This was seen as increasingly important as the Soviets continued a steady buildup of their assets at Cam Ranh Bay. Respondents throughout the region insisted that deterrence and defense against the Soviet regional presence was the responsibility of the United States. The regional contribution to this U.S. capacity is the continuation of current base facilities and the de facto postponement of ZOPFAN as a viable political alternative.

Going beyond the preservation of the status quo, a variety of responses were given to the possibility of alternative locations to the Philippines. Some Thai officials in the Foreign Ministry stated that if the United States were asked to leave the Philippines by a new regime, Bangkok would be favorably disposed to reopen some bases in Thailand for U.S. use. One high-level Foreign Ministry official volunteered that Indonesian officials had told him that if the United States were precipitately forced out of the Philippines, Jakarta might consider providing Natuna island as a Seventh Fleet base. (This is, of course, only an indirect and highly speculative statement of Indonesian interest.) There was no indication from Malaysian officials that Kuala Lumpur would be receptive to the idea of U.S. forces on Malaysian soil. However, Malaysian respondents stated it was unlikely that their government would object if another ASEAN member offered facilities to the United States in the event of a Philippine decision to close the bases. Singaporeans mentioned the possible expansion of U.S. use of their facilities providing there was no objection from neighbors and also suggested that the United States consider approaching Brunei for a facility.

As for U.S. bases in Australia, much would depend on the party in power. A conservative government would probably welcome an expansion of the U.S. air and naval presence as supplementary to Australia's limited capabilities even if there were no change in U.S. deployments from the Philippines. Even the Hawke government might accept an augmented U.S. naval and air presence under certain conditions. These would include the necessity for finding alternatives to the Philippines and that the ships involved not be a component of the U.S. central strategic deterrent—that is, no SSBNs.[59] The problem with the latter stricture is that as the Seventh Fleet deploys nuclear-capable sea-launched cruise missiles (SLCMs) on many of its vessels beginning in the mid-1980s, it could be argued that the whole fleet is becoming part of the central deterrent in addition to its regional responsibilities.

Before leaving the Philippine bases issues, one more alternative should be discussed: their multilateralization, as broached by the U.S. diplomat Robert Pringle.[60] Pringle argues that one way to defuse the bases as a political sore point with Filipino nationalists is to lease them on a commercial basis, thus making U.S. operations there subject to Philippine law. The bases would also be linked to regional development projects. According to Pringle, contract operations would stimulate U.S. planners to consolidate and trim excess base facilities and transfer some maintenance work out to other contractors in the region, possibly Singapore. Thus the benefits of U.S. military spending would be dispersed more widely through ASEAN territory.

Additionally the bases could be opened more for the use of Philippine forces and subsequently other ASEAN states. This multilateralization of the bases would integrate them directly into ASEAN security planning. As the association members develop a regional air and naval capability toward the end of this decade, the Philippine bases could provide attractive training and port call facilities, as well as opportunities for bunkering and provisions. Insofar as the systems used by ASEAN armed forces are compatible, the storage facilities at Clark and Subic could even serve as supply depots. Precedent for this scenario exists in that the Singapore Air Force keeps a permanent detachment at Clark; and the Philippines, Australia, New Zealand, and Thai air forces use the air gunnery range to hone their skills.[61]

In sum, the future of the Philippine bases will probably be determined more by the Philippines domestic political and economic situation in the late 1980s than ASEAN's strategic environment. ASEAN leaders have expressed their preference that the bases be retained. If Aquino can maintain a sufficient balance within the ruling coalition between the left-nationalist forces that dominate the Con-Com and the center-right groups that coalesce with the Philippine Armed Forces, then she will probably agree to a limited renewal of the bases agreement at a much higher rate of compensation with added Philippine jurisdiction over the action of U.S. personnel on Philippine territory. She may also insist on more consultation with respect to the bases in crisis situations and their availability to the AFP for training purposes. These changes would meet some of the nationalists' concerns, help buttress the economy, and sustain a U.S. regional military presence, thus supporting ASEAN solidarity. Closure of the facilities in the early 1990s would strain U.S.-Philippines relations, as well as ASEAN cohesion. The Aquino government prefers neither of these outcomes.

Other ASEAN External Links

Thailand is ASEAN's only other member with direct military links to the United States through treaty (the Manila Pact), executive agreement (the 1962 Rusk-Thanat accord, declared a still-valid basis for security ties by the Reagan administration), and FMS credits—the latter up from $32 million in FY 1979 to $110 million in FY 1986. Although most of the aid goes to support the modernization of Thai ground forces, they still are no match for the Vietnamese, even with improved U.S. weapons.

Thailand's link to an external protector continues a security policy over 150 years old. Initiated in the reign of Rama 3 (1824–1851), the Thais, finding it beyond their capacity to undertake trans-Mekong military operations, have sought an attachment to a larger power that would act as protector of its interests across the Mekong River. From the 1950s to mid-1970s, the United States served in this capacity. However, after the U.S. defeat in Vietnam and a brief experiment with nonalignment, the Vietnamese invasion of Cambodia required a new variation on the old theme. While the United States alone would no longer be sufficient protector, a combination of forces might be. Therefore Thailand has sought to bring together political, military, and economic assistance from the United States, China, Japan, ASEAN, the EEC, and Australia and New Zealand both to back Thailand's case against Vietnam in the United Nations and provide the economic and military aid needed to deter Hanoi without harming economic growth.[62]

In addition to military assistance, U.S. amphibious forces undertake annual joint exercises with the Thai navy and air force—the Cobra Gold maneuvers. In recent years, these exercises have been designed to repel an invader from the South China Sea.[63]

Malaysia, too, is concerned about threats from the South China Sea. Since the early 1980s, Kuala Lumpur has expanded its ability to monitor Soviet activity in and around the Strait of Malacca, particularly submarines. In what may be part of a tripartite surveillance arrangement among Indonesia, Singapore, and Malaysia, the last acknowledged its particular responsibility for monitoring Soviet vessels between the Singapore Strait and the Indian Ocean.[64] Malaysian surveillance is improved by a detachment of Australian P3C Orions that fly legs from Learmoth to Diego Garcia, to Butterworth, to the South China Sea (where U.S. Navy P3Cs pick up the patrol), and then back to Australia. Australian P3C intelligence is shared with Malaysia.[65]

The Malaysian navy by mid-1985 had acquired eight Exocet-armed gunboats, two new corvettes, and two British-built frigates, the latter four armed with sea-skimming ship-to-ship missiles. Six other warships were commissioned at the end of the year as part of a $565 million fleet modernization program. By the middle of the decade, then, the Malaysian navy had acquired a modest bluewater capability—virtually all of it deployed toward the South China Sea.[66]

The FPDA in addition to providing Singapore and Malaysian bases for small contingents of the Australian air force and the New Zealand army, also constitutes an agreement within which training, technical assistance, and consultation are offered. Malaysian and Singaporean pilots regularly train in Australia and New Zealand. For more than twenty years, Royal Australian Air Force (RAAF) fighters have been deployed at Butterworth opposite Penang. Although the old fighter squadrons are being withdrawn, Australia has agreed to rotate some of its newly acquired FA-18 Hornets through Butterworth on a regular basis, thus sustaining a visible and upgraded commitment to the security of Malaysia and Singapore.

Throughout the 1980s, the five powers have held annual joint military exercises and Consultative Council meetings. In 1985, Malaysia sought Australian training for its ASW program, and in Singapore, Canberra proposed the establishment of a joint venture to manufacture naval electronic missile defense systems for ship protection.[67] While Kuala Lumpur continues to nurture its

FPDA ties and a regional U.S. military presence, it nevertheless rankles at a perceived U.S. reluctance to share its top-line technology. The Malaysian decision to explore the possibility of buying Soviet helicopters—the first ASEAN state to consider Soviet weapons in twenty years—should be seen as a sign of dissatisfaction directed at the United States. The unwillingness of the United States to provide its best avionics in the refurbished A-4s it has sold to the Malaysian air force, its refusal to sell M-48 tanks to Malaysia when it provided them to Thailand, and its prohibition on the resale of U.S. equipment irritated the strongly nationalist Mahatir government and led to a public statement of willingness to consider purchasing systems from any supplier that offered the best terms for Malaysia.[68]

The F-16 Issue

The desire for top-line equipment in several ASEAN states concerns a number of defense analysts, for it could portend an arms race in the region not only between Vietnam and ASEAN but even within the association itself. As military technology costs spiral upward, third world states—even those as affluent as ASEAN members—will find their defense budgets ballooning while resources remaining for development expenditures dwindle. Typical of this policy issue is the interest of three ASEAN states, particularly Thailand, in purchasing an early version of the top-line U.S. fighter, General Dynamics F-16A.

In 1979, a Thai request for the F-16 was turned down in Washington, as was a similar Indonesian request three years later. The Philippines also made a tentative bid in 1984, to no avail. The Reagan administration acknowledged in 1984 that it had no strong grounds to reject the Thai request, particularly since it is a frontline state against Vietnamese-dominated Laos and Cambodia, other than the belief that there is no military need for the aircraft and its inordinate expense. (A squadron of sixteen F-16As with training and spare parts would cost approximately $500 million.)[69]

One alternative to the F-16A touted by the United States was the F-16/79, which has the same airframe as the F-16A but is powered by an engine similar to that used in Vietnam War–era F4 Phantoms. Both models carry identical armament, though the F-16/79 has about half the range of the F-16A, meaning that it could not reach Hanoi and return. The F-16/79 also costs $5 million less per aircraft. The other alternative is Northrop's prototype F-20, yet to be built in serial production. It is an upgraded version of the F-5, currently the mainstay of the Thai air force. The F-20 is being offered at a fixed price of $15 million per aircraft. Although no foreign purchases of either alternative aircraft have been made, this situation could change. A major objection to the F-20 by potential buyers is that it is not part of the U.S. Air Force inventory. Partly because of the congressional anger over irregular billing practices of

General Dynamics, the U.S. Air Force agreed in May 1985 to purchase 126 F-20s in the 1987–1991 budgets. F-16 purchases would be accordingly reduced in the same period.[70]

U.S. observers believe that Thai F-5Es are more than a match for Hanoi's MiG-21s. Despite the presence of TU-16 Badger bombers at Cam Ranh Bay and a squadron of MiG-23s deployed in late 1984, there is no indication that they are being provided to the VPA or that any Vietnamese are receiving training to fly them.[71] This assessment should not be construed as a permanent cap on Hanoi's weapons acquisition, however. The USSR has been phasing MiG-23s out of the Warsaw Pact countries and in due course may well provide them to Vietnam, especially if Hanoi offers additional base facilities for the Pacific fleet. (See table 4–5).

The Thai air force, pointing to the success of the Israeli F-16s against numerically superior Arab adversaries and U.S. willingness to sell the aircraft

Table 4–5
Southeast Asian Air Forces

Brunei
 6 combat aircraft

Indonesia
 83 combat aircraft
  2 FGA squadrons with 30 A-4E, 4 TA-4H Skyhawks
  1 interceptor squadron with 11 F-5E, 4 F-5F

Malaysia
 34 combat aircraft
  1 FGA squadron with 13 F-5E, 4 F-5Es
  2 4E-5E
  1 MR squadron with 3PC-130H

Philippines
 82 combat aircraft
  1 FGA squadron with 23 F-8H

Singapore
 167 combat aircraft
  2 FGA squadrons with 41 A-4S/SI, 6 TA-4S, Skyhawks
  1 FGA squadron with 21 Hunter FGA-74
  1 AD squadron with 24 F-5E, 3 F-5F

Thailand
 188 combat aircraft
  1 FGA squadron with 13 F-5A/B
  2 AD squadrons with 34 F-5E, 5 F-5F

Vietnam
 290 combat aircraft
  40 armed helicopters (plus many more in store)
  4 air divisions
  3 FGA regiments with 70 MiG-17, 40 Su-7/-20
  4 interceptor regiments with 180 MiG-21bs/F/PF, MiG-15

Source: *Pacific Defense Reporter* (May 1985): 19.

to South Korea and Pakistan, argues that a squadron would be an effective deterrent against a Vietnamese attack. Superior Thai pilot skills combined with the F-16As avionics would be a potent threat against Vietnam in the event of major hostilities. Moreover, given the constraints on any U.S. president to respond quickly to a friendly country's cry for assistance, the Thais would prefer to have their own, however limited, deterrent.

Of equal importance to military considerations is the political-symbolic value of a U.S. willingness to sell the F-16A to Thailand. In an early 1984 visit to Washington to persuade the Pentagon and Congress to endorse the sales request, Thai armed forces general Arthit Kamlang-ek made it clear that Thailand would regard the U.S. decision as a test of Thai-U.S. friendship.

Thai air force interest in the F-16A is not reciprocated by civilian officials. The Finance Ministry opposed the purchase on the ground that it would worsen an already serious external debt of approximately $11 billion in 1984. The army, too, showed little enthusiasm, pointing out that they could equip a new infantry division—more appropriate for the actual threat along the borders with Laos and Cambodia—for the cost of a single F-16 with spare parts and training—more than $30 million. Even some air force logistics officers have qualms about the shift from F-5s to F-16s, which would entail massive maintenance and operational changes. Moreover, the drain on the air force budget would reduce the number of flying hours for flight crews, of crucial importance for honing the complex skills needed in air combat. Finally, critics claim that the fighter purchase would end the acquisition of additional C-130 cargo planes, harming the military logistics and troop life capability.[72]

By early 1985, the United States cleared the Thai purchase of the F-16As. The Thai air force believes it can overcome financial objections by making the purchases from its own budget entirely. This would mean adopting austerity measures for virtually every other air force category, suspending new recruitment, and curtailing training. Air Force Chief Praphan Dhupatemoya claims that his service need not request any additional resources from the government if the internal reallocation within the air force is approved. Praphan also plans to retire older aircraft to save money, in effect creating a significantly smaller air force by the end of the decade when the twelve to sixteen F-16s become operational.[73]

In June 1985, the Thai cabinet approved the air force purchase of twelve F-16As for $317.8 million, presumably financed from the regular air force budget with no additional allocations. Deliveries will not begin until 1988. Air force planners insist that the F-16 will provide considerable versatility, including the ability to loiter over the battlefield with greater ordnance than either the F-5 or F-20. The F-16s will enter service toward the end of the decade, at about the same time that work is completed on the first phase of an automated air defense system for the surveillance of Thai airspace.[74]

Since the United States approved Thailand's request, Singapore and Indonesia have followed suit. Singapore's offer to buy eight F-16A and F-16B fighters at a cost of $280 million was approved by the U.S. Defense Department with alacrity. Washington emphasized Singapore's strategic location astride the primary route between the Indian Ocean and Pacific Ocean, implying the role F-16s could play in helping to defend that important junction.[75] Only Malaysia and Brunei appear uninterested at this point—the latter because of its small size and the former because of its recent commitment to buy over forty refurbished A-4 Skyhawks to form the base of its air defense into the 1990s.

There is, however, a drawback to the F-16 over and above its expense, especially to governments sensitive to their images of independence and nonalignment. Acquisition of the F-16A requires U.S. maintenance and training personnel in country for three to five years until a sufficient number of local technicians are trained.[76] Ironically, especially for Thailand whose military mission is concentrated along its eastern borders, the F-16 would be much less useful than cheaper, more flexible tactical aircraft such as the A-7, which could be modernized to mission requirements and sold for one-third the cost of even the F-16/79 or F-20. There is, however, no indication of interest in the A-7 by ASEAN air forces.[77]

If the ASEAN air forces acquire the F-16A, they will also be commiting to a high degree of maintenance and downtime per unit of operability. Air force data show that the F-16A requires double the maintenance schedule and provides half the flying time of the F-20 and is also considerably less efficient than the F-16/79 (table 4–6).

ASEAN may be on the verge of a new regionwide air capability. Despite the financial and maintenance drawbacks of the F-16, Thailand, Indonesia, and Singapore will have perhaps three squadrons in their inventories by the early 1990s. With Singapore's four E-2C Hawkeye airborne early warning

Table 4–6
Maintenance Ratios of Advanced U.S. Fighters

	Maintenance/ Man-Hours/ Flying Hour	Mean Time between Failures
F-16A	31.7[a]	2.9
F-16/79	26.4	4.1
F-20	14.9	4.2

Source: U.S. House of Representatives, Committee on Foreign Affairs, Subcommittee on International Security and Scientific Affairs, *Review of Administration's Policy on Sales of Advanced Fighter Planes to ASEAN: Hearings*, 98th Cong., 2d sess., March 28, 1984, p. 37.

[a]Calendar year 1983.

Note: If only recently produced block 15F-16s are considered, mean time between failures is 4.

aircraft, ASEAN would have a significant regional air and sea surveillance and defense capability, a possible first step toward the realization of ZOPFAN based on regional capacities.[78] The expense of these systems could also provide an incentive for the three states to consider a regionwide purchasing arrangement and parts depot. While the best technical location for this depot would be Singapore with its own aircraft industries, the three might agree to Indonesia as the only politically acceptable alternative. The depot would provide spare parts and perhaps even some long-term maintenance. If located in Indonesia, it would also serve as a symbol of Jakarta's commitment to Thailand's security needs, that is, an understanding that Bangkok's military requirements would be met from supplies jointly stocked in Indonesia.[79]

The Southeast Asia Nuclear-Free Zone Proposal

Indonesia's impatience with Thailand's prominence in Cambodian decision making has been manifest on a number of occasions. In 1987, with Malaysia's support, Jakarta revived a proposal for the creation of a Southeast Asian nuclear-free zone (NFZ) and put it on the agenda for the ASEAN summit at the end of the year. The purpose of this move was to place the Indonesian-Malaysian ZOPFAN concept on the association's political list once again. Thailand and Singapore oppose the NFZ idea, arguing its unrealistic character at a time when both the United States and USSR are expanding their forces in the region. The Thais have argued privately that an NFZ would benefit only the USSR since the zone could deprive Southeast Asia of an important deterrent. Indonesia's riposte is that the zone would apply equally to Soviet forces.

The United States, while opposing the zone, is somewhat embarrassed by the initiative. Washington does not want to be on the opposite side of an ASEAN proposal, particularly when the Soviet Union and China have endorsed it. However, as in the South Pacific Nuclear Free Zone Treaty, Washington's opposition is based on the belief that nuclear-free regional pledges will undermine the nation's sea-based global deterrent.[80] Proposals for NFZs cannot be accepted by the United States as its fleets become almost entirely nuclear capable in the 1990s.

At the December 1987 ASEAN summit, the NFZ issue was finessed. While its desirability as a long-term component of ZOPFAN was affirmed, no operational plans for its realization were presented. Nor was any timetable proffered by which the nuclear powers would be asked to remove their nuclear forces from the region. The Southest Asia NFZ has become another symbol of ASEAN's future hope to determine its own regional order.

ASEAN and the Indochina Conflict

The catalyst for ASEAN political solidarity since the end of the second Indochina War in 1975 has been the need to coordinate responses to Vietnam's
regional ambitions and its invitation to the Soviet Union to become a major
security participant in Southeast Asian affairs. Vietnam's alliance with the USSR
violated ASEAN's hopes for creating a regional order free of great power military
activities. The association moved instead to strengthen its own mechanisms
for military consultation and political action, while urging that countervailing
friendly military contingents from the United States, Britain, Australia, and
New Zealand remain in the region's oceans and airspaces.

Although an economic cripple, almost totally dependent upon the Soviet
Union and its COMECON partners for economic sustenance, Vietnam is a
formidable regional power. Although its per capita income is estimated by the
U.S. State Department to be only about $125 a year—one-fourth that of its
ASEAN neighbors—it fields the world's fourth largest army of 1.2 million.
The USSR subsidizes Vietnam by about $2 billion annually, or one-seventh
of its GNP. While the economies of every ASEAN state at least doubled be-
tween the mid-1970s and mid-1980s, Vietnam's showed no growth.[81]

The ASEAN states have at least three major security complaints against
Vietnam. The first is its invasion of Cambodia in open violation of the dictum
of small states that denies legitimacy to the military invasion and occupation
of a neighbor. The second is Hanoi's alliance with Moscow, providing the USSR
an opportunity to become a major Southeast Asian security participant for
the first time. The third, growing from the first two, has been the extension
of both Sino-Vietnam and Sino-Soviet hostilities directly into ASEAN's
neighborhood. Because Thailand faces Vietnamese troops along its frontiers
supplied with Soviet weapons, Bangkok has turned to China as an additional
guarantor against Hanoi. There is little chance that the Chinese will reduce
either their pressure on Vietnam's northern border or their supplies to the Khmer
Rouge component of the Resistance unless and until Hanoi withdraws from
Cambodia and acknowledges the legitimacy of a Chinese security interest in
Southeast Asia. For Hanoi to resist Beijing's threats requires the continuation
of its alliance with the Soviet Union—hence, the vicious circle character of current security relations within Southeast Asia. Each indigenous actor relies on
external mentors to face down its neighbor.

Production from Soviet-funded projects in Vietnam helps repay its debt to the
USSR. The trade pattern between the two countries has created an international
division of labor that places Vietnam in a neocolonial relationship to the Soviet
Union. That is, Vietnamese raw materials and light consumer goods go to the
Soviet Union at Soviet-determined prices in exchange for Soviet military and
economic aid. Over half of Vietnam's exports are sent to the USSR and thought
to be tied up in long-term commitments that restrict Hanoi's trade options.[82]

The only significant diplomatic attempt within ASEAN to break the Chinese and Soviet connections to the latest Indochina conflict was embodied in the 1980 joint Indonesia-Malaysian statement at Kuantan.[83] It was designed to effect an agreement by which Vietnam would cut its ties to the USSR while Thailand gave up its reliance on China. In exchange, ASEAN would recognize Vietnam's security interests in Indochina. The Kuantan Declaration was an attempt to restore the regional balance that existed prior to Vietnam's invasion of Cambodia when neither China nor the Soviet Union was deeply involved in Southeast Asia. Vietnam's hegemonic position within Indochina had been tacitly accepted by ASEAN at that time as long as that position was sustained through political control, not military occupation.

Nevertheless, the Kuantan Declaration proved abortive. Thailand rejected it because it conceded Vietnam's entitlement to Cambodia, removing a historic buffer against a traditional enemy. Hanoi's response was hostile too since Vietnam believed, quite correctly, that it could not sustain its control over Indochina without Soviet aid. The Kuantan experience was the first in a series of efforts by Indonesia to restore its leading role in ASEAN diplomacy. Jakarta has been frustrated by the fact that its "natural" leadership within the association has been subordinated to Thailand's needs as a frontline state. Indonesian opposition to a Chinese role in regional security matters has been particularly adamant. The several contacts between Indonesian and Vietnamese officials and research organizations in 1984 and 1985 reflect Jakarta's search for a special Indonesian role in resolving the Cambodian conflict. Since Indonesia and Vietnam identify China rather than the Soviet Union as the long-term threat to regional security, Indonesian leaders such as General Murdani maintain that Vietnam can be drawn into a structure of regional cooperation if only it will loosen its ties to the USSR. This view, however, is strongly opposed by Thailand, which insists on the restoration of Cambodia's independence.

Thailand's intransigence over Cambodia has proved to be good domestic politics too. A survey of Thai elite opinion by Chulalongkorn University's Institute for Security and International Studies in 1983 revealed overwhelming agreement that Vietnam and the Soviet Union presented direct threats to Thai security through armed tension along the Cambodian border, the refugee influx, and the intensification of regional great power rivalry. Half the respondents called for direct opposition to Vietnam's actions, while the other half—though hopeful that a compromise could be reached—insisted that Vietnamese forces be completely withdrawn from Cambodia.[84]

Until that withdrawal is effected, Thailand will strengthen ties with friendly external powers to increase the pressure on Vietnam. This policy includes links to China, not only because of the latter's promise to aid Thailand in the event of a Vietnamese invasion but also because China is the sole supplier of the Khmer Rouge, by far the strongest military component of the Resistance despite being its political Achilles heel.

Thailand's reliance on external backers may, however, render Vietnam even more stubborn. As Gareth Porter noted, Vietnam has always viewed Thailand as a weak, unstable state, which has preferred to rely on external powers. Despite Bangkok's wealth and Hanoi's poverty, the Vietnamese do not believe Thailand can attain political stability. Moreover, the military balance between the two states strongly favors Vietnam. Indeed, the Thai army is seen as "incapable of serious combat."[85]

Hanoi's Indochina strategy grows from the belief that the three countries are security interdependent. If any one of the three states is subverted by an external adversary, all are threatened. Therefore arises the need for an alliance among them to guarantee their independence. China's efforts to gain a foothold in Cambodia through the Khmer Rouge are seen by Hanoi as the latest in a series of external efforts to annex Indochina, following the French, Japanese, and Americans. Hanoi would not accept the restoration of Laos or Cambodia as buffers, for that would mean their governments would be susceptible to the influence of actors other than Vietnam.[86] The Vietnamese, according to William Turley's interviews in Hanoi, desire to play Moscow to the rest of Indochina's Eastern Europe. Toward this end, they began a program of economic integration in 1983 by organizing national committees for economic cooperation.[87]

Vietnam's reliance on the Soviet Union remains firm. The USSR is the only actor that can play the role of guarantor for the Indochina security arrangement. Therefore Vietnam cannot afford any resolution to the Cambodian conflict that would weaken the security guarantee provided by Moscow against Beijing.

Hanoi's diplomatic minuet around the ASEAN capitals over the past several years is a device to buy time for the consolidation of the pro-Hanoi Heng Samrin regime in Cambodia. Hanoi agrees with ASEAN demands that its troops withdraw from Cambodia. The sticking point is when and under what conditions. At the January 1985 Indochinese Foreign Ministers Conference in Ho Chi Minh City, Hanoi insisted that Vietnamese forces would be withdrawn only after the Khmer Rouge are eliminated as a force within Cambodia. While ASEAN too wishes to see the Khmer Rouge excluded from any political role in an independent Cambodian government, the association wishes to see a Vietnamese military withdrawal precede a political settlement based on internationally supervised elections. By contrast, while the Heng Samrin government is willing to hold future elections, possibly even with the participation of non–Khmer Rouge Resistance elements as individuals, no opposition political organization would be permitted to run.[88] In short, from Vietnam's perspective, elections in Cambodia must not be a device for the restoration of a neutral government but rather to legitimize Hanoi's post-1980 security community.

Nevertheless, in 1987, Hanoi—pressured by the Soviet Union—acquiesced to discussions in France between Prince Sihanouk and the PRK prime minister, Hun Sen. At the time of writing (January 1988), these talks are only in their early stages. The Prince insists on the creation of a parliamentary government for Cambodia after a Vietnamese troop withdrawal. Hun Sen agreed only that the PRK would be willing to talk with all Cambodian factions, including the Khmer Rouge, implying the possibility of some future coalition government.

The spillover of fighting along the Thai-Cambodian frontier into Thailand in 1983, 1985, 1986 and 1987 serves both tactical and strategic ends for Vietnam. Tactically it is designed to sever supply lines and avenues of retreat for the Resistance back into Thailand (to deny the kind of sanctuary the Vietnamese communists themselves had north of the seventeenth parallel during the second Indochina War). Strategically these skirmishes are meant to demonstrate to Thai leaders that their military is no match for the VPA, that China will not come to Bangkok's assistance, and that it is best for Thailand to make peace on Hanoi's terms.

Vietnam is not operating in a cost-free environment. Its military occupation of Cambodia and Laos exacts a considerable price, which includes economic opportunity costs, since the military drains 1.2 million men away from the civilian sector and heavily distorts the national budget. The Resistance shows no sign of collapsing despite the VPA's 1985 dry season devastation of its border base camps and the construction of a Maginot line along the Cambodian-Thai frontier. Hanoi's adversary relationship with China sustains pressure on Vietnam's northern border. Moreover, China can supply the Resistance through Thailand indefinitely at an acceptable cost. Indeed China's burgeoning economic growth actually makes it easier over time to pursue its bleed-Vietnam policy. Vietnam's refusal to offer any significant concessions to ASEAN has embarrassed and alienated Hanoi's most sympathetic member within the association, Indonesia. Both Jakarta and Kuala Lumpur have backed Bangkok more firmly since the Vietnamese incursions across the Thai border in 1985. Finally, there exists a degree of demoralization within the VPA. Although difficult to gauge, desertions from the military appear to be increasing. Defectors who escape to Thailand cite the unpopularity of their occupation duties as a major reason for abandoning their units. Since these conscripts come mainly from the south, they also object to serving under northern officers. The geographical division in Vietnam still prevails in the military as well as in politics.

Vietnam insists it faces a two-front threat from China, the second front being Khmer Rouge actions in Cambodia to destabilize the Heng Samrin regime. Only when China removes its threat will Hanoi consider a nonmilitary alternative to its Cambodian occupation. Hanoi maintains that an end to the current hostilities and withdrawal of VPA forces can occur only when the Resistance disperses and Thailand no longer provides supplies and sanctuary.[89]

The Vietnamese are pessimistic about China's long-term intentions, fearing the PRC in much the same way Thailand is concerned about a "greater Vietnam":

Within the next 20 years, China will be able to fulfill the readjusted targets of its "four modernizations" program. By then it would have increased four times its total industrial and agricultural output value. We would have then to deal with four Chinas instead of the present one. . . . That is the meaning of why China would want to push the whole world, and Southeast Asia in particular, into great disorder so that China alone can enjoy great order.[90]

Vietnam's most important goal is the consolidation of its Cambodian client. VPA forces will remain in Cambodia until that goal is reached—that is, until a sufficiently strong Cambodian bureaucracy and military have been recruited and trained to pacify the countryside without Vietnamese help. That could be a very long time.[91]

The ASEAN states see little alternative to sustaining the Resistance military capability and trying to build up the fighting capacities of the Sihanouk and Son Sann components. The problem, however, is that other than Singapore, no ASEAN member wishes to be seen as directly involved in providing military aid to the Resistance. Such activity would undermine the association's diplomatic position that the Cambodian conflict does not include ASEAN as a participant. Because China has no such qualms, its aid to the Khmer Rouge serves to sustain Pol Pot's forces' dominance on the battlefield. This, in turn, renders it impossible for ASEAN to disengage credibly from political and diplomatic support of the Khmer Rouge. Moreover, so long as the Resistance must rely primarily on Chinese aid, the greater Beijing's political leverage over all components of the Resistance will become.[92]

This dilemma has led to a number of appeals for U.S. assistance to the Shianouk and Son Sann components of the Resistance. First, the asymmetries of guerrilla warfare mean that each dollar contributed to the insurgents would require a $5 to $10 investment from Vietnam to counter it. A fairly modest investment of $100 million could force Hanoi and its Soviet backer to spend as much as an extra $1 billion.[93] Moreover, insofar as the Resistance is seen by Hanoi as exclusively dependent on China, Vietnam's intransigence will only be reinforced. Hanoi will not compromise with a political movement it views as dependent on the PRC. For Vietnam, dependence on China is equivalent to an alliance with China. Nevertheless, Washington remains skeptical about the noncommunist Resistance abilities. Although Congress appropriated a token $5 million for the Son Sann and Sihanouk forces for the first time in 1985, this is probably not a bellwether for the future given adamant U.S. political opposition to military involvement on the Southeast Asian mainland. Because Washington believes the Resistance is essentially "feeble," it will not provide the resources necessary to increase its ability to fight. A "self-fulfilling prophecy" results in which the military weakness of the noncommunists, caused at least in part by lack of resources, becomes a further justification for not supplying any significant additional assistance. Moreover, even if Resistance fortunes improve, the United States would also interpret this development as a reason for not needing to increase its support.[94]

This is not to say that the United States provides no assistance to the guerrillas. Under ASEAN prodding, informed observers report that Washington was probably providing up to $15 million by late 1984 in nonlethal procurement. The United States also provided over $11 million in 1984 to border relief operations, which, in effect, helped to sustain Resistance base camps. None of this is viewed as sufficient by ASEAN. All its members appealed for greater and more public U.S. support.[95] The State Department, in particular, has resisted. Its officials believe that ASEAN pressure for U.S. military assistance to the Resistance is based not on the association's inability to provide more aid but its preference that the U.S. rather than China guarantee Thai security.

After the 1985 Vietnamese dry season campaign devastated the Resistance base camps, Hanoi appeared to take a tougher line. While continuing to invite the Sihanouk and Son Sann elements of the Resistance to give up their struggle and join the People's Republic of Kampuchea (PRK) as individuals, for the first time the offer was coupled with a deadline—1987. After that year, there presumably would be no more role for them in Cambodia. This suggests that by 1987, Vietnam and its Cambodian backers hoped to have the Cambodian bureaucracy and military fully staffed and consolidated. Thus the regime would be able to handle internal security primarily on its own. As for any future regime following the termination of the Resistance, the Vietnamese told Australian foreign minister William Hayden that elections would be held on PRK terms. Only one party would be allowed to run—the Communist party currently in power. Other candidates would stand as independents. This is a far cry from ASEAN's formula, which calls for the dismantling of the PRK and the formation of a government of national reconciliation, which would integrate the Heng Samrin regime and the Resistance, to be followed by U.N.-supervised elections.[96]

Hanoi ceased mentioning the 1987 deadline a year before it was reached, however. Instead, during the "deadline" year, Vietnam—with Soviet backing—renewed a diplomatic offensive for a negotiated settlement that could include the Khmer Resistance minus the Pol Pot leadership. The Vietnamese insist that China's acquiescence is the key to a resolution of the conflict since Beijing arms the Khmer Rouge. Vietnam rejected a March 1986 Cambodian Resistance eight-point initiative, which would include a simultaneous withdrawal of Vietnamese forces and establishment of a four-party government in which the Heng Samrin regime would be one component alongside the Resistance elements, including the Khmer Rouge. For Hanoi and Phnom Penh, any PAVN withdrawal must be coupled with the elimination of sanctuary for and military support of "the Pol Pot clique and other reactionary forces."[97]

Interestingly, Hanoi offered inducements in its proposal to terminate the Resistance in hopes of making it more attractive to the United States and ASEAN. Foreign Minister Nguyen Co Thach told Hayden that Vietnam would no longer demand that Western bases in the region be an agenda topic for discussions of regional security.[95]

The Vietnamese present an optimistic scenario: Co Thach claims that the Cambodian problem "will solve itself in three years time. The year 1987 will be very important. That year we will be able to withdraw at least half of our troops. In 1990 it will be two-thirds."[99] By the summer of 1985, Vietnamese optimism increased even further; Hanoi stated that all PAVN forces would be out of Cambodia by 1990 at the latest.

For the Resistance, after the 1985 destruction of its border base camps, a major problem has been shifting from set piece conventional warfare to roving guerrilla units. Both Son Sann's Kampuchean People's National Liberation Front (KPNLF) and Prince Sihanouk's forces had created fairly elaborate bases just inside Cambodia, which could be used to claim that the coalition government was not an exile organization. The Vietnamese destruction of these camps forced the Resistance to shift to a guerrilla strategy, although the Khmer Rouge had followed this strategy all along. Sihanouk's forces adapted to the changed conditions, although proselytizing for new recruits more than engaging in small-scale military attacks. The larger KPNLF was less successful, however. According to U.S. intelligence, disputes persist among the KPNLF political and military leaders. The destruction of their camps had been a traumatic experience, for they were used as much for black market trading as military bases. KPNLF forces have displayed little enthusiasm for guerrilla life. Earlier they fought to defend the land on which they had relocated their families. Now those families have moved to refugee camps inside Thailand, while the fighters were told they must penetrate far into Cambodia in hit-and-run operations against Vietnamese supply lines. The shift has not been successful.[100]

Equally disturbing to Thailand has been the growing impunity with which Vietnamese forces are violating Thai territory. Perhaps as many as a thousand Vietnamese soldiers pushed into the mountainous strip of southeastern Thailand along the Cambodian border to destroy Khmer Rouge camps in April 1985. It took a month of fierce fighting by Thai marines supported by F-5Es to dislodge them. The combination of Vietnamese willingness to extend hostilities into Thailand and reports of the training of a new pro-Hanoi Thai insurgency in Laos, combined with the absence of any major Chinese military reaction to Vietnam's 1985 dry season offensive, could elicit some rethinking of Thai strategy toward the war.[101]

Increased Vietnamese military pressure also means even greater reliance on Soviet assistance. Visits by Defense Minister Van Tun Dung to Moscow in May and June 1984 ultimately elicited the transfer to Hanoi of new combat helicopters, SU-22 swing-wing fighter aircraft, missile attack boats, tanks, and a variety of surface-to-air missiles. The Soviets were also permitted to upgrade their own military presence in Cam Ranh Bay by adding a squadron of MiG-23s in December 1984 to the Bear and Badger aircraft already there.[102] By 1985, the Soviets were reported to have fourteen MiG-23s, sixteen Badger medium-range bombers capable of striking as far as the Malacca, Lombok, and Sunda straits, and a number of Bear reconnaissance aircraft. It appeared that the Soviets, like the Americans, were concentrating on control of the South China Sea and its access routes to the Indian Ocean.[103] The MiG-23s serve as air defense to protect the Badgers, Bears, and the base. These systems remain under Soviet, not Vietnamese, control; that is, they are part of the USSR's Asian strategy rather than an addition to Vietnam's defense forces.[104]

South China Sea Disputes

While attention has been focused on the Southeast Asian mainland as the primary area of regional confrontation, future conflict zones may well be located on the waters and island groups of the region (figure 4–2). The South China Sea is rife with conflicting jurisdictional claims growing out of overlapping 200-mile EEZs, the potential involvement of external powers as backers of one or another disputant, and the reported existence of vast quantities of undersea mineral and energy resources. This heady mixture is fermented through the growing maritime capabilities of the littoral states, the Soviet Pacific fleet, the U.S. Seventh Fleet, and, most recently, the early stages of a PRC blue-water navy. (See table 4–7.)

The Sino-Vietnam dispute was extended out to the South China Sea toward the end of the second Indochina War. Vietnam's 1974 claim that two-thirds of the Tonkin Gulf were territorial waters in part precipitated Beijing's occupation of the Paracel Islands later that year. Conflicting claims were further staked when Hanoi seized six Spratly islands in 1975, violating Vietnam's earlier recognition of Chinese sovereignty there, according to the PRC. (Interestingly, China had hinted in 1979 that it might be willing to make concessions in its land boundary dispute with Vietnam if the latter would be "reasonable" on the South China Sea issues.)[105] Chinese petroleum exploration in late 1979 had stayed away from the disputed areas in the Gulf of Tonkin, by confining its activities to an area east of the 108 degrees east line claimed by Vietnam as its sea boundary.

Vietnam too has proposed the principle of equal and mutual benefit as a basis for the division of the South China Sea, suggesting that Hanoi might be prepared to divide the Gulf of Tonkin if China agreed to recognize Vietnamese sovereignty over the Spratlys. China's reticence in taking up this offer is at least partly attributable to several ASEAN states' claims to part of the Spratlys too. That is, a Sino-Vietnam condominium in the South China Sea could undermine the PRC's united front with ASEAN against the USSR-Vietnam encirclement. The South China Sea dispute with Hanoi is portrayed as another component of Hanoi's hegemonic designs and has become intertwined with the continuing war in Kampuchea. An ironic footnote to this assessment is

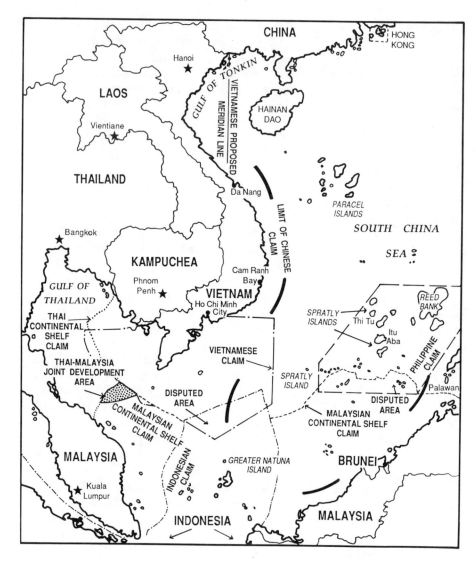

Figure 4–2. Conflict Areas in the South China Sea

China's tacit acceptance of the Kuomintang's occupation of the largest Spratly island, Itu Aba, since 1946, for it gives China a stronger claim to the Spratlys than Vietnam.[106] In late May 1984, the Sixth National Peoples Congress of the PRC discussed incorporating the Spratlys into the Hainan Island administrative region. Possible military action by the PRC and Vietnam around the islands has discouraged oil exploration in the vicinity. China's intransigence contributes to the perception among some ASEAN states that the PRC constitutes a future threat to regional stability.[107]

Table 4-7
East Asia Naval Order-of-Battle Summary

Category	USSR Pacific Fleet	U.S. Pacific Fleet	PRC	Brunei	Democratic People's Republic of Korea	Indonesia	Japan	Malaysia	Philippines	Republic of China	Republic of Korea	Singapore	Vietnam	Thailand
Carrier	2	6	—	—	—	—	—	—	—	—	—	—	—	—
Battleship	—	1	—	—	—	—	—	—	—	—	—	—	—	—
Cruiser	15	17	—	—	—	—	—	—	—	—	—	—	—	—
Destroyer	23	28	21	—	—	—	33	—	—	26	11	—	—	—
Submarine	126	44	114	—	16	3	15	—	—	2	—	—	1–2	—
Frigate	61	46	25	—	4	10	18	2	7	10	8	—	8	5
Major combatants	227	142	160	—	20	13	66	2	7	38	19	—	9–10	5
Patrol/PAC	231	—	962	12	338	16	5	91	90	39	83	30	200	110
Mine warfare	71	—	145	—	—	2	43	4	—	13	11	2	30	10
Amphibious	74	33	363	5	79	19	8	21	114	49	27	12	37	45
Auxiliary	207	58	380	1	7	25	41	24	30	18	11	—	14	10
Total	810	233a	2,170	18	437	75	163	142	241	187	141	44	289	180
Naval aircraft	440b	600b	800b	—	7	42	211	—	23	27	33	—	13	75

Source: *Pacific Defense Reporter* (May 1985): 13.

a U.S. Seventh Fleet afloat consists of about 60 ships and 240 aircraft.

b Approximate.

To dramatize its claims to islands in the South China Sea, China sent elements of its fledgling blue-water Southern Fleet to circumnavigate the region in May 1983. The ships sailed to the southernmost point claimed by China—James Shoal, only about 20 nautical miles north of Sarawak. China's warships were recently equipped with lines for the transfer of supplies at sea, and the Southern Fleet also added an oiler and submarine support ship.[108] Nevertheless, China's ability to project force on a sustained basis as far south as the Spratlys is severely limited. The area is outside the range of its land-based naval air, while the islands are within range of Vietnam's air force and Soviet Badger aircraft operating from Cam Ranh Bay.

As a prelude to its force buildup in the South China Sea, China has been developing the Paracels as a new naval base. Eleven harbors have been constructed on various atolls. In particular, the facilities on Woody Island could be used as a staging point for a future campaign to capture the Spratlys. It contains facilities to service the major warships of the Southern Fleet, projected to become the country's largest.[109] If, however, Vietnam continues to be the beneficiary of Soviet arms transfers, including Petya-class frigates, SU-17 fighter bombers, Koni-class frigates, and Foxtrot submarines, it is extremely unlikely that the PRC will be in a position to enforce its claims.

The conflict core in the South China Sea is the Spratly archipelago of about 100 islands, reefs, and shoals spread over an area of 7,000 square miles. The major concentration, the Central Spratlys, lies about 150 miles west of the Philippines' Palawan island. Sitting astride strategic maritime routes, oil geologists believe that the waters surrounding the islands may contain significant petroleum deposits. In addition to Vietnamese, PRC, and Taiwan claims to the total archipelago, the Philippines and Malaysia claim those portions that overlap their EEZs.

Philippine claims date back to the mid-1950s, when a private Philippine expedition occupied several islands. Philippine troops first occupied five of the islands in 1968 and controlled eight by the mid-1980s, administered through Palawan province. In 1976, oil was found in the Reed Bank northwest of the Central Spratly Group. Over protests from Hanoi and Beijing, the oil has been developed by Manila. Hanoi occupies seven other islands southwest of the Central Group, including Spratly Island. Some of these Vietnamese islands are close to those occupied by the Philippines, Taiwan, and Malaysia. Hanoi has fortified its islands heavily. The most recent claimant to the Spratly stakes is Malaysia. In August 1983, it sent a small group of commandos to the island of Terumba Layong Layong. It also claims the Vietnamese-held island of Amboyna Cay only 40 miles away. The islands would form a natural protective barrier for Malaysian oil and gas fields as part of its EEZ.[110]

The Philippines has approximately 1,000 marines on a half-dozen islands, and Vietnam has about 350. Thailand and Malaysia agreed in 1983 to engage in joint offshore oil exploration in their Gulf of Thailand overlapping EEZs, but there is no indication that Vietnam, the Philippines, and Malaysia are prepared to consider a comparable arrangement for the Spratlys.[111]

Although each claimant has some soldiers on the island(s) it holds, the key capability for any direct confrontation would be naval and air power. Taiwan and the PRC have the best equipped amphibious forces, but they lack the aircraft necessary to support long-range operations. The Malaysian, Vietnamese, and Philippine navies are still essentially coastal defense units. Fighter aircraft from Malaysia (U.S. A-4 Skyhawks), Vietnam (Soviet SU-17s), and the Philippines (U.S. F-8 Crusaders) have sufficient range to reach the Spratlys but could not loiter very long for combat. Thus no single claimant has the ability to enforce its total claim against the others.

Indonesia occupies the Natuna Islands between West and East Malaysia, though the EEZs of Vietnam, Malaysia, and the PRC all intersect with Jakarta's. Surrounding the Natunas is thought to be one of the largest undersea gas deposits in the world. Indonesia has built an airstrip on Natuna Island and plans to develop gas processing facilities there.[112] Vietnam in 1981 protested Indonesia's 1979 announcement of bids for oil exploration around the Natunas, warning foreign corporations that they could be in trouble if they began petroleum surveys. Despite the warning, U.S. companies are exploring for hydrocarbons on behalf of Indonesia's state oil company, Pertimina. Vietnam's oil exploration is being conducted by rigs from the USSR. In effect, Soviet and U.S. petroleum searches go on in adjacent ocean blocs. If Vietnam or the Philippines should engage in hostilities, for example, in the area of their adjacent Spratly island claims, each could presumably invoke the assistance of a superpower mentor. Similarly in the Gulf of Tonkin, it appears that China had U.S. backing in mind when it let contracts to U.S. oil companies for exploration in zones bordering disputed areas with Vietnam.[113]

Stability in the South China Sea depends on a military stalemate if the claimants cannot negotiate a resolution of their differences. Currently the PRC is deterred from action in the Spratlys by both the Soviet and U.S. fleets. Vietnam is deterred from action against Indonesia, Malaysia, and the Philippines by the U.S. Seventh Fleet, and the Philippines is deterred by uncertainty over whether the United States would come to its aid. Noteworthy, however, is the U.S. guarantee to Marcos in an exchange of notes in 1979 that strengthened the U.S.-Philippine Mutual Security Agreement's Article 5. The notes specified that the Philippines could invoke the agreement as a result of an attack on the home islands, on Pacific islands under Manila's jurisdiction, and on Philippine armed forces operating in the Pacific outside the Philippines. Not only do these "clarifications" have implications for U.S. military assistance to Manila in the event of hostilities in the Spratlys, but U.S. support presumably could also be invoked if the Philippines decided to attack bases in Sabah that Manila believed were supporting Muslim rebels in Mindanao.[114]

The South China Sea will remain a region of contention into the 1990s. It is unlikely, however, that the disputes discussed above by themselves would precipitate hostilities among the disputants. Rather, if military force is used, it will result from more basic conflicts among the adversaries. Thus Sino-Vietnamese hostilities in the Spratlys might well occur through a horizontal escalation of fighting along the Sino-Vietnam and/or Cambodian-Thai borders. Hostilities in the South China Sea would raise the costs and risks to both Hanoi and Beijing and could be a type of military pressure by either to force its opponent to settle the conflict on more favorable terms. The rapidity with which China is building a blue-water navy lends credence to this possibility. It also puts considerable pressure on the Soviets to deter such action by China in the event of renewed Sino-Vietnam hostilities on the Southeast Asian mainland. While competitive naval and air buildups throughout the region may invoke caution and hence support stability, the presence of so many competitive, overlapping unresolved maritime jurisdictional disputes ensures that if hostilities do occur, they would be costly and could spread.

5
Australia's Role in Asian Security: Problems of a Middle Power

An Overview

Although historically Australia has looked to external mentors for defense assistance, initially Great Britain and more recently after World War II the United States, the island continent is in fact remote from the major centers of global military tension. It has vast oceans on its eastern, southern, and western sides. Papua New Guinea, the nearest northern neighbor, is 100 miles from the Australian mainland; the next closest neighbor, Indonesia, is 250 miles distant at its nearest point. The Asian mainland is almost 2,000 miles away.

In recent decades, Indonesia has become prominent in Australian strategic thinking. Jakarta's preeminent position in ASEAN, the archipelago's location across major Australian shipping lanes to Japan and Northeast Asia, and the potential for a hostile power to use Indonesia to exert military pressure on northern Australia attest to that country's importance for Australian defense. The concern is not, however, reciprocated by Indonesia. It too looks north for its security needs and finds it difficult to understand Australia's worries.

Papua New Guinea and the islands of the Southwest Pacific are also important for protection and trade. From Papua New Guinea, maritime forces could steam down Australia's east coast and against the sea-lanes to the north. The island countries of the South Pacific also lie across important sea-lanes to Japan and North America. Nevertheless, Australia is in the fortunate position of having no identifiable proximate military threat. (See figure 5–1.)

Australian post-World War II maritime strategy was originally based on the 1950 Radford-Collins Agreement with the United States. The Royal Australian Navy (RAN) with its two carriers was adjunct to the U.S. Seventh Fleet, concentrating particularly on ASW. This division of labor lasted until 1983.[1] Beginning in the 1970s, however, at the end of the second Indochina War, defense planners began to rethink Australia's strategic policy. A focus

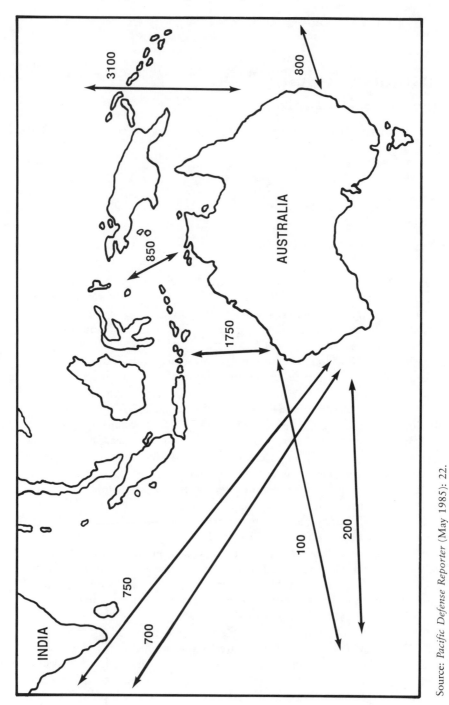

Source: *Pacific Defense Reporter* (May 1985): 22.

Figure 5–1. Australia's Vulnerable Overseas Trade: Number of Sailings Annually

on ASW made sense only if a major maritime conflict with a great power was foreseen. After the mid-1970s, that prospect seemed remote.

Great Britain had drastically reduced its overseas commitments, and the U.S. forces became stretched throughout the globe, giving the Antipodes a relatively low priority because it is so far from the major centers of world conflict.

These developments led Australian planners of both major parties to call for a more self-reliant defense posture. However, the concentration of population and military bases in the southeastern part of the continent renders it difficult to defend the north, where any direct threat to the country would initially occur. The major Australian strategic debate centers on whether the country's limited defense budget should go to the army for continental defense, emphasizing low-level conflict management, or to the navy and air force to ensure the maintenance of open SLOCs. Despite the absence of either an identifiable or imminent threat to Australia, there is nevertheless a feeling of vulnerability in a rich, empty continent with an overpopulated northern neighbor. At the very least, prominent Australian strategists argue, the defense force should build the capacity to protect the country's 200-mile EEZ and the air and maritime approaches to the continent's major centers.[2]

Yet it is difficult to develop the political will for such an undertaking. Since none of Australia's neighbors currently presents a military challenge and because the Soviets do not regularly ply the waters of the southern Indian Ocean and Coral, and Tasman seas, there is little support for a major buildup of either the navy or air force.[3] This does not mean, however, that Australia is retreating into isolationism. Canberra is deeply involved in defense cooperation programs with the ASEAN states, including the provision of training facilities and some military aid. Australia consults regularly with its defense counterparts in ASEAN and engages in joint exercises with both ASEAN states and members of the South Pacific Forum.

More specifically, Australia participates in the integrated air defense system linking Indonesia (informally) with Malaysia and Singapore under the FPDA. Australia maintains an air force presence at Butterworth opposite Penang in Malaysia and rotates some of its new F-18As to that air base as it phases the Mirages out of service. Moreover, Australian P3 Orion patrol aircraft regularly use Malaysian bases as a part of their extended ASW watch over the South China Sea and northeastern Indian Ocean. Nevertheless, the RAN lacks ships with sufficient staying power to participate in conflicts exceeding low-level, sporadic confrontations.

The United States has urged Australia to increase its air and maritime convoy capacity so that it could protect the approaches to Indonesian waters from the eastern Indian Ocean to the reaches north of Papua New Guinea. However, a prominent Australian defense analyst, Paul Dibb, points out that there would be very little to protect against since in the event of crisis, most Soviet submarines from the Pacific fleet would be allocated to important targets in the North Pacific. Thus, there is little reason to develop a force structure based on an unnecessary convoy doctrine.[4]

A counter to this argument is made by analysts who note the buildup of Soviet submarines and surface ships at Cam Ranh Bay, an average of twenty-five daily around the port in the mid-1980s, and the deployment of Badger bombers. These are only 500 miles farther from Darwin than Darwin is to Sydney. The Soviets are developing a regional force projection capability in Southeast Asia to ensure unconstrained passage through the straits between the Indian Ocean and South China Sea. The Liberal party defense minister, Ian Sinclair, stated in November 1982 that Australia should once again develop a forward defense capability, the first time that term had been used since the end of the second Indochina War. Sinclair was concerned about the intimidating effect of a growing Soviet presence on the ASEAN states rather than any direct threat to Australia itself. Australian forces could assist in defending the waters and airspace of their immediate region.[5]

Thus since 1980, initially under the Fraser government and subsequently under its Labour successor, a number of defense initiatives have been taken. These include the deployment of naval forces and air surveillance in the Indian Ocean; provision of facilities for U.S. B-52s at Darwin; the construction of naval bases at Darwin and Cairns; plans to expand the airfield at Derby and build a railway from Alice Springs to Darwin; the improved readiness of the army's operational deployment force based at Townsville; the replacement of the air force's aging Mirage fighters with U.S.-built F-18s; increased defense cooperation with ASEAN, including additional exercises through the FPDA; and the expansion of the army's northern surveillance force.

These growing capabilities, however, have not resolved Australia's strategic debate: should its defense be based exclusively on the protection of the continent and its air and maritime approaches or on some form of power projection to assist its South Pacific and ASEAN neighbors? Some decisions have suggested that Canberra is opting for a continental defense posture. The March 1983 choice by Defence Minister Gordon Scholes not to replace the aircraft carrier *Melbourne* and therefore to disband the fixed-wing component of Australian naval aviation seemed to be an abrogation of force projection. Added to this was a growing conviction in naval circles that the newly purchased smaller, frigate-size ships could not be equipped with modern, long-range, multitarget radar and weapons systems. Therefore they would be less likely to survive intense conflict.[6] Similarly, the Labour government's decision to acquire new diesel electric submarines suggests a coastal defense emphasis. Defence Minister Kim Beazley announced that Stirling Naval Base near Perth is to become a major base for RAN submarines in order to provide Australia with protection on both sides of the continent.

Australia does not maintain large ready forces. Reflecting its small population of 15.5 million and its relatively benign strategic environment, the total military complement is about 72,500 uniformed personnel, with slightly fewer than half of these in the army.[7] Defense planners believe that these forces can be augmented rapidly in the event of a crisis. This belief is, however, problematic given both the limited supplies on hand and a lack of operational readiness. The ever-increasing costs of high technology weaponry mean that fewer units are acquired with each passing year the defense budget remains flat. This has the effect of gradually weakening rather than strengthening the force structure. Canberra's claim that the eastern Indian Ocean and Southeast Asia are of "abiding [strategic] importance to Australia" is questionable in the light of this force structure.[8] Yet Australia remains an important contributor to Asian security because of its linkages as a middle power between the United States on the one hand and the ASEAN and Southwest Pacific states on the other. This relationship is conceptualized in figure 5–2.

The Manila Pact, ANZUS, and the FPDA all intersect. Moreover, since two FPDA members also belong to ASEAN, opportunities for security collaboration exist among Australia, the United States, and virtually all of noncommunist Southeast Asia with the exception of Burma. Indeed Australia's military assistance to its regional neighbors is on the rise. In 1984 more than a thousand officers of regional militaries attended training programs in Australia. The defense cooperation program was budgeted for A$45 million in

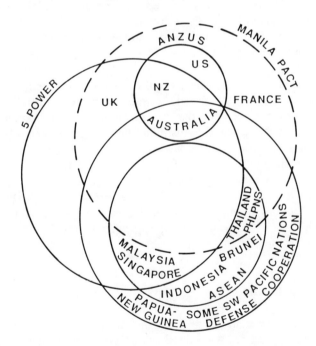

Figure 5–2. Australia's Linkages to Allied and Friendly States in Asia

the same year.[9] Since ASEAN states lack a long-range surveillance capacity, Australia's P3 Orion patrols assist them in regional defense.

The South Pacific is of importance, too, in Canberra's regional plans. An expanding Soviet naval presence south of Vietnam is a distinct possibility as the number of ships using Cam Ranh Bay increases. Vanuatu's establishment of diplomatic relations with Cuba was followed in 1987 by the signing of a fishing agreement with the USSR that provides for port calls.[10]

Because the Southwest Pacific offers an alternative sea-lane to the Malacca Strait, the prospect of Soviet ships deployed in that sea-lane is troublesome. Kiribati signed a fishing agreement with the Soviet Union in August 1985 that permits Soviet fishing boats to operate within Kiribati's 200-mile economic zone. (These ships frequently engage in electronic intercepts.) The treaty allowed sixteen Soviet vessssels to fish for one year for a U.S. $1.5 million fee, although the agreement did not provide for port calls. Australian and New Zealand concern over these developments was displayed in Canberra's sale to New Zealand of a P3B maritime patrol aircraft to monitor Kiribati's resource zone. In return the latter agreed not to allow the Soviets to base fishing vessels there.

By 1986, the United States had become sufficiently concerned about the prospect of Soviet penetration into the Southwest Pacific that it reached an agreement to channel $60 million in fishing fees and developmental aid over the next five years to the island states. The agreement marked the first time U.S. tuna vessels agreed to pay for access to large areas of South Pacific waters. Probably not coincidentally, Kiribati allowed its one-year treaty for Soviet fishing rights to lapse after the Soviet Union asked for a reduction in the $1.5 million fee.[11]

The Australians see, in sum, an essentially nonthreatening immediate security environment. They are concerned, however, with the potential for Soviet interference over time, especially if the latter's relationship with Vietnam is continually strengthened—hence, the Australian Labour government's persistent hopes of weaning Hanoi away from Moscow by suggesting concessions on the future of Cambodia that most of ASEAN are unwilling to consider. Because the Soviets are seen as a maritime problem on the horizon, Australia is involved in contributing to ASEAN and South Pacific security through the FPDA and Manila Pact, as well as through military aid and training programs on a bilateral basis. But what about Australia's ability to project its own military force in the event of a regional crisis?

Australian Capabilities

The emphasis in Australian defense doctrine on protection of the homeland rather than force projection, symbolized by the Labour decision not to acquire a new aircraft carrier to replace the aged *Melbourne* and the Dibb report, does not bode well for a major Australian regional military role. Nevertheless, even a "fortress Australia" policy must include a distant retaliatory capability (or a capacity for preemptive strike) that could be employed in a regional context. Australia's new F-18s with inflight refueling and its submarine force could be used at a distance from the continent to discourage an adversary's escalating a low-level situation. Australia needs additional surveillance and early warning systems, particularly in the north, and air and maritime strike forces to prevent the concentration of enemy assets prior to an attack on the homeland.[12] In 1984, that capacity consisted of six Oberon submarines, three ASW-equipped destroyers, and two FFG-7 frigates with Harpoon SSMs and SAMs. The air force had five ready squadrons with twenty-four F-111s and seventy-one Mirage IIIs. The latter were beginning to be replaced by F-18s, a total of seventy-five planned by decade's end.[13]

If Australia is to focus its defense efforts on keeping the major maritime approaches open, then long-range maritime patrol and a strengthened ASW capacity, including the ability to lay sonobuoy fields and launch helicopters, are necessary. A fixed-wing aircraft carrier is not. These ASW forces should also be capable of amphibious assault and could be integrated into a larger allied effort if need be. The regular Sea Eagle exercises, held in an ANZUS context, are specifically designed for combined ASW operations.[14]

Major items of capital equipment being purchased from the United States but actually built in Australia over the remainder of the 1980s include the F-18 tactical fighters, three guided missile frigates (FFGs), and ten long-range maritime patrol aircraft (P3Cs).[15]

Australia maintains a modest naval presence in the eastern Indian Ocean, homeported at Cockburn South near Perth. It consists of the destroyer escorts HMAS *Stuart* and HMAS *Swan* and two Fremantle-class patrol boats, barely sufficient for diplomatic port calls to friendly countries. In effect, under the Labour government, Australia's Indian Ocean policy is restricted to P3C ocean surveillance with the cooperation of Malaysia. Cockburn Sound has the capacity for rapid upgrading, however, should the government decide to expand its own maritime deployments or invite elements of the U.S. Seventh Fleet, as the previous Liberal government had contemplated. The base has facilities for berthing four destroyers and three submarines.[16]

Defense budget difficulties have delayed the acquisition of helicopters for the recently commissioned FFGs. Indeed it is probable that these ships will not be ready to conduct ASW surveillance until the end of the decade. Similarly, the addition of more Harpoon missiles has been postponed because of the country's economic condition.[17] In sum, financial stringency means that the addition of new equipment for the navy and air force commissioned by the Liberal government after 1979 has been stretched out by Labour so that it will not be fully operational until the early 1990s. Although Australia is reorienting its military to the north and west, it will take several years for such new projects as the U.S. $150 million air base at Tindal in the Northern Territory to be completed. Tindal is to be the main air base in a series of facilities around the northern coastline to ensure that the F-18s have adequate offshore operational range for both the eastern Indian Ocean and Southeast Asia.[18]

The Dibb Report and Subsequent 1987 Defence White Paper

In 1985 the Labour government commissioned an extensive review of Australian defense policy of Paul Dibb, a former intelligence officer and at the time of the study strategic analyst at the Australian National University. Tabled in parliament in June 1986, the Dibb report endorsed trends that had begun several years earlier and provided a rationale for their acceleration.[19] Arguing that there are no imminent great power threats to Australia and that neither the country's resources nor population permit the creation of armed services with a significant power projection capability, Dibb proposed that Australia concentrate on the defense of its continent and adjacent Pacific protectorates (the Cocos and Christmas islands).

Labeling this a strategy of denial, Dibb recommended that Australia allocate defense spending toward a capability to detect and strike against possible attackers in the vast northern approaches. Canberra's contribution to U.S. defense strategy for the Asia-Pacific region would consist of continued U.S. transit use of Australian naval and air bases and the maintenance of three highly sensitive communications and electronic surveillance facilities at the Northwest Cape, Pine Gap, and Nurrungar.

Dibb stressed the importance of submarines and air force fighter bombers (F-111s) for his strategy. They would patrol a thousand-mile zone of denial beyond the country's northern boundary. Additionally Dibb urged the acquisition of ten all-weather light patrol frigates to guard sea approaches. He opposed the navy's requests for a dozen destroyers based on the traditional doctrine of Australian operations as part of an allied fleet, claiming that convoy-escort scenarios are improbable in today's Pacific strategic situation.[20]

Dibb proposed a layered defense screen operating across the continent's sparsely populated north, using the Australian-designed Jindalee OTH radar. This system, according to Defence Minister Beazley, will permit Australia to monitor aircraft and shipping for 1,000 nautical miles offshore. It is expected to be operational by the late 1990s.[21] Strike forces will include air force P3Cs equipped with Harpoon antiship missiles, as well as ASW weapons, and seventy-five new F-18 fighters to be stationed at the new Tindal Air Base near Darwin beginning in late 1988.[22] RAN ships would operate under cover from the land-based F-18s.

U.S. reaction to the Dibb report was not enthusiastic. Criticism from Washington centered on the improbability of any attack on Australia through the Indonesian archipelago and the report's apparent lack of concern over a Soviet threat—either directly or by proxy—from other directions. Nevertheless, the United States was relieved that Dibb endorsed the continued use of Australian territory by the U.S. Navy and Air Force and applauded his recommendations for greater mine warfare capability, as well as the idea of a thousand-mile Australian defense perimeter.[23]

Australian critics of the report see it as a disguised retreat into a "fortress Australia" policy. The abrogation of a power projection capability will leave the island countries of the Southwest Pacific defenseless. Since the report identifies Southeast Asia, the eastern Indian Ocean, and the Pacific islands as strategically important to Australia, should not Canberra develop the force structure to operate in these areas?[24] Most disturbing are the implications of the Dibb strategy for the end of the century. If Dibb's recommendations are adopted, Australian defense forces at that time would be limited to a thousand-mile defense perimeter. The Soviets, by contrast, would have at least one nuclear-powered aircraft carrier in the Pacific. If anything, Australia would be even more dependent on U.S. protection rather than self-reliant.[25]

Many observers were surprised that the Labour government rejected many of the Dibb report's recommendations in a Defence White Paper released in March 1987. To Washington's relief, the new report reaffirmed Australia's position in the Western alliance and a strong regional role for Australian armed forces. The government confirmed the continuation of P3 and F/A-18 flights from Malaysia, released plans to expand the naval base at Cockburn Sound to provide a genuine eastern Indian Ocean capability, and announced the construction of a new SIGINT station in Western Australia.

The shift back to a more traditional relationship with the Western alliance followed consultations not only with Washington but also with Tokyo and the ASEAN states.[26] Unlike the Dibb report's call for light coastal patrol frigates, Beazley plans eight new ocean-going FFGs designed to operate at a range of 3,000 nautical miles (1,000 more than had been recommended by Dibb). The F-111s will be upgraded rather than phased out as Dibb suggested. To implement these plans, the Labour government has tabled the largest defense equipment program in Australia's history, projecting a cost of A$25 billion through the mid-1990s. Acknowledging the growing Soviet regional capability as a motivating factor, Beazley stated that new surveillance aircraft and combat ships will "deny an adversary effective use of the sea-air gap to the north." Soviet assets in Vietnam and the USSR's ability to interdict Southeast Asian sea-lanes give "added importance to our defense cooperative activities . . . , particularly our maritime surveillance of the South China Sea and the northeast Indian Ocean and our naval deployments to these regions."[27]

The White Paper defines the area of direct security interest for Australia to be from the Cocos Islands and Indian Ocean approaches in the west to the islands of the Southwest Pacific in the east and from the archipelago and island chain to Australia's north to the Southern Ocean. Australia's ability to control these reaches will be increased in the 1990s by six new Australian-built submarines, half of which would be based on the west coast, and the new F/A-18s supported by four modified Boeing-707 aircraft for inflight refueling. These systems would be augmented by Jindalee OTH radars, which will be able to monitor air and sea traffic from Southeast Asia. Given sufficient lead time, Australia's F-111s for long-range interdiction and F/A-18s for medium and short range should provide an effective air defense.[28]

While Canberra will terminate permanent air force deployments at Butterworth, Malaysia, beginning in 1988, the aging Mirages will be replaced by a squadron of new F/A-18s for four months annually. Moreover, Australian F-111C jets will continue to exercise each year under the FPDA, thus maintaining the integrated air defense system with Singapore, Malaysia, and Indonesia.

In sum, although the Dibb report's fortress Australia policy has been rejected by the Labour government, many of Dibb's ideas are incorporated in its new defense policy. The emphasis on increased mobility, layered defense, early identification of an aggressor, and engagement of the enemy in the air-sea gap around the continent emanate from the Dibb document.

ANZUS: New Questions of Security Capability

Because Australia is an insulated island continent 1,500 miles from Asia, it is not a potential ignition point for a general conflict. Australia has the capacity to defend itself against most plausible low-level challenges. Indeed, as Henry Albinski points out, the argument heard most frequently in Australia itself is that the greatest threat grows out of the close security links to the United States, particularly U.S. military communications facilities at the Northwest Cape, Pine Gap, and Nurrungar, as well as frequent ship visits to Cockburn Sound. Through ANZUS, Australia has accepted a troublesome burden that could lead to entanglements in conflicts not of its choice and to the targeting of its territory for nuclear attack.[29] Nevertheless, both the Liberal and Labour governments, as well as the vast majority of Australians, are prepared to accept these risks of alliance, for they believe on balance that a substantial U.S. military presence is necessary for regional deterrence and that Australian locations for U.S. strategic communications constitute Canberra's contribution to global deterrence.

ANZUS is an ambiguous treaty. It does not designate a precise area of coverage. This ambiguity has enabled Australia and New Zealand to disassociate from politically or geostrategically inconvenient situations from time to time. However, continued U.S. adherence to ANZUS is contingent, among other considerations, on the willingness of the Antipodean states to exercise at least a minimal forward defense posture in Southeast Asia and the Southwest Pacific. The participation of Canberra and Wellington in the FPDA demonstrates their acceptance of the U.S. view that ANZUS should be a component of regional collective defense.[30]

Although the Liberal party has been the most forthcoming to U.S. regional defense requests—for example, offering the use of Cockburn Sound as a site for U.S. naval units patroling the Indian Ocean in 1980—even the Liberals balk at the prospect of integrating Australian forces with those of the United States. At the 1980 ANZUS Council meeting when U.S. officials proposed the addition of Australia's soldiers to the Rapid Deployment Force, Prime Minister John Malcolm Fraser demurred on the ground that Australia's regional defense contributions must operate through "independent, national efforts."[31]

Insofar as there is a specific Australian–New Zealand responsibility within ANZUS, it is sea-lane protection. Under the Radford-Collins Agreement, last revised in 1978, the Australian responsibility for maritime protection lies generally south of the equator between the mid-Pacific and mid-Indian oceans, with the area east of New Zealand allotted to Wellington.[32] Although Australian P3s regularly patrol much of this area, the RAN has neither the submarine nor surface combatant capacity to secure this vast area or convoy merchant ships. Nor are there plans for Australia to acquire the capability to do so.

Instead, Australia augments its own limited regional forces by providing facilities for U.S. naval forces deployed in the Indian Ocean by the provision of staging facilities at Darwin for B-52 aircraft engaged in Indian Ocean surveillance and by placing RAN vessels deployed on surveillance missions in the Indian Ocean under the operational control of the U.S. Navy.[33] (See figure 5–3.)

From the perspective of the United States, access to Australian and New Zealand ports is viewed as a most important contribution to ANZUS, more significant even than their relatively limited military commitment.[34] Washington's emphasis on access to strategic locations has become the crux of a significant ANZUS crisis centering on New Zealand. At this point, it should be noted that the U.S. concern with location more than allied force contributions typifies the structural asymmetries of an alliance between a great power and smaller states. Because the latter have only limited manpower and weaponry, their primary utility to the strategic interests of their great power partner lies in their strategic locations or bases, a situation that automatically makes them a target of their larger partner's adversaries.

The importance of U.S. access to ports and airfields was reemphasized in the joint communiqué concluding the July 1984 ANZUS Council meeting (after the New Zealand Labour government had won the election but before it assumed office). More than sixty U.S. naval vessels visit West Australian ports each year. These ports, combined with their counterparts in eastern Australia, give protection to an alternate route from the Persian Gulf to Northeast Asia

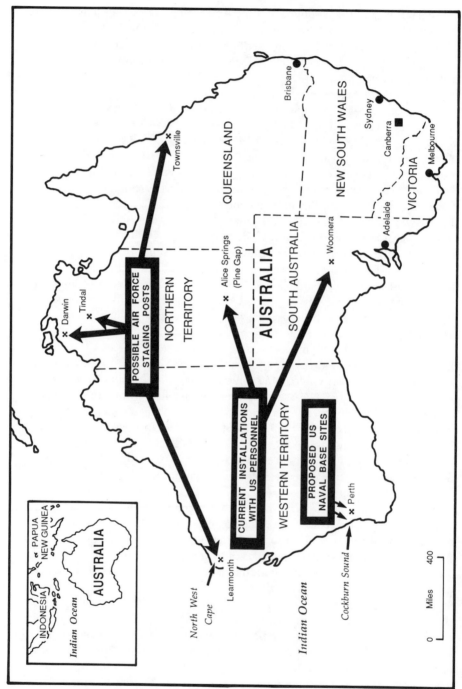

Source: *Christian Science Monitor* (International Edition), August 18, 1980.

around Australia. This route avoids the choke points of the South China Sea, including the Strait of Malacca, and permits allied shipping to transit far from the Soviet forces deployed out of Cam Ranh Bay. This alternate route in the event of a Southeast Asian crisis involving Soviet forces would be crucial, just as it was between 1941 and 1943 when the Japanese Imperial Navy controlled the South China Sea.

Australia and New Zealand have generally considered ANZUS an attractive arrangement because the United States has not put heavy demands upon them. Until the 1980s, U.S. strategic preeminence meant that burden sharing was not a major consideration for ANZUS. Currently, however, Australian officials wonder whether the pressure being exerted by Washington on its NATO allies and Japan to shape their forces to fit U.S. global strategy will extend to the Antipodes as well. The Labour governments of both Australia and New Zealand have explicitly abandoned forward defense doctrines to avoid being drawn into distant conflicts. Their armed forces are configured for action within their own territories and the air and maritime approaches to them. Insofar as Washington sees an indigenous regional defense capability to be Australia–New Zealand's major role in Asian security as well as continued U.S. access to their bases, the future of the alliance seems secure; however, there are clouds on the horizon.

U.S. Facilities in Australia

By the 1980s, U.S. facilities on Australian soil were well established, with purposes that could be classified under three or four broad categories. The first was direct support available to U.S. air and naval operations at Cockburn Sound and Darwin. These arrangements were directly beneficial to Australia by improving the latter's ability to maintain the air and SLOCs vital for Australian international commerce. A second group consists of communications systems that support U.S. air and naval operations. The most significant facility for this task is the North West Cape Communication Station, which, among other tasks, communicates with submerged submarines in the Indian and Pacific oceans through very low frequency transmitters. Additionally, high frequency communications go to Clark Field and Subic Bay, as well as Guam. The North West Cape station also serves British and Australian naval traffic, thus carrying Australian defense communications with its allies. A third group of facilities gathers intelligence information through electronic, photographic, and seismological monitoring. The Tennant Creek and Alice Springs facilities, for example, have monitored Chinese and Soviet nuclear tests for over twenty years. The facilities that have proved the most controversial are the electronic and satellite support stations at Pine Gap and Nurrungar. They appear to have four main tasks: intelligence gathering by satellite photography and infrared sensing, the latter particularly important for early warning of missile launches; the interception of communications, including radar emissions; analyzing and dispatching this information to the United States; and assisting scientific activities through the U.S. National Aeronautics and Space Administration (NASA). It is in the area of surveillance and electronic intelligence where Australian facilities are of greatest importance. Early warning to the United States of Soviet nuclear launch activities depends on the Australian facility because of global geography and the characteristics of the earth's magnetic field.[35]

One of the strongest arguments for Australian acceptance of the risk attendant upon the monitoring and command-and-control stations at Pine Gap and Nurrungar is their important surveillance role in determining Soviet compliance with SALT (Strategic Arms Limitation Treaty) II and any future nuclear arms control agreements between the superpowers. Opponents of these facilities warn that in the event of a superpower showdown, the Pine Gap and Nurrungar stations would be high-priority Soviet targets because of the early warning time they would provide the United States in the event of a Soviet ballistic missile launch. According to Desmond Ball, one of Australia's leading strategic thinkers, the U.S. satellite surveillance system makes a critical contribution to Washington's global second-strike capability because it determines which Soviet missile silos would be used in a first strike and therefore need not be targeted.[36]

Perhaps even more politically sensitive than concern over whether the U.S. communications facilities are probable Soviet targets is whether these facilities are involved in external military activities without the knowledge or consent of the Australian government. Desmond Ball cites two such occurrences: one was the use of North West Cape transmitters in the U.S. mining of North Vietnamese harbors in 1972. The second concerned satellites controlled by Australian ground stations that were used to develop targets for U.S. bombers in Cambodia in 1973. Furthermore, during the Middle East War of October 1973, all three major Australian ground stations were placed on alert.[37] According to Ball, Australian ground stations were apparently used for relaying intelligence information about the Middle East conflict to the United States and through Washington to the Israelis, all without the knowledge and consent of Canberra.

Since these installations are used by the United States for both strategic and regional intelligence and command and control, it is necessary to keep Australia fully informed of any operational changes and policy decisions that could affect that country's security if the U.S.-Australian alliance is to remain firm. Instead the Australians are still excluded from the major communications and control sections at both Pine Gap and Nurrungar. Apparently much of the monitored material is not shared with the Australian military. Unless Australian monitors have access to these facilities, not only do they not determine which intelligence information is of use to their country but there is also no confidence that domestic Australian transmissions are not being intercepted. Ball contends that if Australia is to accept the risks attendant upon hosting U.S. communications facilities that would be a high-priority target in the event of superpower confrontations, then authorized Australian representatives should have access to these facilities and relevant information they acquire.[38] This is particularly important if Washington expects a larger Australian role in protecting the SLOCs between the Indian Ocean and South Pacific and because of Australia's security links to Southeast Asia through the FPDA. U.S. expectations of Australian burden sharing should be reciprocated through the sharing of information and participation in its acquisition from Australian territory.

Further complications have arisen from the U.S. Strategic Defense Initiative (SDI) program. Australia has refused to permit the operation of SDI electronics from its territory. Yet Nurrungar, because it is a principal ground station for the U.S. early warning system, could automatically become part of the SDI program regardless of Australian wishes.[39]

The Australian contribution to the strategic deterrent, arms control, and regional stability in partnership with the United States is significant. It is also pragmatic in that the alternative of going it alone would be more expensive yet less effective in ensuring the country's safety.

It is inevitable and proper that there should be regular consultations over the use of U.S. installations on Australian territory and the possible changes in the strategic situation that could affect Australian security. At the same time, it is probable that the United States will resist the prospect of giving Australia any kind of veto over the use of these facilities that could vitiate some of their purposes. As Harry Gelber noted, these tensions are built in to the situation, although they can be managed with goodwill on both sides.[40]

The "Kiwi Disease" and the Nuclearization of the U.S. Navy

The Reagan administration has equated the modernization of the U.S. Navy with its nuclearization as a means of propulsion and as a platform for weapons. Nuclear power plants aboard ships can perform for years before they require refueling. The deployment of SLCMs on the Seventh Fleet beginning in 1985 means that virtually any ship could become a nuclear weapons launching pad. These developments presumably render the U.S. strategic deterrent more secure by making it virtually impossible for the Soviets to conduct a successful preemptive strike; at the same time, they create new difficulties between the United States and its alliance partners. A major policy question for the United States must be whether the additional increment to the U.S. deterrent created by the new platform outweighs alliance strains with those allies that perceive themselves as potential targets if a superpower crisis occurs.

Nuclear-armed surface vessels transform a navy into much more than a force for sea-lane protection and interdiction and power projection from sea to land. Regional naval deployments become part of the central deterrent. As such, regional allies of the United States that have associated with it for the security of their own territories and surrounding areas may find themselves at risk not because of regional troubles but because they provide bases for U.S. nuclear-equipped forces. In Asia, this concern has been part of the political debate for a number of years in Japan and the Philippines. It became a major issue in the Antipodes in the mid-1980s.

The most politically controversial change in U.S. naval weapons is the Tomahawk cruise missile with a 200-kiloton warhead, more than nine times more powerful than the atomic bomb that devasted Nagasaki in 1945. The projectile has a range of 2,500 kilometers with a low trajectory, using a computerized guidance system to avoid enemy air defenses. By 1991, the United States plans to have both conventional and nuclear-tipped Tomahawks on 137 warships, cruisers, destroyers, and submarines, some of which will be in the Seventh Fleet. The Japan Self Defense Agency has welcomed the deployment of cruise missiles as a necessary deterrent to the stationing of over 130 SS-20 missiles in the Soviet Far East. China, however, has condemned the deployment of SS-20s and U.S. cruise missiles as a major escalation of the nuclear arms race in Asia.[41]

The issue of nuclear-powered ships is much less difficult. Such vessels have called at world ports for over twenty years, beginning with Polaris submarines, with no apparent safety problems or environmental damage. Both Australia and New Zealand have conducted extensive environmental monitoring when U.S. nuclear ships are in port and have detected no adverse results. Even nonaligned countries such as India have permitted U.S. nuclear vessels to make port calls.[42]

Weapons are another matter. Of the 342 major warships in the U.S. Navy, 289 have been declared capable of carrying cruise missile launch tubes.[43] Because the Lange government in New Zealand purports to ban all nuclear-capable ships from its ports, New Zealand will have excluded most of the Seventh Fleet by the early 1990s if the ban is maintained.

The New Zealand Labour government's antinuclear posture did not originate with the Lange government. Earlier, between 1972 and 1975, the Labour government had banned nuclear-powered ships from its territorial waters and ports. The ban David Lange instituted in 1984 should be seen as a continuation of and extension to weapons of the earlier Labour policy. It also reflects the strength of the left wing of the Labour party in that party's councils.

Lange's firm stand on the nuclear force issue is explained as a means of ameliorating left-wing critics in the Labour party who have balked at the prime minister's domestic economic reforms. The unpopular reforms include the privatization of many nationally owned industries and anti-inflationary measures that particularly hurt Labour party constituents.[44]

The practical effect of the ban on U.S.–New Zealand relations within ANZUS is severe. By mid-1985, the United States had cancelled all military exercises planned with New Zealand and stopped sharing intelligence data with Wellington. In May of that year, Australia and the United States decided to cancel the annual meeting of ANZUS foreign ministers.[45] Washington's most important concern is the contagion factor (the "Kiwi disease"): that other countries might adopt the New Zealand policy of insisting on statements that U.S. ships are not carrying nuclear weapons before permitting port calls. When the PRC insisted on such assurances, the United States dropped plans for a ceremonial visit of three destroyers to Shanghai in May 1985, which would have been the first such port call since 1949. Agreement was subsequently reached for a U.S. Navy port visit in November 1986, finessing the nuclear issue.

Lange's policy is not so much the result of strategic thinking but rather a moral antipathy to nuclear weapons that characterizes opinion within the Labour parties of both New Zealand and Australia. The New Zealand government feels freer to act on its scruples because it is too small to merit concern in the geopolitical balance. There is also something of the free rider in Wellington's policy. Because of New Zealand's proximity to Australia, should there be any threat by the Soviets in the vicinity, both Washington and Canberra would automatically include the smaller country under their protective umbrella. The former would have no choice since the protection of New Zealand is necessary to the security of Australia, the South Pacific, and the southern sea route to the Indian Ocean. Thus, New Zealand's obstinacy is not unlike de Gaulle's withdrawal from NATO in the early 1960s. Just as NATO geographically surrounds France, so New Zealand could not be abandoned by its ANZUS partners. This perception prevails in Wellington despite U.S. moves in 1986 to end its security commitments to New Zealand under ANZUS. Prime Minister Lange stated in response to the U.S. decision to suspend security obligations that New Zealand remained ready to play its conventional defense role in the alliance.[46]

Moreover, New Zealand does not believe the Soviets will target its territory as long as Wellington refrains from providing port facilities for nuclear vessels. To the extent that Labour has an alternative policy, it centers on support for a nuclear-free zone in the South Pacific, a status endorsed in principle by other members of the South Pacific Forum.

Prime Minister Lange in no way considers his government's policy to be anti-American. He points out to those who so accuse him that he reversed the 1984 New Zealand Labour party conference demands to withdraw from ANZUS and close the U.S. air base in the country. Lange also reaffirmed New Zealand's continuing commitment to active participation in conventional defense arrangements with the United States and the maintenance of a battalion in Singapore as part of the FPDA.[47] For New Zealand, nuclear weaponry is seen as irrelevant in the South Pacific, a remote, tranquil region outside the boundaries of great power competition. Lange insists that his policy is antinuclear, not anti-American.

Washington has also appeared to limit the damage incurred by the ANZUS rupture. The United States continues to support Australia's bilateral defense relationship with New Zealand. A spokesman for the Reagan administration, U.S. Senate Foreign Relations Committee chairman Richard Lugar, stated in Wellington that both countries performed "a very excellent service" for South Pacific security.[48]

While Australia has expanded intelligence sharing with New Zealand and has slightly increased the number of joint exercises, Canberra is the first to admit that it cannot replace the U.S. role in ANZUS. New Zealand has lost supplies no longer available from the United States and the quality of training that can occur only with a highly modernized navy such as the U.S. Seventh Fleet. Moreover, Australia is not investing heavily in the new joint exercises with New Zealand, preferring to put its resources in the more important U.S. military relationship. No longer able to use the U.S. Air Force Cope Thunder range in the Philippines or participate in the biannual RIMPAC naval maneuvers, New Zealand's forces are falling behind in combat capability.[49]

The United States had hoped that New Zealand would follow a variation of the Japanese approach to the issue of nuclear weapons on board U.S. ships in which a certain amount of ambiguity is tolerated. U.S. officials are particularly annoyed that Lange has insisted on having it both ways: an antinuclear policy and full status in ANZUS. If the United States were to make an exception for New Zealand, a precedent would be set that could lead to reduced access to ports in Europe, Japan, and elsewhere. Therefore, the U.S. decision to abrogate its ANZUS obligations to New Zealand and the cancellation of joint exercises in 1985 signaled not only to New Zealand but to other U.S. allies as well that the disruption of alliance arrangements cannot be cost free.[50] New Zealand's military chiefs have publicly voiced their concerns about the effects of the termination of defense cooperation with the United States. They claimed that New Zealand's operational standards have been lowered and that the loss of U.S. intelligence has left them with an incomplete picture of ship movements in the South Pacific.[51]

Lange has countered U.S. arguments by noting that curtailing defense cooperation with New Zealand harms U.S. interests only in the long run. New Zealand's ability to assist the island states of the South Pacific in monitoring those waters will be diminished if U.S. assistance through ANZUS does not resume. Moreover, Lange has stated that, unlike NATO, which plays a central role in the nuclear deterrent strategy of the United States, ANZUS is a regional defense pact, not a component of a global strategy:

> What we have done in New Zealand is to state unequivocally that New Zealanders want no part of nuclear weapons. . . . We do not ask, we do not

expect the United States to come to New Zealand's assistance with nuclear weapons or to present American nuclear capability as a deterrent to an attacker.[52]

Here lies the crux of the dispute: U.S. officials insist that their country's regional alliances are more than separate, local defense pacts: "Collectively, these alliances deter aggression and prevent an outbreak of global conflict by creating mutually reinforcing links between the respective national interests and security capabilities of the Western states."[53] Assistant Secretary of State Paul Wolfowitz singled out Australia as an example of a Pacific alliance partner that accepts the heightened risk of the U.S. relationship because it believes that risk to be outweighed by increased deterrence. Nuclear arms control agreements can be verified from Australian monitoring sites.[54]

The United States has only one navy, not separate conventional and nuclear groups. Because that navy has both regional and global roles, all U.S. allies are at least indirectly associated with Washington's global deterrent, as well as the regional protection provided by the presence of these vessels in their vicinity. In reality, Prime Minister Lange's objection to U.S. nuclear ship visits making New Zealand a Soviet target is not persuasive. Given much higher-priority targets in other parts of the world and the infrequency of U.S. ship visits, it is improbable that New Zealand ranks very high in Soviet targeting priorities. Moreover, in the contingency of a possible nuclear war following international tension, U.S. warships would be at sea on alert rather than remain in port.[55]

Worst of all, acceptance of New Zealand's restrictions would undermine Washington's primary defense policy for Asia: burden sharing. Wellington's constraints would have a chilling effect on mutual defense for they would exclude primarily the vessels on which Asian states depend for maintaining the SLOCs against an ever-growing Soviet navy in Southeast Asia and the Indian Ocean.

Curiously, there has been at least one unexpected benefit for South Pacific defense in New Zealand's position. Because the Lange government lost U.S. assistance in 1985—at least for the time being—it has had to beef up its own defense budget to pick up the slack. Thus, New Zealand plans to acquire more Orions for sea surveillance. In 1985 alone, its defense spending on procurement went up by $19 million. Another $75 million is planned over the next few years.[56] Greater New Zealand capability, for whatever reason, can only improve the overall ANZUS situation.

Australia and Southeast Asia

Southeast Asia is Australia's near north. Its strategic importance is embodied in Canberra's membership in the FPDA and Manila Pact, which links it to four of ASEAN's six members. Thus Australian forces could be asked to help defend the integrity of Thailand, the Philippines, Malaysia, and/or Singapore in the event of external attack. Although there are no direct legal or political linkages between ANZUS and the FPDA, any potential aggressor in Southeast Asia must take into account that an attack involving Australian forces could activate ANZUS, bringing the United States into the fray.

The FPDA umbrella is best seen as part of a post-Vietnam network of security arrangements in which U.S. forces, through a variety of bilateral and multilateral linkages, cooperate with several national military establishments throughout the Asian-Pacific region. The FPDA provides a framework, too, in which two nonaligned countries, Malaysia and Singapore, can cooperate militarily with Western states without jeopardizing their political status in relation to the superpowers. ANZUS, the Manila Pact, and the FPDA provide a diplomatic justification for the U.S. military presence in Southeast Asia, the Indian Ocean, and the Southwest Pacific without compromising the political status of Malaysia, Singapore, and Indonesia.

In the 1980s, the FPDA has become a more active military arrangement in response to the Vietnamese invasion of Cambodia and the inexorable Soviet naval and air buildup at Cam Ranh Bay. Multinational air and naval exercises involving all five partners were revived for the first time since 1970. These included exercises in the South China Sea designed to maintain control over the Strait of Malacca. Integrated air defense system exercises have been enlarged and held annually. In 1980, the Australian and Malaysian governments also agreed to the regular deployment of Australian P3 maritime patrols from Butterworth both eastward to the South China Sea and westward to the Indian Ocean. These planes sometimes have Malaysian copilots.[57] The long-term goal may well be for Malaysia to take over responsibility for these patrols. But for now, the ASEAN states rely on Australia and the United States for long-range surveillance.

Because of Malaysia's own budget difficulties in the mid-1980s, it has welcomed Australia's decision to rotate a detachment of its newly acquired F-18s through Butterworth when it phases out the last of the Mirages from the air base in 1988. Thailand and Singapore have also lobbied for the maintenance of Australian air forces at Butterworth.[58]

Southeast Asia's importance to Australia is also reflected in the major beneficiaries of its Defense Cooperation Program. Papua New Guinea and Indonesia are the largest recipients, Jakarta receiving A$10 million in 1982–1983. Most of this program goes for Australian equipment. Current projects include the supply of two Attack-class patrol boats, the conversion of Indonesian Sioux helicopters to gas-turbine engines, and the provision of Australian army technicians to support eighteen Australian Nomad maritime surveillance patrol aircraft.[59]

Australia's attitude toward Indonesia is ambivalent. On the one hand, Canberra worries about possible Indonesian designs on Papua New Guinea,

Jakarta's apparent willingness to use force, and its long-term goal of removing Western military influence from Southeast Asia. On the other hand, Indonesia's importance as ASEAN's putative leader, its focus on internal security concerns, and its expressed desire to keep Australia and the United States involved in regional security arrangements for the foreseeable future make Jakarta an important political partner. With regional security guaranteed by the U.S. (and, to a smaller extent, Australian) presence, Indonesia need not place priority on the development of a force projection capability. This, in turn, helps to reassure Canberra of Indonesia's essentially defensive posture.[60]

Until 1987, New Zealand too maintained a strong Southeast Asian orientation. Of its two active army battalions, one was deployed in Singapore and the other constituted as a ready reaction force, capable of being deployed anywhere it is needed. New Zealand forces engage in close coordination with their Australian counterparts. Common equipment acquisition procedures are being planned through the 1982 Closer Economic Relations Agreement (CER), which has laid the foundation for a common market between the two countries. As long as Australia maintains a Southeast Asian military presence, New Zealand can augment it. Indicative of this were the largest ever FPDA naval exercises held off Singapore in August 1986 in which two New Zealand frigates and a P3 ASW plane participated.[61] In addition to deploying their own forces to Malaysia and Singapore, Australia and New Zealand provide training facilities for some ASEAN members as well. Singapore has sent detachments of A-4 Skyhawks, F-5Es, and Hunters to Australian bases for four to five months at a time for training and joint exercises. Elements of the Singapore army have maneuvered in the Queensland Shoalwater Bay training area.[62]

In December 1986, however, New Zealand decided to reduce its Southeast Asian deployments in a defense review that identified the Southwest Pacific islands as Wellington's priority security zone. By 1989, New Zealand will withdraw its small force of 700 from Singapore. Nevertheless, Lange has stressed that the troop withdrawal will not diminish New Zealand's commitment to the FPDA, which will continue to take the form of training and joint exercises.[63] The rationale for reduced concern about Southeast Asia in both Australia and New Zealand centers on the belief that the ASEAN states have developed sufficient military capacities to provide for their own security so long as FPDA commitments remain in force. The Southwest Pacific, by contrast, is seen as more vulnerable and therefore more in need of military aid from its larger, more developed neighbors.[64]

Officials and analysts in all of the ASEAN countries I visited in the spring of 1984 (Brunei excepted) viewed an increased Australian air and maritime presence in Southeast Asia as at least acceptable and, in several instances, preferable to any portended Japanese naval role in the region. Australia's intentions were seen as benign and its cooperation in the Integrated Air Defense System (IADS) with Singapore and Malaysia evidence of a positive role in regional security. At the same time, my interviews demonstrated that little thought had been given to an Australian role in regional security beyond its limited air force deployments. For example, joint patrols with the U.S. Seventh Fleet had not been discussed, nor, for that matter, had Australian participation in ASEAN navy missions been considered. Malaysian officials, in particular, expressed an interest in the possibility of Australian ships in the South China Sea but were skeptical about Canberra's willingness to provide them. They believed that, to the contrary, Australia was reversing its forward defense policy, and, insofar, as it still maintained regional military interests, these were oriented more toward the Indian Ocean than Southeast Asia.[65]

Because Australia's P3 Orion patrols are the only long-range surveillance capacity whose results are regularly available to ASEAN members, it is probable that demands for more of these patrols will increase as Soviet naval activity grows around the Malaysian and Indonesian straits.[66] The F-18s and Australia's inventory of F-111 medium bombers provide a fairly formidable maritime strike force, however, if they are stationed at Butterworth. This is particularly true since the Soviet Pacific fleet has no air cover at sea.[67] Noteworthy too is that F-18s at Tindal in northern Australia could also reach Southeast Asia.

The only ASEAN member that might not welcome a larger Australian regional presence is Indonesia, not because of any anti-Australian feeling particularly but because of a more fundamental objection to the presence of external forces in Southeast Asia. Insofar as external military strength is necessary for ASEAN security, no new forces should be invited; rather reliance on U.S. ships and planes from Clark and Subic should be sufficient. From Jakarta's point of view, the long-term goal of ZOPFAN would be easier to implement if only one or two external militaries are involved rather than several.

The ASEAN states are concerned, however, about the strains within ANZUS caused by the New Zealand Labour government's refusal to permit U.S. nuclear-armed ship visits. Because the Seventh Fleet is such an important component of regional maritime defense, any policy that would diminish its capability to deploy is viewed with alarm. Both Singapore and the Philippines have openly expressed dismay at the ANZUS disagreements, noting that they could undermine security arrangements elsewhere in the region. If the ANZUS treaty is reviewed and altered, it is feared, Wellington's and Canberra's resolve under the FPDA could also be affected. Even Indonesia, normally sympathetic to manifestations of small state independence, has privately voiced concern over the removal of the ANZUS umbrella that covers the region to its south, permitting Jakarta to focus its defense attentions on the north and east.[68]

The ANZUS row is not the only issue affecting Antipodean-ASEAN relations. There is some friction, too, over the manner in which the Australian Labour government has tried to serve as interlocutor over the Cambodian conflict. This problem began in 1983 when Canberra refused to continue to cosponsor the ASEAN resolution in the United Nations endorsing the anti-Vietnam Coalition Government of Democratic Kampuchea (CGDK) government. Thailand and Singapore took particular objection to any weakening of the strong international-united front ASEAN had created behind Thailand on the issue. Although the Hawke government explained that its intentions were merely to provide good offices for ASEAN-Vietnam negotiations, the association resented Canberra's presumptions. Hard-line members, such as Singapore and Thailand, disagreed with Australia's view of Vietnam as a potential regional security collaborator, and Indonesia, which had no quarrel with Canberra's strategic view, was angry that it had tried to preempt what Jakarta viewed to be its major role as facilitator for any regional rapprochement with Vietnam.

The crisis subsided in late 1983 when Prime Minister Robert Hawke in Thailand condemned the Vietnamese occupation of Cambodia and called for the withdrawal of its forces. Nevertheless, Hawke has continued to appeal for an end to Hanoi's isolation as the only hope of reducing the further entrenchment of the USSR in the region. Hawke avoided any mention of China's entrenchment, however, through its relationship to Thailand, a fact that worries both Indonesia and Malaysia.[69] Subsequently the prime minister belittled any regional threat from China, insisting that its energies would be focused on economic modernization for several generations. For Vietnam, however, opportunities must be found to "diversify its relations and achieve a more satisfactory relationship with its neighbors."[70]

Australia's commitments to Southeast Asia elicit some ambivalence. Although the Manila Pact and the FPDA are generally favored by ASEAN states because of the Soviet presence in the area, these arrangements, which provide for external power intervention, are seen as part of the problem, as well as a temporary solution. Foreign forces and bases in Southeast Asia undoubtedly conflict with ASEAN's declared aim of creating a ZOPFAN. Moreover, their existence has been cited by Hanoi as justification for the Soviet use of Vietnamese facilities.

The Labour government believes that Australia's principal military assets, including six Oberon-class submarines, twenty-four F-111 strike-reconnaissance aircraft, twenty P3 Orion ASW-surveillance aircraft, and seventy-five F-18 interceptors (to be added by 1990) create, in effect, a fortress Australia capacity by which Canberra could defend its northern shores from its own territory. While this is not to say that Australia would choose unilaterally to withdraw from either the FPDA or the Manila Pact, should Southeast Asian politics lead to an ASEAN call for ZOPFAN in the next decade, Australia could withdraw its forward-deployed forces with relative equanimity. This situation puts Canberra at odds with Washington in Southeast Asia since the United States does not view its access to regional facilities as either temporary or local but as part of the necessary global deployments of a superpower protecting its economic and strategic interests along with those of friends and allies.

In all probability, however, this potential confrontation among Western-oriented Southeast Asian states will not occur. The dynamics of a continued Soviet military buildup in the region portend the continued acceptability of U.S. and Australian forces as a second choice for ASEAN. There is, therefore, a symbiotic relationship between the Soviet and Australia–New Zealand–U.S. presence in Southeast Asia. Western forces remain not merely acceptable but necessary in the light of additional Soviet deployments at Cam Ranh Bay. Should the Soviets genuinely desire to generate regional pressure for the withdrawal of the U.S. Seventh Fleet and Thirteenth Air Force, their best policy would be to close down their Vietnamese facilities and withdraw to Vladivostok, an unlikely scenario.

6
Cross-Regional Security Collaboration:
A Balance Sheet

E ach perspective, as Nietzsche once said, is like casting a new set of eyes on the subject. The ability to shift perspectives and to recognize and relate the different unfolding views, rather than the illusory quest for an impossible "objectivity," is the best way to understand complex social phenomena. U.S. strategic policy and its interface with its counterparts among Asian allies and adversaries is just such a complex social phenomenon. That extended containment could involve the United States in multitheater wars simultaneously was never reconciled in post–World War II U.S. strategic doctrines. Instead, contingency planning posited uncertainties about abstract "half-wars" that could break out in third world regions without attaching scenarios, probabilities, force sizes or durations to those half-wars. Indeed the decade-long commitment to the second Indochina "half-war" so skewed U.S. military budgets and logistics arrangements that Washington would have been hard-pressed to respond anywhere else in the world if a comparable crisis had developed.[1]

In retrospect, U.S. strategic doctrine has fluctuated widely between administrations from the selected response formulae of the Eisenhower and Carter years to the more global designs of Truman's National Security Council memorandum 68 and Kennedy's flexible response doctrine down to President Reagan's horizontal escalation prescription, which assumes intertheater spread in any future Soviet-U.S. confrontation.

Yet the Reagan doctrine does not seem to fit the political preference of the U.S. Congress. Although defeat in Vietnam, humiliation in Iran and, more recently, Lebanon, and the Soviet invasion of Afghanistan have produced a yearning among many Americans for a reassertion of U.S. power and preeminence, there nevertheless remains strong opposition to the commitment of U.S. power to any open-ended conflict in the third world. Americans responded positively to the invasion of Grenada—a short, swift action with a decisive outcome and relatively low financial costs and casualties—but heaved a sigh of relief when the U.S. Marines were pulled out of Beirut after hundreds were killed in a single suicide car bomb attack. Although Reagan's overall popularity remained high through his second term of office, public opinion surveys showed four out of five Americans opposing his policy of pressuring Marxist Nicaragua. The prospect of direct U.S. military involvement in the third world still holds little appeal.

Despite the president's seeming assertiveness in military affairs, he has acknowledged when asked about the lessons in Vietnam, "I think if I had to say one thing we learned it would be that never again must the government of the United States ask young men to go out and fight and die for a cause it is unwilling to win."[2] That the lesson of Vietnam has been applied to Central America is evidenced by the limit imposed on the number of U.S. military personnel, only fifty-five of whom are stationed in El Salvador to supervise counterinsurgency there. Yet in the debate between former Secretary of Defense Weinberger and Shultz over coercive diplomacy, a strategic view that requires total commitment to military victory or no participation at all violated the main Clausewitzian dictum that war must be subordinated to politics. If the military cannot be used in limited and low-level contingencies, then a whole range of coercive diplomatic actions will be surrendered by default to U.S. adversaries, and the credibility of U.S. security relationships will be severely eroded in the third world.

To avoid this all-or-nothing dilemma, the United States emphasizes burden sharing as an integral part of its Asian strategic policy and urges that the use of U.S. forces be considered only as a last resort to counter an overwhelming external attack against friendly states. The presence of U.S. forces in Asia is meant as a deterrent to external aggression. They are not deployed to intervene at the first sign of trouble, with the exception of the Korean peninsula where U.S. casualties would occur immediately if war broke out.

An examination of U.S. military budgets between 1981 and 1985 reinforces this view. While the number of personnel has increased only by 317,000 since 1980 to 3.2 million, with the biggest increase in the National Guard and reserves, the budget grew annually at an average rate of 9 percent. The bulk of that budget has gone for weapons procurement, research, and military construction, which in 1985 consumed 47 percent of the military budget. Given the importance of the navy for U.S. strategy in the Pacific, it is hardly surprising that the navy has been the most favored service during the Reagan years, with Congress granting its request in 1982 for $7 billion to build two new aircraft carriers. Even these substantial appropriations may not be sufficient, however, to complete a 600-ship navy by the 1990s. A 1985 Congressional Budget Office study estimated that navy budgets must grow 5 percent faster than the rate of inflation through the mid-1990s if the 600-ship target is to be reached. Yet substantial additions have been made to U.S. naval and air forces between 1981 and 1985. The Seventh Fleet added fifteen Perry-class frigates, eight Spruance-class destroyers, and six Los Angeles-class submarines. The refitted U.S. *Missouri* joined the Seventh Fleet in 1986. The air force has acquired 112 F/A 18s and two new squadrons of F-16s.[3]

Former Secretary of Defense Weinberger enunciated "six pillars" of U.S. security policy in East Asia, designed to reassure friendly states and provide guidelines for U.S. priorities:

1. U.S. determination to remain a Pacific power.

2. The U.S. security relationship with Japan.

3. The U.S. commitment to stability on the Korean peninsula.

4. U.S. efforts to build an enduring relationship with China.

5. U.S. support for the political and economic viability of ASEAN and the defense efforts of its members.

6. The ANZUS alliance.[4]

All appear compatible with the possible exception of the potential strategic cooperation of the United States with China. From Washington's perspective, a tacit strategic relationship already exists between the two countries. China restrains North Korea, aids the Cambodian guerrillas against Vietnam, has stopped supporting insurgents in Southeast Asia against ASEAN governments, and ties down one-third of the Soviet armed forces along its northern and western borders. Nevertheless, U.S. assistance for the PRC's economic and military modernization is a potential source of friction in U.S. relations with other Asian states.

Although South Korea, Japan, Thailand, Singapore, Australia, and New Zealand welcome closer Sino-U.S. cooperation and see China as a useful addition to a regional anti-Soviet coalition, this view is not held by Indonesia or Malaysia. Kuala Lumpur and Jakarta are apprehensive of the U.S. propensity to incorporate every regional security issue into the competitive context of the central balance with the Soviet Union. To engage China as a strategic partner in this quest unnecessarily provokes the Soviet Union and gives undue rein to China's own regional ambitions. China's role as guarantor to Thailand is particularly disturbing in this context, for it has introduced the Sino-Soviet conflict directly into ASEAN security matters via Vietnam.[5]

Ironically, the reduction of Sino-Soviet tension may be equally worrisome to Asia. Even if it does not lead to a rapprochement between Asia's two largest military establishments, it could permit Beijing to redirect its power from a Siberian–Central Asian orientation outward toward Northeast, Southeast, and South Asia. Thus, the United States could be caught in a competitive arms race, assisting both China and its neighbors, possibly against each other. A better way out of this dilemma would be to help allay mutual suspicions through diplomacy.

U.S. Strategy and Burden Sharing

U.S. defense strategy in the Pacific depends on maintaining the security of key air and naval routes and blocking Soviet forces in eastern Siberia from moving south to attack U.S. bases and forces traversing sea and air routes to Korea and Japan through the Southwest Pacific, Southeast Asia, and the Indian Ocean. The United States hopes to accomplish these objectives through its own air and naval assets, particularly those stationed in Korea and Japan, and with the cooperation of its allies. Because the U.S. Pacific Command has operational responsibility for the Indian Ocean and Persian Gulf and has committed two carrier task groups to that theater, the cooperation of allies has become increasingly important in the East Asian balance.

In Northeast Asia, air and naval defense cooperation among the United States, Japan, and South Korea would complicate Soviet air attack plans and the Pacific fleet's ability to move from the Sea of Japan to the Pacific. Soviet Backfires would have to fly down the Sea of Japan through the Tsushima Strait to attack U.S. bases in Okinawa and the Philippines as well as naval forces in between. Larry Niksch of the Congressional Research Service has postulated:

> Currently, U.S. F-15 fighters on Okinawa comprise a single echelon of defense covering these routes. The South Korean air force could establish a forward defense line from facilities in the southern part of South Korea or, better yet, from Cheju Do off Korea's southern coast. An air defense screen based on Cheju Do would cover both routes, including an arc from the Korea Strait westward and then southwest to the approaches to Taiwan. Air bases on Cheju Do would allow South Korean interceptor aircraft the maximum operation range for both routes and place ROK aircraft outside the range of most North Korean and Soviet fighters.
>
> . . . The F-16 fighter, which Seoul currently is acquiring, could do the job. It has the speed and weaponry to intercept and shoot down the *Backfire*. It has a combat radius of about 500 miles and therefore could cover most of the distance to Taiwan.
>
> Early warning aircraft would constitute an essential component of a South Korean air defense screen. U.S.-operated AWACs from Okinawa and/or ROK-operated E-2Cs from Cheju Do, for example, could cover the approaches from the Sea of Japan, the Yellow Sea, and the East China Sea.
>
> . . . South Korea and Japanese air defenses would block three potential routes of Soviet bombers: across Japan, down the Sea of Japan, and over the Yellow Sea and East China Sea. U.S. interceptors on Okinawa or at Clark Air Base in the Philippines would provide a second and possibly a third echelon. The defense system of U.S. aircraft carriers would add to this. Japan could contribute to a second echelon by stationing interceptor fighters on Iwo Jima, thus blocking the route toward Guam and the Marianas.[6]

While an expanded South Korean defense role would probably improve the ROK's image in the United States and create a greater sense of mutuality in the defense treaty, the notion of trilateral cooperation with Japan is more problematic. From a purely military standpoint, considerable benefit would be derived from joint mining operations in the Tsushima Strait. Japanese air defense from Kyushu could be coordinated with similar efforts from South Korea's Cheju Do. Such cooperation, however, would be politically difficult in both countries. Japanese policy limits its military cooperation exclusively to the United States. Moreover, Japanese general antipathy toward South Korea would guarantee strong opposition to any proposed defense collaboration. Further, an expanded South Korean role in western Pacific defense would be a source of Korean leverage on Japan to be more generous in its economic aid. From the other side of the relationship, the prospect of joint defense efforts would conjure up the prospect of a future Japanese military role on the Korean peninsula—anathema to both Koreas as well as China.

There is even some question over how much burden sharing the United States really needs in the Pacific with Washington's emphasis on freedom of maritime movement. The capability of the U.S. Navy with its massive lead in carrier forces and heavy combatants such as destroyers and cruisers far exceeds that of the Soviet Pacific fleet (table 6–1). The United States has considerable air and amphibious assault capacity; the USSR has virtually none. The Soviets do have a large numerical edge in attack submarines, but the older models that

Table 6–1
Superpower Force Levels in the Asia-Pacific Region, 1985

	U.S. Pacific Forces	Soviet Far East Forces
Aircraft carriers		
Attack	7	0
Helicopter	6	3
Cruisers	17	13
Destroyers	31	20
Frigates	45	55
Submarines		
Strategic	3	31
Attack	40	91
Replenishment and support	40	85
Navy/marine forces	259,000	134,000
Long-range bombers	12	355
Tactical aircraft	990	1820
Army	47,000	450,000

Source: Based on figures from CINCPAC and U.S. Defense Intelligence Agency as reported in *Armed Forces Journal International* (April 1984): 384. See also Charles Waterman, "Soviets Scale Back Expansionist Tendencies," *Christian Science Monitor*, September 10, 1986.

dominate the fleet are much louder and therefore more easily detected than their U.S. counterparts. Moreover, the Soviet submarines have limited access to the open seas from their bases.

The Reagan administration's emphasis on complex, expensive nuclear air-craft carrier battle groups has been criticized. A number of naval strategists believe a more realistic configuration for SLOC control would consist of larger numbers of smaller, less expensive ships and improved ASW capacity.[7] Never-theless, the U.S. posture provides a force projection capability over an extended maritime environment from the western Pacific to the Indian Ocean and beyond. Friendly regional navies can facilitate the U.S. surveillance role through the shar-ing of information acquired on their own patrols, but they cannot replace the United States as guarantor of open sea-lanes across this vast region. Washington's encouragement of air and naval buildups in the ASEAN states should be inter-preted within the strategic framework of providing local permanent supplements to intermittent U.S. patrols across subregions. That is, regular surveillance of local air and sea-lanes by ASEAN armed services, if coordinated with the movements of larger U.S. vessels, can provide intelligence on naval and air activity throughout East Asia.

If the ASEAN partners see the growth of Soviet sea power and airpower in Southeast Asia in collaboration with Vietnam as a threat to their security, they may well increase both their own informal defense cooperation and assist U.S. Seventh Fleet patrols from Subic. If Soviet military forces in Vietnam con-tinue to increase in number and variety in the last half of the 1980s as they have in the first half, then Manila's ASEAN partners will strongly lobby the Philippine government to permit U.S. forces to remain at Clark and Subic Bay. The alternative, deemed highly desirable by the USSR, would be a decision by a left-leaning nationalist regime in Manila to ask U.S. forces to leave the Philippines. This, in turn, could lead to a Finlandization of ASEAN and the subsequent regional dominance of the Soviets and their Vietnamese ally.

To forestall such a development, the United States must support the reform-ist Aquino government in the Philippines. Aquino faces the enormous political task of bringing both the center and left wings of the polity into her govern-ment. Washington should respond with a large program of loan credits, trade concessions, development aid, and outright grants to help rebuild the Philip-pine economy. Even if a massive aid program of this scope could be passed by the U.S. Congress, however (an unlikely prospect in the Gramm-Rudman era), it might still flounder on the shoals of Philippine nationalism, which would view large-scale U.S. economic intervention as neocolonialism. The task for U.S. diplomacy is delicate indeed: to encourage a coalition of reformist democrats and its economic efforts without at the same time creating the im-pression that it is merely a lackey of the United States.

A new Philippine government must be able to justify the retention of U.S. bases on the grounds of its own security needs. ASEAN support for the regional deployment of U.S. forces is an important component of this justification, and the multilateralization of the bases could be another way of legitimating their continued operation. Indeed the expanded use of Philippine base facilities by ASEAN militaries might actually increase their overall contribution to regional air and naval surveillance. Politically, the bases must be seen as helping to meet the security needs of the region's members and not simply as part of the accoutrements of a superpower's global strategy. Thus, the Philippine bases could accelerate greater security cooperation among the ASEAN states as their militaries trained together using, for example, the sophisticated facilities for air warfare simulation.

Just as ASEAN's cooperation is necessary for the maintenance of a loosely spread Asia-Pacific security net, so is Australia's. The U.S. forward deployment network stretches from Japan through Southeast Asia into the Indian Ocean's Diego Garcia islet, which has become almost a $1 billion air and naval facility, and onto East Africa where the United States has access to bases in Kenya, Somalia, and Oman. Because Diego Garcia is the only permanent U.S. base between the Philippines and the Persian Gulf, access for U.S. Navy ships to Sydney, Melbourne, Brisbane, and Perth is crucial for the maintenance of a two ocean posture. The certainty of this access becomes even more important in the light of the uncertain political future of the Philippine bases. Since the Labour government in Canberra has decided against a forward deployment strategy for its own forces, Australia becomes that much more dependent on the Seventh Fleet to maintain SLOCs. Thus, its contribution to regional security can be effective only by operating in tandem with the United States.

The Soviet Position

The only significant imminent external threat to Asian security is seen by Washington and most of its Asian allies to be the Soviet Pacific fleet and Moscow's subregional ally, Vietnam. Yet from the Soviet perspective, its military forces are limited in scope and range, geographically vulnerable at key choke points, and surrounded by hostile states. Soviet merchant ships traveling the Indian Ocean–western Pacific route run a gauntlet among a succession of unfriendly states through waters controlled primarily by the USSR's major adversary.

Strikes from the Pacific and U.S. bases in Japan would pose serious threats to concentrations of Soviet forces in eastern Siberia and to the large economic investments made in this region since the mid-1970s. Nevertheless, it is improbable that China, Japan, or the United States would ever initiate a war against the Soviet Union in East Asia. Territorial disputes in the region are long term, characterized by a low level of conflict, and susceptible to diplomatic resolution or prolonged stalemate. If war were to come to this region, it would more likely occur as a counteraction against attack in other parts of the world. (Recall

Secretary of the Navy John Lehman's view of horizontal escalation discussed in chapter 1.) The Soviet view of U.S. strategy was summed up succinctly in a *Pravda* article reviewing Washington's Asia policy:

> According to the designs of Washington's ruling circles, east Asia and the Pacific and Indian Oceans which wash its shores must become a line for the deployment of forward-based nuclear systems, just as West Europe and the adjacent Atlantic area. What they have in mind is to bring first-strike weapons as close as possible to the Soviet borders along their entire length, and at the same time to use the allies in the West and in the East as lightning conductors to attract retribution to themselves.
>
> American strategists, having declared the goal of U.S. military policy in the region to be confrontation with the Soviet Union "from the Persian Gulf to the Aleutians," are backing up this plan with a new military-political structure. They want to "natoize" Japan, that is, entrust it with the same military commitments as the West European NATO members have; to form Washington's bilateral agreements with Tokyo and Seoul into a triangle; to involve their ANZUS bloc partners—Australia and New Zealand—more closely in the Pentagon's plans, and in particular in the militarization of the Indian Ocean; and lastly, to pave the way for the creation of a "Pacific community" in which they plan to involve—in addition to the United States, Japan, Canada, Australia, New Zealand, and South Korea—the members of ASEAN.[8]

While Soviet military assets are impressive in the geographical zone consisting of the Sea of Japan, Sea of Okhotsk, and several hundred miles off Petropavlovsk, they become rapidly degraded as one moves south and west away from land-based aircraft. Soviet air and naval forces remain concentrated in northeast Asia. Those deployed in the South China Sea have minimal combat capabilities against the U.S. forces stationed at Clark and Subic, although if the Soviets added Backfire bombers to the MiG-23 interceptors at Cam Ranh Bay, they could develop a significant offensive thrust in time. Nevertheless, the Soviets lack the forces to carry out a sustained interdiction of SLOCs unless they alter their strategy to deploy most of their attack submarines away from Northeast Asia. Within 300 to 500 miles of their home bases on the northern Sea of Japan and Sea of Okhotsk, however, the Soviets have built a capacity to conduct air, surface, and submarine operations that conceivably could overwhelm Japan and South Korea. (In 1985, the Soviets had deployed some 80 Backfires with a range of 4,000 kilometers and 120 SS-20 IRBMs east of Lake Baikal, as well as 24 SSBNs in the Sea of Okhotsk.)[9]

On closer examination, however, the concern of U.S. Pacific military commanders seems less with present Soviet military capabilities than with the steady pace of the USSR's Asian military expansion. This trend is particularly unnerving because of the belief held in the United States that Asian security has depended on the undisputed superiority of U.S. arms since the end of World

War II. From this perspective, the Soviet "threat" lies not so much in the ability of its Pacific fleet to challenge the United States in combat but rather in the fact that the Soviets have deployed a force large enough to deprive the United States of its long-accustomed naval dominance throughout the Pacific.

The Soviets are not in an enviable political position, however. By choosing to ally with Vietnam for strategic reasons, they have separated themselves from one of the region's most important groups, ASEAN. Moreover, even the long-term relationship with Vietnam may be problematic. The Vietnamese must come to terms with China. When they do, much of the rationale for dependence on the Soviets will disappear.

These considerations lie behind Gorbachev's 1986 and 1987 Asian initiatives, first at Vladivostok and one year later in an interview with the Indonesian newspaper *Merdeka*. Concerned about the combined ability of U.S. nuclear naval forces operating with Japan's cooperation around the choke points in the Sea of Japan, the general secretary hopes to effect a U.S. withdrawal from these waters in exchange for a freeze on current levels of nuclear-capable aircraft in the Asian part of the Soviet Union. Gorbachev has also raised the prospect of negotiating limits on antisubmarine activity in the northern Pacific, thus removing forward deployed U.S. ships from the Soviet bastion.

Japan's Position in Asian Security Cooperation

Japan's evolution toward a postindustrial services-oriented society could affect its security policy in unusual ways. On the one hand, because it will become less dependent on raw materials for manufacturing and will ship fewer actual products abroad from the home islands, the need for sea-lane defense could diminish beginning in the 1990s. (Japan already derives 60 percent of its balance of payments surplus from services. By the turn of the century, that figure may be around 90 percent.) This is not to say that Japanese capital will no longer be involved in major manufacturing and fabrication but rather that these activities will be undertaken in third world countries where factor costs are more favorable. On the other hand, because Japan will be on the cutting edge of communication technology and information processing, the dependence of the United States on Japanese research in defense-related areas will probably increase. The security relationship between Washington and Tokyo will become more symmetrical, then, in the 1990s.

There are other reasons for Japan to raise its military profile in Northeast Asia. If the United States perceives Japan to be uninterested in sharing SLOC surveillance and control responsibilities in the Northwest Pacific at the same time the Japanese bilateral trade surplus protected by U.S. forces keeps growing, there could well be a U.S. reaction in the 1990s to retreat to the mid-Pacific and reduce defense burdens so that its economy becomes more competitive.

To avoid this outcome, Japan must sustain the gradually developing defense contribution it began to the United States in the 1980s. This development will grow only by degrees since political leaders must reconcile the requirements for the maintenance of open sea-lanes with the generally antimilitary outlook of the Japanese population.

The Nakasone government established some useful precedents for burden sharing by interpreting Article VI of the Japan-U.S. Mutual Security Treaty on the purpose of U.S. forces in Japan to mean that Japan's security is tied to U.S. responses to threats from a variety of locations in the Pacific–Indian Ocean region. Japan's survival may be threatened not only by Soviet actions in Northeast Asia but also by the possible closure of oil routes through Southeast Asia or the Persian Gulf. In September 1984, a small detachment of U.S. Special Forces was permitted to be stationed in Okinawa. The detachment could deploy from Japanese territory in response to a potential crisis in the Middle East.[10] In effect, the Nakasone government recognized by this gesture that U.S. forces in the western Indian Ocean were protecting Japan's trade routes. Along these same lines, joint Japan-U.S. studies have been conducted since 1982 on the availability of Japanese seaports for U.S. ships in the event of war outside the home islands.[11]

The idea of Japanese burden sharing with the United States is increasingly acceptable to other Asian states, particularly if confined to the Northwest Pacific. But what about the possibility of a broader security role that would encompass the three subregions of this study? Soviet commentators have alleged for some time that the ANZUS countries and Japan are in the process of creating a "JANZUS" treaty, which would be the first step toward a Pacific pact incorporating ASEAN as well. These Soviet allegations reflect a concern that the USSR is being outflanked in the Pacific by the superior economic power of the West and Asian newly industrializing countries and that Washington's next step will be to form these same states into an anti-Soviet entente. U.S. Congressman Paul Findley proposed a variant of this idea on October 31, 1979, before the House Foreign Affairs Committee when he urged the creation of a Pacific patrol fleet consisting of vessels from the United States, Japan, Australia, New Zealand, and the five ASEAN states designed to secure the trade routes in the Indian and Pacific oceans.

Legally Japan is probably unable to engage in such joint military action because it would constitute a type of collective self-defense, prohibited under Article IX of the country's constitution.[12] Nevertheless, if the Asian-Pacific states were to divide up the western Pacific, China and the Philippine Seas, and the eastern Indian Ocean into subregions for surveillance by the adjacent littoral states with a strong U.S. role as coordinator, Japan could probably participate in such an informal arrangement. This kind of cooperation would be least threatening to those in the Philippines and Indonesia who fear that unrestrained Japanese armament would be the first step toward its political and military domination of Southeast Asia.[13]

ASEAN apprehensions about Japanese military plans should be further eased by an examination of the weapons being acquired by Tokyo in its current defense buildup. Destroyers, frigates, submarines, P3C maritime patrol aircraft, E-2C air warning aircraft, and surface-to-surface, surface-to-air, and air-to-air missiles do not constitute a force projection capability. These systems are designed for defense of the air and maritime space around the home islands. With no significant sea and airlift capability, Japan poses no direct military threat to its neighbors.

Australia too should be reassured by the subregional focus of Japan's military buildup. While the Labour government has expressed concern about a Japanese military role in Southeast Asia and Oceania, it has voiced support for the Japan-U.S. security relationship, and Australian forces participate alongside the MSDF annually in the RIMPAC exercises in the North Pacific. At the same time, Foreign Minister Bill Hayden has emphasized that Japan's most effective contribution to Asian security lies in its economic assistance to those countries striving for growth.[14]

A Japanese navy and air force confined to the Northwest Pacific, patroling a radius of 1,000 miles from Honshu to the Bashi Channel, poses no threat to the rest of Asia, does not complicate ASEAN's long-term hopes for the creation of ZOPFAN, but still assists the Seventh Fleet in its surveillance of Soviet movements between Vladivostok and Cam Ranh Bay. The thousand-mile sea-lane patrol goal fits well into an informal Asia-wide strategy of information sharing. It is also essentially nonprovocative to both friend and adversary.

Added to this should be a continuation of Japan's comprehensive approach to security, whereby Tokyo identifies countries to aid because of their strategic location or because they border on areas of conflict. Since 1980, Japan has targeted Egypt, Turkey, Pakistan, Sudan, Thailand, Kenya, and Jamaica for special aid programs to increase their economic prospects and, in some cases, improve their strategic setting. Japanese financial assistance to Egypt to widen the Suez Canal, for example, has made it possible for U.S. aircraft carriers from the Sixth Fleet to move from the Mediterranean to the Red Sea and Indian Ocean.[15]

ASEAN, U.S. Goals, and Cross-Regional Collaboration

In many ways, the decade after the end of the second Indochina War has witnessed the development of considerable stability in East Asia. The United States has always called for a region of many actors and the dominance of none. That situation has been achieved. The powerful forces of Asian nationalism are perhaps the best assurance to Washington that no new hegemony will be permitted to emerge unopposed. The emotional appeal of ASEAN's ZOPFAN ideal actually helps guarantee that the intrusive Soviet enclave in Vietnam will at most remain confined to Indochina.

By supporting subregional autonomy, the United States can take advantage of local nationalism for its own broader strategic purposes; however, this requires a policy sensitive to Asian concerns about future threats. Thus, the United States would be unwise to encourage Japan to develop the military capability to move beyond the thousand-mile sea-lane surveillance promised by Prime Ministers Suzuki and Nakasone. Washington must also be cautious about arms sales to China. Systems such as antitank missiles useful only in a defensive mode against a Soviet ground attack present no problem; however, any effort to develop China's longer-range conventional military capability, particularly its air force and navy, will raise doubts in Southeast Asia about both the wisdom and priorities of U.S. policy.

A number of ASEAN intellectuals believe that the greatest threat to Southeast Asia is neither Vietnam nor the Soviet Union but the symbiotic relationship created by all great power efforts to block one another. According to Kraisak Choonharan, an adviser to Thai Prime Minister Prem Tunsulanond, the Soviet position in Southeast Asia is limited and vulnerable. Resolution of the Cambodian conflict and rapprochement (or at least détente) between China and Vietnam would result in a drastic reduction in the Soviet position in Indochina. This, in turn, could lead to a reduction in the U.S. military presence, as well as bring ZOPFAN as the region's preferred security posture closer to realization.[16] Kraisak's position is not consensual. At least as many analysts fear the prospect of a Sino-Vietnam rapprochement and are concerned that a reunified Asian communist coalition would create a much more threatening environment for the region than the current Cambodian stalemate.

Nevertheless, open alliance with the United States is not seen as an attractive option by the ASEAN states. Nationalist governments view a formal link to any great power as an infringement on their independence and an invitation to the great power's adversary to engage in subversion. Alliance with the United States against a perceived Soviet threat, then, becomes a self-fulfilling prophecy. Particularly if the partners host U.S. bases, these countries may well become new frontline states and possible targets of a Soviet attack.[17] A high-level Malaysian official complained at an international conference on Asian security:

> The big powers take small powers for granted. Big powers expect small powers to support the formers' global dispositions. The United States defines security too narrowly from a global balance and military hardware perspective. Security is much more than this. More emphasis should be placed on the creation of a just international system, including the reduction of trade barriers and an increase in technology transfer, investment, and educational opportunities from the industrial states to the third world.[18]

Minister V.B. Dato Khalil Yaakob's argument is the other side of the security debate: that for much of Asia, the real threats to social and political stability are internal, requiring economic development and external investment.

Resources allocated to defense buildups must be subtracted from productive resources. In this view, the Soviet and Chinese "threats" are both seductive and subversive, diverting political decision makers from the real challenges to their societies: economic growth and equity. Increasing defense expenditures increase the military's importance, reduce opportunities for the rise of civilian elites, restrict the international competitiveness of local manufactures, and heighten dependency on Western military supplies.

Despite these reservations, the ASEAN states on balance accept the necessity of a U.S. military guarantee against the Soviets (and by implication, Vietnam) no matter how ambiguously it is articulated. They also grudgingly acknowledge the utility of Japanese forces in Northeast Asian waters and those of Australia and New Zealand to the south. None of these military deployments threatens ASEAN. All help to maintain the freedom of movement necessary for international commerce.

Furthermore, ASEAN foresees a long period of low-level conflict in Indochina, testing Thailand's resolve and ASEAN solidarity. Hanoi will constantly probe for fissures among the six. Indonesia particularly hopes to arrange a compromise with Hanoi over Cambodia so that good relations with an important buffer against China can be restored. The Marcos government sent rice to Vietnam. Even Singapore has traded Thai goods to Vietnam. ASEAN is increasingly nervous about occasional direct conflict between Thai forces and Vietnam. Because the Khmer bases of all three resistance factions were destroyed in the 1985 dry season offensive, Thailand is now directly responsible for maintaining supply routes into Cambodia. Thus, Vietnamese attacks against Cambodian guerrillas project the fighting across the border into Thailand to sever logistics lines and to provoke direct confrontations with Thai troops. Hanoi hopes these actions will convince Thailand to reconsider its backing for the resistance and hasten an ASEAN compromise.[19]

In all probability, however, Vietnam will not be successful in either splitting Thailand from ASEAN or eliciting acceptance of Vietnamese hegemony in Cambodia. Maintenance of the resistance in Cambodia and international pressure on Vietnam for a troop withdrawal ensures that political and military disputes among China, the Soviet Union, and Vietnam will persist in Southeast Asia. Animosity among the three major communist actors in Southeast Asia appears preferable to the alternative: a negotiated solution in Cambodia that could lead to rapprochement among Moscow, Hanoi, and Beijing. Any movement toward renewed cooperation among these states and their communist parties would be perceived as much more threatening to ASEAN than the continuation of guerrilla warfare in Cambodia.

Assuming a growing Soviet naval presence, the Soviet-Vietnam alliance, continued China suspicion of Soviet armies on its borders, and support for Vietnam to the south, what kind of security arrangements appear on the horizon among the United States and its Southeast Asian friends?

Growing nationalism in noncommunist third world states makes it increasingly difficult for the United States to maintain exclusive control of military bases in these countries by the 1990s. Moreover, the political and military effectiveness of overseas bases would be undermined if the United States were to operate from them in conditions of local hostility, as in Guantanamo, Cuba. The alternative is not necessarily a complete exodus from these facilities, however. Even those who are unhappy with U.S. forces on their soil in Asia do not want to see a U.S. withdrawal from the region. In the Philippines, for example, such a withdrawal could provide opportunities for direct Soviet and Vietnamese aid to the communist NPA. The problem is, rather, to make the base facilities politically palatable to nationalist elites. This can be accomplished by reducing the proportion of the facilities used exclusively by the United States and inviting other ASEAN states plus Australia and New Zealand forces to use Clark and Subic as part of a regional defense effort. The Philippines could charge a user's fee for the bases, continuing their role as a revenue generator. Use of the bases by a number of friendly states would also reinforce the international stake in sustaining a noncommunist Philippines.

U.S. naval and air forces would remain at the bases; however, they would be reduced in size. Other regional facilities might be opened to them, including possibly Singapore, Thailand, Brunei, Australia, and perhaps expanded facilities in Guam, Okinawa, and Tinian. The U.S. Defense Department has drawn up detailed contingency plans to move navy and air force units from the Philippines to Guam, Okinawa, and other Pacific locations. While the Pentagon fully expects to continue to use the Philippine facilities at least through 1991, it realizes the necessity of planning alternatives that would require a dispersal of forces. Among the locations cited in the plans are air and naval facilities on Guam, an air base on Okinawa, airstrips on the Marianas island of Saipan, and U.S. bases in Korea. Washington has also leased 18,000 acres on Tinian, which could become a bombing range, according to a senior Pentagon official.[20]

With the decentralized base arrangements, U.S. forces may have to remain on station for longer periods before returning to home ports for major repairs and maintenance. Nevertheless, that should present no serious problem with the new systems scheduled for introduction into the U.S. fleet in the 1990s. By the end of the century, the U.S. Navy should have lighter, faster, more fuel-efficient ships, with modular surveillance and fire-control systems. These could be snapped out and replaced at regular intervals, a procedure that could be done at sea.

With the foregoing changes in mind, renegotiation of the Philippine bases agreement in 1991 could become the centerpiece of a new U.S.-backed Asian security strategy. Without any additional formal security arrangements, increased military cooperation among Japan, Australia, the ASEAN states and the United States would develop. Shared surveillance tasks through contiguous areas; joint exercises, particularly at maritime choke points; ASW, mining, and minesweeping exercises; and possibly joint air patrols such as those already conducted with Malaysian crews in Australian P3 aircraft from Butterworth could become routine.

New arrangements of this kind in the 1990s would honor nationalist sentiments antithetical to exclusive foreign bases on one's territory, increase regional security collaboration, yet still provide facilities for U.S. air and naval forces to patrol Asian air and maritime space and coordinate the activities of friendly armed services beyond their own regional capabilities. Both burden sharing and nationalist sensitivities are taken into account in this scheme. The question to be answered is whether the United States and its Asian partners are willing to exercise the political will to bring about these alterations in security arrangements by the end of the century.

Notes

Chapter 1

1. See the discussion by Indonesian strategist Jusuf Wanandi, "Security Issues in the ASEAN Region," in Karl D. Jackson and M. Hadi Soesastro, eds., *ASEAN Security and Economic Development* (Berkeley: University of California Institute of East Asian Studies, 1984), pp. 298, 299.

2. These figures may be found in the address by U.S. Secretary of State George Shultz to the Asia Foundation in San Francisco, "Economic Cooperation in the Pacific Basin" (Washington, D.C.: Department of State, Bureau of Public Affairs, Current Policy No. 658, February 21, 1985), p. 3, and in Admiral James A. Lyons, Jr.'s, interview in the *Proceedings of the U.S. Naval Institute* 113/7/1013 (July 1987): 67.

3. These data are summarized from several recent studies in Richard Higgott, "The Dilemma of Interdependence: Australia and the International Division of Labor in the Asia-Pacific Region" (paper prepared for the twenty-sixth annual meeting of the International Studies Association, Washington, D.C., March 5–9, 1985), pp. 14, 15.

4. Bernard K. Gordon and Lloyd R. Vasey, "Security in East Asia-Pacific," in Charles E. Morrison, ed., *Threats to Security in East Asia-Pacific* (Lexington, Mass.: Lexington Books, 1983), pp. 33–49.

5. An excellent review of this debate is found in Henry Albinski, *The Australian-American Security Relationship* (New York: St. Martin's Press, 1983), pp. 39–43.

6. This assessment is drawn from Richard K. Betts, "Washington, Tokyo, and Northeast Asian Security: A Survey," *Journal of Strategic Studies* (December 1983): 23. Also see Peter Grier, "Pentagon Faces Tough Choice," *Christian Science Monitor,* December 16, 1985.

7. Secretary of State George Shultz, address before the Commonwealth Club, San Francisco, "America and the Struggle for Freedom" (Washington, D.C.: U.S. Department of State, Bureau of Public Affairs, February 22, 1985), p. 3.

8. *New York Times*, February 7, 1985.

9. Richard Halloran, "Shultz and Weinberger: Disputing Use of Force," *New York Times*, November 30, 1984. The analysis of this issue is drawn from Halloran's article and that of Brad Knickerbocker, "Weinberger Spells Out Conditions for Deployment of U.S. Troops," *Christian Science Monitor*, November 30, 1984.

10. *Security and Arms Control: The Search for a More Stable Peace* (Washington, D.C.: U.S. Department of State, Bureau of Public Affairs, September 1984), pp. 11, 12.

11. Cited by *Far Eastern Economic Review,* January 12, 1984, p. 15.

12. Former U.S. Deputy Secretary of State David Newsom makes this argument in "ASEAN and U.S. Foreign Policy: The Future," in Jackson and Soesastro, *ASEAN Security and Economic Development,* p. 310.

13. Deputy Assistant Secretary of Defense Richard Armitage made this assessment in 1981. Cited by Gareth Porter, "The United States and Southeast Asia," *Current History* 83, no. 497 (December 1984): 403.

14. Tun-hwa Ko and Yu-ming Shaw, eds., *Sea Lane Security in the Pacific Basin* (Taipei: Asia and World Institute, 1983), p. 12.

15. This exercise was discussed by Japan Defense Agency official Kenichi Kitamura in ibid., p. 45.

16. The maritime strategy's effects on U.S. Pacific alliances is discussed in Sheldon W. Simon, "The Maritime Strategy and America's Pacific Allies" (paper presented to the Naval Postgraduate School conference, "The Navy in the Pacific," Monterey, August 13–14, 1987).

17. This discussion draws heavily upon Mark Valencia, "ZOPFAN and Navigation Rights: Stormy Seas Ahead?" *Far Eastern Economic Review,* March 7, 1985, pp. 38–39.

18. Lewis P. Young, "The 1983 Japanese White Paper: An Assessment," *Asian Defense Journal* (December 1983).

19. For an excellent brief discussion of the Orion's capabilities, see Desmond Ball, "Ocean Surveillance," Reference Paper No. 87 (Canberra: Strategic and Defense Studies Centre, November 1982), pp. 11, 46–49.

20. Donald Daniel, "Antisubmarine Warfare in the Nuclear Age," *Orbis* 28, no. 3 (Fall 1984): 529.

21. Wayne Biddle, "The Cruise Missile Comes of Age," *New York Times,* January 6, 1985.

22. Louis C. Finch, "Nuclear Armed SLCMs: Contribution to American Security" (paper prepared for the twenty-fifth annual meeting of the International Studies Association, Atlanta, March 28, 1984), p. 5.

23. Nayan Chanda, "American Big Stick," *Far Eastern Economic Review,* June 20, 1985, p. 46.

24. Bill Keller, "Reagan Military Budget Aims to Expand Forces and Modernize Weapons," *New York Times,* February 4, 1985.

25. See, for example, the arguments made by Nicholas Lemann, "The Peacetime War," *Atlantic Monthly* (October 1984): esp. 92–94; and PBS-TV, "Battle for the Norwegian Sea," *Frontline,* January 2, 1985.

26. Lemann, "Peacetime War," pp. 92–93.

27. PBS-TV, "Battle for the Norwegian Sea."

28. Stansfield Turner, "A Strategy for the '90s," *New York Times Magazine,* May 6, 1984, pp. 42–49.

29. Ibid., pp. 48–49.

30. Nautilus Research, *Pacific Command: The Structure and Strategy of the U.S. Military in the Pacific* (Leverett, Mass., July 1983), p. 65.

31. Sang-woo Rhee, "The Roots of South Korean Anxiety about National Security," in Morrison, *Threats to Security,* p. 74.

32. This information is drawn from a statement by then CINCPAC Admiral Robert L.J. Long in "United States–Philippines Relations and the New Base and Aid

Agreement," *Hearings before the House Foreign Affairs Subcommittee on Asian and Pacific Affairs,* 98th Cong., 1st sess., June 17, 23, 28, 1983, pp. 7–10.

33. Statement by Assistant Secretary of Defense Richard Armitage in ibid., p. 33.

34. This concern was pointed out to me by a high-level Philippine Foreign Ministry official based on that official's meetings with ASEAN counterparts in 1983. The interview occurred in Manila on May 25, 1984.

35. Quoted in Thomas B. Modly, "The Rhetoric and Realities of Japan's 1000-Mile Sea-Lane Defense Policy," *Naval War College Review* 38, no. 1 (January–February 1984): 27.

36. This discussion is drawn from Jeffrey Record, "Can the U.S. Honor Its Military IOUs?" *Wall Street Journal,* October 25, 1984.

37. Ibid.

38. *Far Eastern Economic Review,* November 10, 1983, p. 19.

39. Nayan Chanda, "Friend-ship Calls," *Far Eastern Economic Review,* December 13, 1984, p. 18.

Chapter 2

1. John Stephan, "Soviet Approaches to Japan: Images behind the Policies," in Jae Kyu Park and Joseph M. Ha, eds., *The Soviet Union and East Asia in the 1980s* (Seoul: Kyungnam University Press, 1983), p. 123.

2. These Soviet goals are summarized in Joseph G. Whelan, *The Soviets in Asia, An Expanding Presence* (Washington, D.C.: Congressional Research Service, March 27, 1984), pp. 11–13.

3. Typical allegations are found in the "International Situation" broadcast of the Radio Moscow Domestic Service, April 3, 1986, in Foreign Broadcast Information Service (FBIS), *Daily Report/USSR,* April 8, 1986, CC3-CC4.

4. *New York Times* excerpts of the *Merdeka* interview, July 23, 1987.

5. Soviet government statement on the Asia-Pacific region, *Tass,* April 23, 1986, in FBIS, *Daily Report/USSR,* April 23, 1986, CC1-CC3.

6. "International Observers Roundtable," Radio Moscow Domestic Service, April 27, 1986, in FBIS, *Daily Report/USSR,* April 30, 1986, CC4. See also *Krasnaya Zvezda Observer,* May 4, 1986, in FBIS, *Daily Report/USSR,* May 12, 1986, CC5.

7. Statement by Akil Salimov, deputy president of the Supreme Soviet, in Kuala Lumpur, carried by *Agence France Presse,* June 5, 1986, in FBIS, *Daily Report, Asia Pacific,* June 6, 1986, O1.

8. Susuma Awanohara, "The Bear at the Door," *Far Eastern Economic Review,* March 26, 1987, pp. 18–19.

9. Statement by Donald Zagoria in Joint Subcommittees on Europe and the Middle East and on Asia and Pacific Affairs of the Committee on Foreign Affairs, *The Soviet Role in Asia: Hearings,* 98th Cong., 1st sess., July 19, 21, 26, 28, August 2, September 27, October 19, 1983, p. 37.

10. A useful Soviet view of why the USSR fears U.S. capabilities in Asia is found in Alexei G. Arbatov, "Arms Limitation and the Situation in the Asian-Pacific and the Indian Ocean Regions," *Asian Survey* 24, no. 11 (November 1984): 1108–1116.

11. Ibid., p. 1111.

12. See the commentaries by *Kransnaya Zvezda,* May 23, 1986, Radio Moscow, in Japanese, May 28, 1986, and *Izvestiya,* August 23, 1986, in FBIS, *Daily Report/USSR,* May 29, 1986, CC14-16, C3, and August 23, 1986, C2.

13. Paul Dibb, "The Soviet Union as a Pacific Military Power," Working Paper 81 (Canberra: Strategic and Defense Studies Centre, Australian National University, August 1984), p. 5.

14. Ibid., pp. 6, 7.

15. These figures are drawn from the study by F.A. Mediansky, "The Superpowers and Southeast Asia" (paper prepared for the conference "Destiny in Asia? Australia and ASEAN," Australian National University, Canberra, October 31–November 2, 1984), pp. 5, 6, 7, 9, 20, 21. Submarine data were given to me during a briefing aboard the Seventh Fleet command ship, U.S.S. *Blue Ridge,* February 26, 1986.

16. This discussion draws extensively from Walter K. Andersen, "Soviets in the Indian Ocean: Much Ado about Something—But What?" *Asian Survey* 24, no. 9 (September 1984): 913–915.

17. "The Soviet Art of Naval Warfare," in *Strategic Survey: 1979* (London: International Institute for Strategic Studies, 1980), p. 20.

18. James J. Tritten, "Soviet Naval War Fighting Capabilities," P-6917 (Santa Monica: Rand Corporation, October 1983), p. 5. Also see Norman Polmar, "Soviet Surface Combatant Development and Operations in the 1980s and 1990s" (paper prepared for the annual meeting of the International Studies Association, Atlanta, March 30, 1984).

19. Polmar, "Soviet Surface Combatant Development," p. 12.

20. Ibid., p. 14.

21. *Kyodo* (Tokyo) April 5, 1985, in FBIS, *Daily Report, Asia Pacific,* April 5, 1985, C4; *New York Times,* August 17, 1986.

22. Benjamin F. Schemmer, "The Pacific Naval Balance," *Armed Forces Journal International* (April 1984): 32–43.

23. Dibb, "Soviet Union as a Pacific Military Power," pp. 10, 13.

24. Research Institute for Peace and Security, *Asian Security 1984* (Tokyo: Nikkei Business Publishing, 1984), p. 138.

25. Denis Warner, "Point, Counterpoint in the South China Sea," *Pacific Defense Reporter* (August 1984).

26. Dibb, "Soviet Union as a Pacific Military Power," p. 8.

27. Stuart D. Goldman, "Soviet Policy toward Japan and the Strategic Balance in Northeast Asia" (Washington, D.C.: Congressional Research Service, February 27, 1984), p. 20. See also Marian Leighton, "Soviet Strategy towards Northern Europe and Japan," *Survey* 118–119 (Autumn–Winter 1983): 138–139.

28. Hiroshi Kimura, "Soviet Policy toward Japan," Working Paper 6, (Providence, R.I.: Brown University, Center for Foreign Policy Development, August 1983), pp. 13, 25, 26.

29. Typical are the commentaries in the Moscow Domestic Service in Russian, October 14, 1983, in FBIS, *Daily Report/USSR,* October 17, 1983, C11; *Red Star,* November 3, 1983, in FBIS, *Daily Report/USSR,* November 8, 1983, C6.

30. Interview with Deputy Chief of the International Department of the CPSU Central Committee Ivan Kovalenko, NHK-TV (Tokyo), February 3, 1984, in FBIS, *Daily Report/USSR,* February 6, 1984, C2.

31. Joseph M. Ha, "Soviet Perception of North Korea," in Park and Ha, eds., *Soviet Union and East Asia in the 1980s,* p. 49.

32. Ibid., p. 59.

33. Richard Nations, "Militant Brotherhood—Kim Tilts to Moscow," *Far Eastern Economic Review,* June 20, 1985, pp. 32–33.

34. Richard Nations, "Love Boat to Wonsan," *Far Eastern Economic Review,* August 29, 1985, pp. 22, 23. See also *Agence France Presse,* October 7, 1985, in FBIS, *Daily Report, Asia Pacific,* October 7, 1985, D1; Robert Karniol, "South Korea: Keeping a Fighting Edge," *Far Eastern Economic Review,* June 26, 1986, p. 46.

35. Nayan Chanda, "Pyongyang Revisited," *Far Eastern Economic Review,* November 7, 1985, pp. 18–19; Jonathon Pollack, "Peking Stands Back as Moscow Courts Kim," *Far Eastern Economic Review,* December 5, 1985, pp. 48–49.

36. Murray Hiebert, "Broadening Trade Horizons," *Far Eastern Economic Review,* July 23, 1987, p. 28.

37. These figures are cited in testimony by Evelyn Colbert of the Carnegie Endowment for International Peace in *The Soviet Role in Asia: Hearings,* pp. 193–196. Also see Richard D. Fisher, Jr., "Moscow's Growing Muscle in Southeast Asia," *Asian Studies Center Backgrounder* (Washington, D.C.: Heritage Foundation, April 4, 1984), p. 6; and Research Institute for Peace and Security, *Asian Security 1984,* p. 168.

38. F.A. Mediansky and Dianne Court, "The Soviet Union in Southeast Asia," Canberra Papers on Strategy and Defence, No. 29 (Canberra: Strategic and Defence Studies Centre, Australian National University, 1984), pp. 28–30; Edmund F. McWilliams, Jr., "Hanoi's Course in Southeast Asia: A Source of Growing Regional Instability," *Asian Survey* 24, no. 8 (August 1984): 881–882. For a report on the number of Badgers at Cam Ranh Bay, see "Soviets Beefing Up Air Power in Vietnam," *New Straits Times* (Kuala Lumpur), November 14, 1984; Admiral James A. Lyons, Jr.'s, interview in *Asian Wall Street Journal Weekly,* March 30, 1987, p. 14; and the articles by Hamish McDonald and Sosuma Awanohara in the *Far Eastern Economic Review,* June 18, 1987, pp. 34–35.

39. Marian K. Leighton, "Soviets Still Play Dominoes in Asia," *Wall Street Journal,* October 14, 1983.

40. Mediansky and Court, "The Soviet Union in Southeast Asia," p. 32.

41. Leif Rosenberger, "The Soviet-Vietnamese Alliance and Kampuchea," *Survey* 27, nos. 118–119 (Autumn–Winter 1983): 214–215.

42. Ibid., pp. 218, 221.

43. MacAlister Brown and Joseph Zasloff, "Laos: Gearing Up for National Development," *Southeast Asian Affairs, 1985* (Singapore: Institute for Southeast Asian Studies).

44. Rosenberger, "Soviet-Vietnamese Alliance and Kampuchea," pp. 224–225.

45. Eighth Indochina Foreign Ministers Conference communiqué, Vientiane Domestic Service in Laos, January 29, 1984, in FBIS, *Daily Report Asia Pacific,* January 30, 1984, p. 17.

46. *Nation Review* (Bangkok), March 17, 1985, in FBIS, *Daily Report Asia Pacific,* March 18, 1985, J1.

47. Comments by Haji Ahmad Zakaria, deputy director, Institute for Strategic and International Studies, Kuala Lumpur, at the March 31, 1984, annual meeting of the International Studies Association, Atlanta.

48. This viewpoint was articulated by Thai Foreign Ministry official Sarasin Varaphol at the Third U.S.-ASEAN Conference, Chiangmai, Thailand, January 10, 1985.

49. Nayan Chanda, "United We Stand," *Far Eastern Economic Review,* August 11, 1983, pp. 24–25.

50. *Tass,* March 19, 1985, in FBIS, *Daily Report/USSR,* March 21, 1984, A4; *New Times* (Moscow), March 1985, in FBIS, *Daily Report/USSR,* March 20, 1985, E1-E3.

51. Michael Ong, "Malaysia in 1983: On the Road to Greater Malaysia," *Southeast Asian Affairs, 1984,* p. 228.

52. Unpublished paper by U.S. Defense Intelligence Agency Soviet analyst, Leif Rosenberger, "Philippine Communism and the Soviet Union," February 26, 1985, p. 23. See also Paul Quinn-Judge, "Philippine Insurgents Are Turning Down Soviet Support," *Christian Science Monitor,* November 26, 1985.

53. Marian K. Leighton, "Soviets Still Play Dominoes in Asia," *Wall Street Journal,* October 14, 1983.

54. Michael Leifer, "The Security of Sealanes in Southeast Asia," in Robert O'Neill, ed., *Security in East Asia* (New York: St. Martin's Press for the International Institute for Strategic Studies, 1984), p. 171.

55. *Shijie Zhishi* (Beijing) (No. 6), March 16, 1985, in FBIS, *Daily Report/PRC,* March 26, 1985, C1.

56. Richard K. Betts, "Washington, Tokyo, and Northeast Asian Security: A Survey," *Journal of Strategic Studies* (December 1983): 20.

57. Remarks by Admiral Ito in Tun-hwa Ko and Yu-ming Shaw, eds., *Sea Lane Security in the Pacific Basin,* no. 29 (Taipei: Asia and World Institute, September 1983), pp. 81–82.

58. PBS-TV, "Battle for the Norwegian Sea," *Frontline* (KAET-TV, Phoenix), January 2, 1985. Also see Donald C. Daniel, "Antisubmarine Warfare in the Nuclear Age," *Orbis,* 28, no. 3 (Fall 1984): 548.

59. Author's briefing by analysts in the U.S. Defense Intelligence Agency, Washington, D.C., May 2, 1984.

60. The remainder of these discussions is drawn extensively from Dibb, "Soviet Union as a Pacific Military Power," pp. 10, 11, 15.

61. The Gorbachev July 28, 1986, address may be found in the *Supplement to Soviet Life* (October 1986). The citations are from pages III and IV.

Chapter 3

1. Bruce Roscoe, "The Long and Short of It," *Far Eastern Economic Review,* April 17, 1985, p. 83.

2. Larry Niksch, "Japanese Attitudes toward Defense and Security Issues," *Naval War College Review,* 36, no. 4 (July–August 1983): 63.

3. Edward A. Olsen, *U.S.-Japan Strategic Reciprocity* (Stanford: Hoover Institution Press, 1985), p. 44.

4. Ibid., pp. 14, 102.

5. Mike M. Mochizuki, "Japan's Search for Strategy," *International Security* 8, no. 3 (Winter 1983–1984): 154–156.

6. Masashi Nishihara, "Expanding Japan's Credible Defense Role," *International Security* 8, no. 3 (Winter 1983–1984): 183.

7. Olsen, *U.S.-Japan Strategic Reciprocity,* p. 96.

8. Ibid., p. 17.

9. R. Nishijima, "History and Future of Japan's Self Defense Forces," *Asia-Pacific Community* 26 (Fall 1984): 128; K.V. Kesavan, *Japanese Defense Policy since 1976: Latest Trends,* Papers on Strategy and Defence, No. 31 (Canberra: Strategic and Defence Studies Centre, 1984), p. 18.

10. Murray Sayle, "The Siberian Cruise of the USS Enterprise," *Far Eastern Economic Review,* June 16, 1983, p. 73.

11. Cited by Kesavan, *Japanese Defense Policy,* p. 35.

12. Author's discussion with a research analyst from the U.S. Air University, Maxwell Air Force Base, Alabama, November 3, 1983.

13. Richard Nations, "Japan's 'Omni-Direction,' Is Now Dead and Gone," *Far Eastern Economic Review,* December 20, 1984, p. 27.

14. Nishihara, "Expanding Japan's Credible Defense Role," pp. 184, 195.

15. *Kresnaya Zvezda,* July 15, 1984, in FBIS, *Daily Report/USSR,* July 19, 1984, C2. Also see the *Tass* warning of increased Soviet "countermeasures" on April 15, 1985, in the FBIS of the same date, C1.

16. Richard Nations, "Chores of Deterrence," *Far Eastern Economic Review,* April 11, 1985, pp. 36, 37.

17. Author's interview with U.S. embassy Officials, Tokyo, May 7, 1984.

18. October 1984 *Yomiuri* poll results cited by William T. Tow, "Japan's Security in an East Asian Context: Some Considerations" (paper presented to the twenty-seventh annual meeting of the International Studies Association, Washington, D.C., March 5–9, 1985), p. 10.

19. Author's interview with Hisiao Iwashima, National Defense College, Tokyo, May 7, 1984. Robert Y. Horijuchi, "U.S. Backpedals on Japan's Defenses," *Pacific Defense Reporter* (April 1986): 25.

20. Richard Nations, "Hot and Cold Shoulder," *Far Eastern Economic Review,* May 10, 1984, p. 15.

21. Qian He, "Sino-Japanese Relations and the Security of Asia," *Journal of Northeast Asian Studies* 3, no. 1 (Spring 1984): 77. The author is a research associate in the Chinese Academy of Social Sciences, Beijing.

22. *Asian Wall Street Journal Weekly,* April 15, 1985, p. 6; "U.S.-Japan Trade," *Gist* (Washington, D.C.: U.S. Department of State, April 1985).

23. Research Institute for Peace and Security, *Asian Security 1983* (Tokyo: RIPS, 1983), p. 238.

24. Tow, "Japan's Security," p. 19; Mike Tharp, "Defense—The Nuts and Bolts," *Far Eastern Economic Review,* June 16, 1983, p. 77.

25. Commander James Auer, USN, in Robert W. Barnett, *Beyond War: Japan's Concept of Comprehensive National Security* (New York: Pergamon Braisey's, 1984), pp. 24, 33–35.

26. Gregg Rubinstein, U.S. Department of Defense, in ibid., p. 30.

27. Erik Fromm, analyst for Boeing Aircraft, in ibid., p. 42.

28. Antonio Kamiya, "Booming Domestic Defense Industry Examined," *Foreign Media,* September 24, 1984, pp. 54, 55.

29. Tsuneo Akaha, "The Threat of Shipping Disruptions in the Middle East and Asia: The Nexus of Japanese Comprehensive Security" (Bowling Green State University, Department of Political Science, unpublished paper, September 1984), p. 21.

30. Murray Sayle, "The Siberian Cruise of the 'U.S. Enterprise,' " p. 77; and Joseph F. Bouchard and Douglas J. Hess, USN, "The Japanese Navy and Sea-Lanes Defense," *U.S. Naval Institute Proceedings* (March 1984): 94–95.

31. Hideo Sekino and Sadao Seno, "Japan: Will the Giant Shed Its Fetters?" *Pacific Defense Reporter* 9 (March 1983): 15–23.

32. Ikeuchi Fumio, "The 1986–90 Medium-Term Defense Plan," *Japan Quarterly* (November–December 1984): 394.

33. U.S. Defense Department, *Defense '87* (May–June 1987): 18.

34. Lawrence E. Grinter, "Strategy in East Asia: New Realities, New Requirements" (paper presented to the twenty-seventh annual meeting of the International Studies Association, Washington, D.C., March 5–9, 1985), pp. 20, 21.

35. Statement by JSDF Defense Bureau director, Toru Hara, to the Diet in 1980, cited in Niksch, "Japanese Attitudes," p. 68.

36. Marian Leighton, "Soviet Strategy toward Northern Europe and Japan," *Survey* 118–119 (Autumn–Winter 1983): 138–139.

37. Martine-Amice Matyas, "Japan Still Claims 'Its' Northern Territories," *Le Figaro* (Paris), December 2, 1983 in FBIS, *Daily Report/Asian Pacific,* December 8, 1983, C1–2.

38. Mochizuki, "Japan's Search for Strategy," pp. 172–174.

39. Nishihara, "Expanding Japan's Credible Defense Role," p. 195.

40. Tetsuya Kataoka, "Japan's Northern Threat," *Problems of Communism* 33, no. 2 (March–April 1984): 7; *Kyodo,* February 20, 1984, in FBIS *Daily Report/Asia Pacific,* February 21, 1984, C2.

41. Edward A. Olsen, "Japan and Korea," in Robert S. Ozaki and Walter Arnold, eds., *Japan's Foreign Relations: A Global Search for Economic Security* (Boulder: Westview Press, 1985), p. 181.

42. Major Tom Linn, USMC, "On Soya Strait and Soviet Pacific Deployment," *Defense and Foreign Affairs* (December 1983).

43. International Institute for Strategic Studies, *The Military Balance, 1983–1984* (London: IISS, 1983), pp. 92, 94. See also Tun-hwa Ko and Yu-ming Shaw, eds., *Sea Lane Security in the Pacific Basin,* (Asia and World Monograph Series, 29, Taipei: Asia and World Institute, September 1983), pp. 75, 76; *Kyodo,* April 6, 1985, in FBIS, *Daily Report/Asia/Pacific,* April 8, 1985, C3.

44. *Kyodo* (Tokyo) March 30, 1984, in FBIS, *Daily Report Asia/Pacific,* April 2, 1984, C4; *Nodong Sinmun,* editorial, April 8, 1985, in ibid., April 10, 1985, P2.

45. Yatsuhiro Nakagawa, "The WEPTO Option: Japan's New Role in East Asia/Pacific Collective Security," *Asian Survey* 24, no. 8 (August 1984): 833, 834, 838.

46. Lee W. Farnsworth, "Japan and the Third World," in P. Taylor and G. Raymond, eds., *Third World Policies of Industrial States* (Westport, Conn.: Greenwood Press, 1982), p. 175.

47. Lee W. Farnsworth, "Japan-ASEAN Relations: Changing Patterns" (paper presented to the Western Political Science Association, Las Vegas, Nevada, March 28–30, 1985), pp. 15, 21.

48. Akaha, "Threat of Shipping Disruptions," p. 13.

49. Ibid., pp. 16, 17.

50. Typical are statements by Thai Foreign Minister Sitthi and Singapore's Foreign Minister Dhanabalan carried in *Nation Review,* January 25, 1984, and on the Singapore Domestic Service, January 16, 1984, in FBIS, *Daily Report Asia/Pacific,* January 18, 1984, O8.

51. Willard H. Elsbree and Khong Kim Hoong, "Japan and ASEAN," in Ozaki and Arnold, eds., *Japan's Foreign Relations,* p. 129.

52. Zakaria Haji Ahmad, "ASEAN and the Major Powers" (paper prepared for the Third U.S.-ASEAN Conference, Chiangmai, Thailand, January 7–11, 1985), p. 6.

53. Frances Lai Fung-wei, "Japan's Defense Policy and Its Implications for the ASEAN Countries," in *Southeast Asian Affairs 1984* (Singapore: Southeast Asian Studies Institute, 1984), p. 62.

54. Nations, "Japan's 'Omni-Direction' Is Now Dead and Gone," p. 28.

55. Poll data cited in Research Institute for Peace and Security, *Asian Security 1984* (Tokyo: Research Institute for Peace and Security 1984), p. 162.

56. Elsbree and Hoong, "Japan and ASEAN," p. 128.

57. Research Institute for Peace and Security (Tokyo), *Asian Security, 1986* (London: Brassey's Defence Publishers, 1986), pp. 179–181. See also Frank Langdon, "The Security Debate in Japan," *Pacific Affairs* 58, no. 3 (Fall 1985): 397–410.

Chapter 4

1. The term is Donald Weatherbee's in his "ASEAN Regionalism: The Salient Dimension," in Karl D. Jackson and M. Hadi Soesastro, eds., *ASEAN Security and Economic Development* (Berkeley: University of California Institute of East Asian Studies, 1984), p. 264.

2. Donald Weatherbee, "ASEAN Military Capacities and Security Concerns" (paper prepared for the twenty-sixth annual meeting of the International Studies Association, Washington, D.C., March 5–9, 1985), pp. 2, 3.

3. U.S. House of Representatives, Subcommittee on Foreign Affairs, *The Soviet Role in Asia, Hearings,* 98th Cong., 1st sess., July 19, 21, 26, 28, August 2, September 27, October 19, 1983, p. 218.

4. A very good discussion of ASEAN objections to Western alignment is found in Robert C. Horn, "U.S.-ASEAN Relations in the 1980s," *Contemporary Southeast Asia* 6, no. 2 (September 1984): 119–134.

5. Comments by Noordin Soipee, director of the Institute for Strategic and International Studies, Kuala Lumpur, at the *Southeast Asia Security Conference,* Port Dickson, Malaysia, November 13, 1984. Also see J. Soedjati Djiwandono, "The Long-Term Strategies of the Southeast Asian Countries: The Case of ASEAN," *Indonesian Quarterly* 12, no. 2 (April 1984): 196.

6. Johan Saravanamuttu, "ASEAN Security For the 1980s: The Case for a Revitalized ZOPFAN," *Contemporary Southeast Asia* 6, no. 2 (September 1984): 188.

7. Bernard K. Gordon and Lloyd R. Vassey, "Security in East Asia-Pacific," in Charles E. Morrison, ed., *Threats to Security in East Asia–Pacific* (Lexington, Mass.: Lexington Books, 1983), p. 44. This chapter is drawn from Gordon and Vassey's extensive interviews with regional officials.

8. Jusuf Wanandi and M. Hadi Soesastro, "Indonesia's Security and Threat Perceptions," in Morrison, *Threats,* p. 96.

9. Lau Teik Soon, "National Threat Perceptions of Singapore," in Morrison, *Threats,* p. 123.

10. Robert O. Tilman, *The Enemy Beyond: External Threat Perceptions in the ASEAN Region,* Research Notes and Discussion Paper No. 42 (Singapore: Institute of Southeast Asian Studies, 1984), pp. 48–49.

11. Wanandi and Soesastro, "Indonesia's Security and Threat Perceptions," p. 96.

12. Jusuf Wanandi, "Seeking Peace amid Cambodia's Conflict," *Far Eastern Economic Review,* March 8, 1984, pp. 34–36.

13. "Malaysia's Doctrine of Comprehensive Security," *Foreign Affairs Malaysia* 17, no. 1 (March 1984): 95.

14. "Southeast Asia in the '80s," address by Foreign Minister Ghazalie Shafie, March 16, 1984, in *Foreign Affairs Malaysia* 17, no. 1 (March 1984): 22.

15. For a good brief review of the Philippine situation in 1985, see Larry Niksch, "Special Report on the Philippines," *Asian News and Analysis* (Wharton Pacific Basin Economic Service) 2, no. 5, March 15, 1985.

16. Seth Mydans, "Philippine Communists Are Spread Widely . . . ," *New York Times,* September 14, 1986.

17. Cited by Weatherbee, "ASEAN Military Capacities," pp. 4, 5.

18. Larry Niksch, "Philippine Domestic Politics and Foreign Policy" (paper prepared for the Third U.S.-ASEAN Conference, Chiangmai, Thailand, January 7–11, 1985), pp. 20, 21.

19. Author's interviews with Regional Command officers in Mindanao and Cebu, as well as U.S. embassy officials, May 1984. Also see J.V.P. Goldrick and P.D. Jones, RAN, "The Far Eastern Navies," *Proceedings* (Washington, D.C.: U.S. Naval Institute, March 1984), p. 64.

20. Weatherbee, "ASEAN Military Capacities and Security Concerns," pp. 26–27.

21. Chulacheeb Chinwanno, "Thailand in 1983: The Parliamentary System Survives," *Southeast Asian Affairs, 1984* (Singapore: Institute for Southeast Asian Studies, 1984), p. 322.

22. Weatherbee, "ASEAN Military Capacities," p. 28.

23. International Institute for Strategic Studies, *The Military Balance, 1983–84* (London: IISS, 1984), p. 101.

24. Reports of these offers may be found in the *Far Eastern Economic Review,* March 19, 1987, p. 16, and in FBIS, *Daily Report Asia-Pacific,* March 9, 1987, J2, March 24, 1987, J2-J3, and August 3, 1987, M1-M2.

25. Chandran Jeshurun, "The Evolution of Malaysian Strategic Policy and Regional Security in Southeast Asia," *Asia-Pacific Defense Forum* (Summer 1983): 11.

26. Most of these data are drawn from Harold Crouch, "A Strict Division," *Far Eastern Economic Review,* October 20, 1983, p. 48, and Goldrick and Jones, "The Far Eastern Navies," p. 63.

27. Weatherbee, "ASEAN Military Capacities," p. 10.

28. Ibid., p. 13. Also see Zakaria Haji Ahmad, "Malaysia in 1984: No More Free Lunches?" *Asian Survey* 25, no. 2 (February 1985): 212.

29. Author's interviews with Malaysian Wisma Putra (Foreign Ministry) officials, May 29, 1984.

30. Crouch, "Strict Division," p. 49.

31. Author's discussion with Mak Joon Num of the Malaysian Institute for Strategic and International Studies, Port Dickson, November 12, 1984.

32. Goldrick and Jones, "The Far Eastern Navies," p. 64. A.W. Grazebrook, "Indonesian Frigate Buy Upstages Australia," *Pacific Defence Reporter* (May 1986): 29–30.

33. Harold Crouch, "No Enemy in Sight," *Far Eastern Economic Review,* February 14, 1985, p. 32.

34. *Agence France Presse* (Hong Kong), September 15, 1986, in FBIS, *Daily Report Asia Pacific,* September 16, 1986, N1.

35. Weatherbee, "ASEAN Military Capacities," pp. 19, 21–25.

36. For a discussion of the types and purposes of ASEAN states' military cooperation through the early 1980s, see Sheldon W. Simon, *The ASEAN States and Regional Security* (Stanford: Hoover Institution Press, 1982), chap. 3.

37. B.A. Hamzah, "ASEAN Military Cooperation without Pact or Threat," *Asia Pacific Community* 22 (Fall 1983): 40–42.

38. Author's discussion with a Malaysian member of the ASEAN Secretariat, Kuala Lumpur, May 28, 1984.

39. Author's discussion with Wisma Putra, Southeast Asia specialist, Kuala Lumpur, May 29, 1984.

40. Kuala Lumpur Domestic Service in English, June 29, 1987, in FBIS, *Daily Report East Asia,* June 30, 1987, H1.

41. *Far Eastern Economic Review,* August 16, 1984.

42. Author's discussions with Professor Chan Heng-chee of the National University of Singapore and Jusuf Wanandi, director of the Center for Strategic and International Studies in Jakarta at the Third U.S.-ASEAN Conference, Chiangmai, Thailand, January 8, 1985.

43. *Agence France Presse,* Hong Kong, March 31, 1985, in FBIS, *Daily Report Asia Pacific,* April 1, 1985, O3.

44. Weatherbee, "ASEAN Military Capacities," p. 32.

45. John McBeth, "Open-Arms Cache," *Far Eastern Economic Review,* April 24, 1986, pp. 44–45.

46. *Bangkok Post,* January 12, 1987. For a dissenting view on the munitions stockpile, arguing that it could draw Thailand into conflicts not of its making, see *Maitchon Sut Sapda* (Bangkok), February 1, 1987, in FBIS *Daily Report Asia Pacific,* February 11, 1987, J1-J2.

47. Research Institute for Peace and Security, *Asian Security 1983* (Tokyo: RIPS, 1983), pp. 28, 29.

48. Address by Malaysian Foreign Minister Tan Sri Ghazalie Shafie at the National University of Malaysia, March 16, 1984, in *Foreign Affairs Malaysia* (Ministry of Foreign Affairs) (March 1984): 22.

49. Zakaria Haji Ahmad, "ASEAN and the Major Powers" (paper presented to the Third U.S.-ASEAN Conference, Chiangmai, Thailand, January 7–11, 1985), p.4.

50. For extensive descriptions of the bases, see Lawrence E. Grinter, *The Philippine Bases: Continuing Utility in a Changing Strategic Context,* National Security Affairs Monograph Series 80-2 (Washington, D.C.: National Defense University Research Directorate, 1980); William R. Feeney, "The United States and the Philippines: The

Bases Dilemma," *Asian Affairs* 10, no. 4 (Winter 1984): 63–85; Alvin J. Cottrell, "The U.S. Philippine Security Relationship," in James Gregor, ed., *The U.S. and the Philippines: A Challenge to a Special Relationship* (Washington, D.C.: Heritage Foundation, 1983), pp. 55–56; F.A. Mediansky, "U.S. Security Assets in the Philippines and Their Role in the Pacific Balance" (paper presented to the annual meeting of the American Political Science Association, Washington, D.C., August 28–31, 1986); U.S. Congress, Subcommittee on Asian and Pacific Affairs, Committee on Foreign Affairs, *United States–Philippines Relations and the New Base and Aid Agreement: Hearings,* 98th Cong., 1st sess., June 17, 23, 28, 1983. For a negative view of the bases as contributory to the repressive policies of the Marcos government and an instrument of U.S. neocolonialism, see Walden Bello, "The U.S. Military Bases in the Philippines," *Southeast Asia Chronicle* 89 (April 1983): passim. Enrile is cited in FBIS, *Daily Report, Asia Pacific,* May 30, 1986, p. 5.

51. *Business Day* (Manila), July 18, 1986; Seth Mydans, "U.S. Aid Doesn't Ease Philippine Doubts," *New York Times,* October 5, 1986.

52. *Philippine Daily Inquirer,* June 12, 1986.

53. William R. Feeney, "The United States and the Philippines: The Bases Dilemma," p. 71; *Bulletin Today* (Manila), January 25, 1985, in FBIS, *Daily Report, Asia Pacific,* January 28, 1985, p. 5.

54. George McT. Kahin, "Remove the Bases from the Philippines," *New York Times,* October 12, 1983.

55. Cottrell, "U.S.-Philippine Security Relationship," pp. 60, 61, 63; *Hearings,* pp. 16, 40.

56. *Hearings,* pp. 226, 242.

57. Author's interview with the manager of the Sembawang Shipyards, Singapore, May 30, 1984.

58. The following discussion is drawn from a number of interviews in the ASEAN countries with government officials and other specialists. All government interviews were provided on a nonattribution basis. They occurred primarily with middle-level officials in foreign affairs and defense matters in May 1984.

59. Author's interview with Alan Rix, director, Center for the Study of Australian-Asian Relations, Griffiths University, Brisbane, June 8, 1984.

60. This discussion was drawn from Pringle's book, *Indonesia and the Philippines: American Interests in Island Southeast Asia* (New York: Columbia University Press, 1980), pp. 83–84.

61. Denis Warner, "Point, Counterpoint in the South China Sea," *Pacific Defense Reporter* (August 1984).

62. This argument was made in Suchit Bunbongkarn and Sukumbhand Paribatra, "Thai Politics and Foreign Policy in the 1980s" (paper prepared for the Third U.S.-ASEAN Conference, Chiangmai, Thailand, January 7–11, 1985), pp. 31, 32.

63. *Nation Review,* July 6, 1983, in FBIS, *Daily Report, Asia Pacific,* July 6, 1983, J1.

64. *New Straits Times* (Kuala Lumpur), October 1, 1983, in FBIS, *Daily Report, Asia Pacific,* October 7, 1983, O2.

65. "Asian Aerospace '84," *Asian Wall Street Journal Weekly,* January 9, 1984.

66. *Agence France Presse,* (Hong Kong), May 20, 1985, in FBIS, *Daily Report, Asia Pacific,* May 24, 1985, O1.

67. Kuala Lumpur International Service, February 25, 1985, in FBIS, *Daily Report, Asia Pacific,* February 28, 1985, O2; *Agence France Presse* (Hong Kong), April 3, 1985, in FBIS, *Daily Report, Asia Pacific,* April 4, 1985, O1.

68. *New Sunday Times* (Kuala Lumpur), September 9, 1984, in FBIS, *Daily Report, Asia Pacific,* September 12, 1984, O2, O3.

69. John McBeth, "Reach for the Sky," *Far Eastern Economic Review,* December 29, 1983, p. 16; Nayan Chanda, "Countdown on F-16s," *Far Eastern Economic Review,* April 5, 1984, pp. 42, 43.

70. David Clark Scott, "The Salvos Fired at General Dynamics," *Christian Science Monitor,* May 13, 1985; "Air Force Set to Buy Controversial F-20 Jet," *Washington Post,* May 10, 1985.

71. Author's discussions with U.S. Defense Intelligence Agency analysts, Washington, D.C., May 8, 1985.

72. John McBeth, "F-16 Counter-Attacked," *Far Eastern Economic Review,* October 25, 1984, pp. 50, 51.

73. *Bangkok Post,* March 15, 1985, and *Siam Rat* (Bangkok) April 11, 1985, both in FBIS, *Daily Report, Asia Pacific,* March 15, 1985, J3, and April 12, 1985, J2, respectively.

74. John McBeth, "Cheaper by the Dozen," *Far Eastern Economic Review,* May 30, 1985, pp. 44–45; *Asian Wall Street Journal Weekly,* June 24, 1985, p. 9.

75. *New York Times,* July 9, 1985.

76. U.S. House of Representatives, Committee on Foreign Affairs, Subcommittee on International Security and Scientific Affairs, *Review of Administration's Policy on Sales of Advanced Fighter Planes to ASEAN: Hearings,* 98th Cong., 2d sess., March 28, 1984, pp. 21, 22.

77. Ibid., p. 104.

78. *Merdeka* (Jakarta), editorial, March 1, 1984, in FBIS, *Daily Report, Asia Pacific,* March 12, 1984, N1.

79. Author's discussion with Indonesian ambassador to the United States, General Habib, at the Council on Foreign Relations Conference, "1985: A Critical Year for ASEAN," Phoenix, Arizona, May 2, 1985. Nayan Chanda, "F16 Wins Sales Dogfight," *Far Eastern Economic Review,* September 25, 1986, pp. 29–30.

80. Paisal Sricharatchanya, "Milestone or Mirage?" *Far Eastern Economic Review,* March 12, 1987, p. 16; *Jakarta Post,* May 26, 1987, in FBIS, *Daily Report East Asia,* June 1, 1987. J2; Jusuf Wanandi, "ASEAN: Time for More Political Cooperation," *Far Eastern Economic Review,* June 11, 1987, pp. 48–50; and Jakarta International Service, in English, July 18, 1987, in FBIS, *Daily Report East Asia,* August 17, 1987, J1.

81. "After Vietnam, U.S. A Power in Asia," *New York Times,* April 18, 1985. Also see Thai Quang Trung, "The Moscow-Hanoi Axis and the Soviet Military Buildup in Southeast Asia," *Indochina Report* 8 (October 1986): 13–14.

82. Paul Keleman, "Soviet Strategy in Southeast Asia: The Vietnam Factor," *Asian Survey* 24, no. 3 (March 1984): 345.

83. For a good, brief overview of the strategic dynamics leading to the Kuantan statement, see Michael Leifer, "ASEAN under Stress over Cambodia," *Far Eastern Economic Review,* June 14, 1984, pp. 34–36. A statement indicating Indonesian Foreign Minister Mochtar's relaxed view of the Soviet-Vietnam alliance was reported by the

Agence France Presse (Hong Kong), April 28, 1986, in FBIS, *Daily Report, Asia Pacific,* April 29, 1986, N1.

84. Sukhumbhand Paribatra, "Strategic Implications of the Indochina Conflict: Thai Perspectives," *Asian Affairs: An American Review* 11, no. 3 (Fall 1984): 33, 34.

85. Cited by ibid., p. 38.

86. An excellent discussion of Hanoi's security conception is found in William S. Turley, "Vietnam's View of Regional Order" (paper presented to the twenty-sixth annual meeting of the International Studies Association, Washington, D.C., March 8–11, 1985).

87. Ibid., p. 10.

88. Barbara Crossette, "Now Vietnam Deals from Strength," *New York Times,* May 5, 1985.

89. Pham Binh, "Prospects for Solutions to Problems Related to Peace and Stability in Southeast Asia," *Indonesian Quarterly* 12, no. 2 (April 1984): 216–218. This paper was presented at the first Indonesian-Vietnamese Bilateral Seminar in Hanoi, February 25–26, 1984. The author is director of Hanoi's Ministry of Foreign Affairs Institute of International Relations.

90. Ibid., p. 221.

91. See Pham Van Dong's interview with Walter Cronkite, *Vietnam News Agency,* April 29, 1985, in FBIS, *Daily Report, Asia Pacific,* May 1, 1985, K17.

92. This argument was made by Donald Weatherbee in his edited volume, *Southeast Asia Divided: The ASEAN-Indochina Crisis* (Boulder: Westview Press, 1985), pp. 4, 5, 14.

93. This argument is made by Karl D. Jackson, "U.S.–Southeast Asian Relations" (paper presented to the Third U.S.-ASEAN Conference, Chiangmai, Thailand, January 10–13, 1985), pp. 16, 17.

94. Ibid., p. 21.

95. Nayan Chanda, "CIA No, US Aid Yes," *Far Eastern Economic Review,* August 16, 1984, pp. 16–18.

96. Paul Quinn-Judge, "Vietnam Presents Khmer Guerrillas with a Catch-22," *Christian Science Monitor,* March 13, 1985.

97. The quotation is taken from an interview with PRK President Heng Samrin in *Patriot* (Delhi), July 15, 1987, in FBIS, *Daily Report East Asia,* August 3, 1987. I1. Also see the interview with Vietnamese Foreign Minister Nguyen Co Thach in *Le Monde* (Paris), May 10–11, 1987.

98. Paul Quinn-Judge and Hamish McDonald, "Deadline on Compromise," *Far Eastern Economic Review,* March 21, 1985, pp. 50, 51.

99. *Le Monde* (Paris) April 6, 1985.

100. Author's interview with U.S. Defense Intelligence Agency analysts, Washington, D.C., May 8, 1985.

101. *Nation Review* (Bangkok) March 17, May 5, 1985, in FBIS, *Daily Report, Asia Pacific,* March 19, May 6, 1985, J2 and J1, respectively.

102. Donald S. Zagoria, "The USSR and Asia," *Asian Survey* 25, no. 1 (January 1985): 26, 27.

103. Report by the director of the Japanese Defense Agency to the Diet Budget Committee, *Nippon Keizai Shimbun,* February 22, 1985, and Richard Nations, "The Reason Why," *Far Eastern Economic Review,* May 9, 1985, p. 44.

104. Author's interview with analysts of the U.S. Defense Intelligence Agency, Washington, D.C., May 8, 1985. See also Trung, "The Moscow-Hanoi Axis," pp. 21–28.

105. See the excellent discussion of these issues in Cheng Pao-min, "The Sino-Vietnamese Territorial Dispute," *Asia Pacific Community* 24 (Spring 1984): 37–48.

106. Ibid.

107. Richard D. Fisher, Jr., "Brewing Conflict in the South China Sea," *Asia Studies Backgrounder* (Washington, D.C.: Heritage Foundation, October 25, 1984), p. 4; Robert Rau, "Present and Future Maritime Security Issues in the Southeast Asian and South China Seas," *Contemporary Southeast Asia* 8, no. 1 (June 1986).

108. George Lauriat, "Bluewater on a Budget," *Far Eastern Economic Review,* July 28, 1983, p. 38.

109. Fisher, "Brewing Conflict," pp. 7–8; *Pacific Defense Reporter* (May 1985): 14.

110. Fisher, "Brewing Conflict," pp. 3–4.

111. Robert Trumbull, "5 Nations Dispute Rights to an Asian Archipelago," *New York Times,* August 28, 1983; Clayton Jones, "Law of Sea Runs Aground amid 26 Tiny Coral Isles," *Christian Science Monitor,* June 10, 1983.

112. Fisher, "Brewing Conflict," p. 8.

113. An excellent discussion is found in Mark Valencia, "Oil under Troubled Waters," *Far Eastern Economic Review,* March 15, 1984, pp. 30–33.

114. *U.S.-Philippines: Hearings,* pp. 213–215.

Chapter 5

1. The following discussion of Australian maritime strategy is based on my discussion with Alan Behm, assistant secretary, Strategy and International Policy Division, Australian Department of Defense, at Arizona State University, May 14, 1986.

2. See particularly the chapter by Desmond Ball and J.O. Langtry in Ball, ed., *Strategy and Defence: Australian Essays* (Boston: George Allen and Unwin, 1982).

3. The Hon. Gordon Scholes, Australian minister of defense, "Australia's Strategic Outlook and Defense Policy," *Australian Outlook* 38, no. 3 (December 1984): 137–141.

4. Paul Dibb, "Issues in Australian Defence," *Australian Outlook* 37, no. 3 (December 1983): 161, 162.

5. Sinclair's statements are cited by Ray Sunderland, "Australia's Changing Threat Perceptions," Working Paper No. 78 (Canberra: Australian National University, Strategic and Defence Studies Center, March 1984), p. 9.

6. Joseph M. Siracusa and Glen St. J. Barclay, "The Historical Influence of the United States on Australian Strategic Thinking," *Australian Outlook* 38, no. 3 (December 1984): 157; Melbourne Overseas Service, December 13, 1985, in FBIS, *Daily Report, Asia Pacific,* December 18, 1985, M6; Brigadier P.J. Greville, "Hawke Government Has Handled Defense Well, But . . . ," *Pacific Defence Reporter* (November 1985): 18, 19.

7. International Institute for Strategic Studies (IISS), *The Military Balance, 1983–1984* London: IISS, 1983), pp. 87, 88.

8. Scholes's 1983–1984 defense budget statement cited by Ray Sunderland, "Australia's Emerging Regional Defense Strategy," Working Paper No. 80 (Canberra: Australian National University, Strategic and Defense Studies Center, July 1984), pp. 25, 26.

9. Ibid, p. 30.

10. Wellington Overseas Service, March 15, 1985, in FBIS, *Daily Report, Asia Pacific,* March 18, 1985, E4. Also see *Pacific Defense Reporter* (May 1985): 50, and Hamish McDonald, "Tangled Fishing Lines," *Far Eastern Economic Review,* June 13, 1985, pp. 30, 31.

11. Melbourne Overseas Service, August 23, 1985, in FBIS, *Daily Report, Asia Pacific,* August 23, 1985, M1; "Soviet Pact Stirs Fears in Pacific," *New York Times,* November 10, 1985; "Pacific Nations Sign Tuna Deal," *New York Times,* October 22, 1986; Barbara Crossette, "South Pacific Comes of Age in Global Politics," *New York Times,* October 26, 1986.

12. Dibb, "Issues in Australian Defense," p. 164.

13. IISS, *The Military Balance, 1983–1984,* p. 88.

14. Michael MacGuire lays out the requirements for an ASW-oriented Australian navy in "Australia as a Regional Seapower: An External View," Working Paper No. 11 (Canberra: Australian National University, Strategic and Defence Studies Center, February 1979), esp. pp. 14, 16, 24. See also Research Institute for Peace and Security, *Asian Security 1984* (Tokyo: RIPS, 1984), p. 175.

15. MacGuire, "Australia as a Regional Seapower."

16. Jacqueline Rees, "Australia: The Navy Looks West," *Far Eastern Economic Review,* March 22, 1984, p. 36.

17. Derek Woolner, "Funding Australia's Defense," Working Paper No. 77 (Canberra: Australian National University, Strategic and Defence Studies Center, December 1983), pp. 52–53.

18. Jacqueline Rees, "Canberra Approves Bases for Northern Territory, *Far Eastern Economic Review,* August 23, 1984, p. 10.

19. Paul Dibb, *Review of Australia's Defense Capabilities* (Canberra: Australian Government Publishing Service, 1986). The following discussion is drawn from this document.

20. Hamish McDonald, "Australia: Back to Basics," *Far Eastern Economic Review,* June 18, 1986, pp. 32–33.

21. Melbourne Overseas Service, October 14, 1986, in FBIS *Daily Report, Asia Pacific,* October 15, 1986, M1.

22. Hamish McDonald, "High-Tech and Super Fast," *Far Eastern Economic Review,* June 18, 1986, p. 34.

23. Howard Handleman, "Whither Australia? U.S. Has Major Reservations about the Dibb Report," *Pacific Defense Reporter* (August 1986): 45. For an Australian critique of the Dibb report, see Ross Babbage, "Would the Dibb Strategy Work?" (paper presented to the Victorian Fabian Society Conference on Australia's Defense, August 2–3, 1986, Melbourne).

24. "The Dibb Report," *Pacific Defense Reporter* (July 1986): 4–5.

25. This argument is made by Richard J. Fisher, Jr., "Responding to New Zealand's Challenge to Western Security in the South Pacific," in *Asian Studies Center Backgrounder* (Washington, D.C.: Heritage Foundation, July 24, 1986), p. 12.

26. Peter Samuel, "Australia's Reversal on Defence Policy," *Asian Wall Street Journal Weekly,* April 6, 1987, p. 15.

27. Melbourne Overseas Service, March 19, 1987, in FBIS, *Daily Report Asia-Pacific,* March 20, 1987, M1-M3.

28. Ian Hamilton, "The Defense White Paper," *Pacific Defense Reporter* 13, no. 10 (April 1987): 19–23. Also see Andrew Mack, "Defence vs. Offense: The Debate over Australia's Defense Policy," (paper presented to the Annual Meeting of the International Studies Association, Washington, D.C., April 15–18, 1987), pp. 6–7.

29. Henry Albinski, "Australia and the United States: An Appraisal of the Relationship," *Australian Journal of Politics and History* 29, no. 2 (1983): 293.

30. William T. Tow, "ANZUS and American Security," in Robert O'Neill, ed., *Security in East Asia* (New York: St. Martin's Press for the International Institute of Strategic Studies, 1984), p. 175.

31. Cited by ibid., p. 178.

32. "The Strategic Basis of Australian Defence Policy" (an official Australian government assessment), excerpted in *National Times,* March 30–April 5, 1984, p. 24.

33. Ibid., p. 25.

34. Statement by U.S. Assistant Secretary of State for East Asian and Pacific Affairs, Paul Wolfowitz, "The ANZUS Relationship: Alliance Management," *Australian Outlook* 38, no. 3 (December 1984): 151.

35. This discussion and much of the ensuing analysis is drawn from the following sources: Harry Gelber, "Australia, the U.S. and the Strategic Balance: Some Comments on the Joint Facilities," *Australian Outlook* 36, no. 2 (August 1982): 16–18; Dibb, "Issues in Australian Defence"; Robert Catley, "Australia and the Great Powers," *Australian Outlook* 37, no. 3 (December 1983); Jane Ford, "US Bases—What Hawke Didn't Say," *Weekend Australian,* June 9–10, 1984, p. 17; and the following studies by Desmond Ball: "The U.S. Naval Ocean Surveillance Information System (NOSIS): Australia's Role," Reference Paper No. 77; "The ANZUS Connection: The Security Relationship between Australia, New Zealand, and the United States," Reference Paper No. 105; "U.S. Installations in Australia: Agenda for the Future," Reference Paper No. 119—all published by the Strategic and Defence Studies Center of the Australian National University, February 1983, May 1983, and August 1983, respectively.

36. Ford, "US Bases."

37. Ball, "ANZUS Connection," p. 43.

38. Ball, "U.S. Installations in Australia," esp. pp. 15–24.

39. Desmond Ball interview on the Melbourne Overseas Service, February 7, 1985, in FBIS, *Daily Report, Asia Pacific,* February 8, 1985, M1-M2.

40. Gelber, "Australia, the U.S. and the Strategic Balance," pp. 18, 19.

41. Michael Richardson, "Cruising the Pacific," *Far Eastern Economic Review,* September 6, 1984, pp. 42, 43.

42. Ralph A. Cossa, "New Zealand: Friend or Ally?" *Pacific Defense Reporter* (June 1984): 2, 3.

43. Robert Y. Horiguchi, "Kiwi Disease—Japanese Version," *Pacific Defense Reporter* (June 1985): 48.

44. Henry S. Albinski, *ANZUS, The United States and Pacific Security* (Washington, D.C.: University Press of America for the Asia Society, 1987), p. 29.

45. "New Zealand Leader Won't Meet Shultz," *New York Times* May 23, 1985.

46. David Barber, "New Zealand Shrugs as U.S. Scraps Joint Defense Treaty," *Christian Science Monitor,* August 13, 1986; Colin James, "Adrift from ANZUS," *Far Eastern Economic Review,* August 20, 1986, pp. 15–16.

47. *Agence France Presse,* September 10, 1984, in FBIS, *Daily Report, Asia Pacific,* September 10, 1984, M2. See also "New Zealand Premier Cautions U.S. on Economic Sanctions," *New York Times,* February 12, 1985.

48. David Barber, "U.S. Senator Goes to New Zealand to Mend Some Fences," *Christian Science Monitor,* August 29, 1986.

49. Thomas Durrell-Young, "Australia Can't Fill U.S. Shoes," *Pacific Defense Reporter* 13, no. 12 (June 1987): pp. 49–50.

50. Robert Manning and Colin James, "ANZUS All at Sea . . . ," *Far Eastern Economic Review,* February 14, 1985, p. 12; Bernard Gwertzman, "U.S. Plans Actions to Answer Rebuff by New Zealand," *New York Times,* February 6, 1985.

51. David Barber, "New Zealand Military Says Defense Rift with U.S. Hurts," *Christian Science Monitor,* October 14, 1986.

52. *Agence France Presse* (Hong Kong), February 26, 1985, in FBIS, *Daily Report, Asia Pacific,* February 28, 1985, M1–M2; National Public Radio, "All Things Considered" (Washington, D.C.), February 27, 1985; and Bernard Gwertzman, "U.S. Retaliation in New Zealand Dispute," *New York Times,* February 27, 1985.

53. Remarks by Assistant Secretary of State for East Asia and the Pacific, Paul Wolfowitz, before the Subcommittee on Asian and Pacific Affairs of the U.S. House of Representatives Foreign Affairs Committee, published as "The ANZUS Alliance," Current Policy No. 674 (Washington, D.C.: Bureau of Public Affairs, U.S. Department of State, March 18, 1985), p. 1.

54. Ibid., p. 2.

55. Ramesh Thakar, "Toward a Nuclear Free New Zealand?" *Asia Pacific Community* 27 (Winter 1985): 20.

56. Wellington Overseas Service, May 3, 1985, in FBIS, *Daily Report, Asia Pacific,* May 6, 1985, M2, M3. See also Dora Alves, *Anti-Nuclear Attitudes in New Zealand and Australia* (Washington, D.C.: National Defense University Press, 1985), pp. 39–40.

57. Michael Richardson, "The Influence on the ASEAN Community of Australian-American Security Relations," *Australian Outlook* 38, no. 3 (December 1984): 196, 197; and the author's interview with an Australian Defense official in Canberra, June 1982.

58. James Clad and V.G. Kulkarni, "Keeping the Flag Flying," *Far Eastern Economic Review,* June 7, 1984, p. 28.

59. Tim Huxley, "Southeast Asia and Australia's Security," *Asia Pacific Community* 23 (Winter 1984): 42.

60. "Strategic Basis of Australian Defense Policy," p. 5.

61. Robert A. Brand, "Defense Down Under: An American View," *Pacific Defense Reporter* (June 1985): 13; *Agence France Presse* (Hong Kong), in FBIS, *Daily Report, Asia Pacific,* August 18, 1983, O3.

62. Michael Richardson, "Singapore, the Poison Shrimp," *Pacific Defense Reporter* (June 1985): 21.

63. Singapore Domestic Service, December 23, 1986, in FBIS, *Daily Report Asia-Pacific,* December 24, 1986, O2.

64. Interview with Australian Defence Minister Beazley on the Melbourne Overseas Service, February 20, 1987, in FBIS, *Daily Report Asia-Pacific,* February 25, 1987,

M4. Also see J.H. Beaglehole, "Defense White Paper Lacks Strong Commitment to Western Stance," *Pacific Defense Reporter* (May 1987): 31–34.

65. Author's interview with Wisma Putra (Foreign Ministry) officials, Kuala Lumpur, May 29, 1984.

66. Author's interview with Australian Department of Defense, Asia Branch officials, Canberra, June 15, 1984.

67. Author's interview with Australian defense expert Paul Dibb, Australian National University, Canberra, June 18, 1984.

68. A good review of ASEAN concerns over the ANZUS difficulties is found in "ASEAN, ANZUS, FPDA, ZOPFAN, or Complete NWFZ?" *Far Eastern Economic Review,* March 7, 1985, pp. 22, 23.

69. For a semiofficial Indonesian view of the Hawke government's policy on Cambodia, see C.P.F. Luhulima, "Australia and ASEAN" (paper presented to the Third Australia-Indonesia Seminar, Griffiths University, Brisbane, July 16–17, 1984), esp. p. 14.

70. Melbourne Overseas Service, April 15, 1985, in FBIS, *Daily Report, Asia Pacific,* April 16, 1985, M2.

Chapter 6

1. John Lewis Gaddis, *Strategies of Containment* (New York: Oxford University Press, 1982), p. 267.

2. *Far Eastern Economic Review,* May 2, 1985, p. 39.

3. "Billions For Defense: The Spending Debate," *New York Times,* May 14, 1985. See also Secretary Shultz's address to the July 12, 1985, ASEAN Postministerial Conference (Washington, D.C.: U.S. Department of State, Current Policy No. 722), p.2.

4. Nayan Chanda, "American Big Stick," *Far Eastern Economic Review,* June 20, 1985, p. 46.

5. For Indonesian suspicions about the affect of Sino-U.S. relations on Asian security, see the editorial in *Merdeka,* May 3, 1985, as published in FBIS, *Daily Report Asia-Pacific,* May 16, 1985, N1-N2.

6. Larry A. Niksch, "South Korea in Broader Pacific Defense," *Journal of Northeast Asian Studies* 2, no. 1 (March 1983): 95.

7. Typical is the article by Richard Stubbing, "The Defense Program: Buildup or Binge?" *Foreign Affairs* 63, no. 4 (Spring 1985): esp. pp. 854, 855, 857, 861, 862.

8. *Pravda,* June 22, 1985, in FBIS, *Daily Report/USSR,* June 26, 1985, CC9.

9. These figures are cited by William T. Tow, "Japan's Security Role and Continuing (Policy) Debates," in Young-hwan Kihl and Lawrence Grinter, eds., *Asia-Pacific Security* (Boulder: Lynne Rienner Publishers, 1986), p. 9.

10. Ibid., p. 30.

11. Robert W. Barnett, *Beyond War: Japan's Concept of Comprehensive National Security* (Washington, D.C.: Pergamon-Brassey's, 1984), p. 65.

12. Masashi Nishihara, "Expanding Japan's Credible Defense Role," *International Security* 8, no. 3 (Winter 1983–1984): 197.

13. R.B. Byers and Stanley C.M. Ing, "Sharing the Burden on the Far Side of the Alliance: Japanese Security in the 1980s," in Joshua D. Katz and Tilly C. Friedman-Lichtschein, eds., *Japan's New World Role* (Boulder: Westview Press, 1985), p. 172.

14. Cited by Alan Rix, "Japan and Oceania: Strained Pacific Cooperation," in Robert S. Ozaki and Walter Arnold, eds., *Japan's Foreign Relations: A Global Search for Economic Security* (Boulder: Westview Press, 1985), p. 60.

15. Reinhard Drifte, "The European Community and Japan: Beyond the Economic Dimension," in Katz and Friedman-Lichtschein, *Japan's New World Role,* p. 159.

16. "Threats to ASEAN Security," *Asiaweek,* June 21, 1984, p. 90.

17. This view is expressed by J. Soedjati Djiwandono of the Center for Strategic and International Studies in Jakarta, in "The Soviet Presence in the Asian Pacific Region: An Indonesian Perspective," *Asian Affairs* 11, no. 4 (Winter 1985): esp. pp. 26–31.

18. Remarks by V.B. Dato'Khalil Yaakob, minister attached to Malaysian Prime Minister Mahathir's Office, at the Conference on Stability, Development, and Security in East and Southeast Asia, Port Dickson, Malaysia, November 12, 1984.

19. *Wongchon Kan Thut,* in Thai, June–July 1985, in FBIS, *Daily Report Asia Pacific,* July 19, 1985, J3-J4; John McBeth, "Bangkok's High Risk," *Far Eastern Economic Review,* August 8, 1985, pp. 12, 13; and Foreign Minister Sitthi's reply to a parliamentary question on the magnet effect of Khmer resistance bases on Thai soil for Vietnamese cross-border assaults, *Bangkok Post,* July 19, 1985.

20. "U.S. Plan to Quit Manila Bases Reported," *New York Times,* January 25, 1986.

Index

About the Author

Sheldon Simon is professor of political science and faculty associate of the Center for Asian Studies at Arizona State University. A specialist on Asian security issues, he is the author or editor of five books and sixty scholarly articles and book chapters. His most recent book is *The ASEAN States and Regional Security* (1982). Professor Simon is a member of the Southeast Asia Council of the Asia Society and has been a consultant to the United States Information Agency, the U.S. Department of State, and the Department of Defense. He travels through the Asia-Pacific region regularly for research and lectures on Asian security issues.